"Sing to the Lord a new song; play skillfully, and shout for joy."
Psalm 33:3

On October 15, 1948,
a mother brought unto this earth a baby
— one destined to become a star.
Not just any star, as there are many in the sky
that shine brightly on a clear night,
but a star that brings emotion, passion, thought, even tears,
to the words given him in song.
The mother gave the child a guitar and said,
"Sing... Sing loud... Sing strong..."

And thus, he screamed.

The child grew to a youth and then a man,
then a man with dreams, hope, and the love of music.
His stardom may not have come to be what he dreamed,
but in truth, his stardom touched so many lives
in so many ways — including his own.
From encounters with future music greats,
to being a loving son, brother, and friend
the young man, Pat Liston, not only became a star,
he became a galaxy.

I close this in saying, in my 20 years in the music business — from John Hartford to Leon Russell to Richie Havens — I have not known a more passionate, caring, and loving man than my friend and the best musician, songwriter, artist… Pat Liston.

Lovingly,
Bob Bell

13 Notes to Life
A Life of Poetry and Melancholy Rhyme

by Pat Liston

Cover image: by Dawn Liston

I have tried to recreate events, locales, and conversations from my memories of them. I have tried to mention every person I have worked with musically. I have included only part of my personal life because this is a music memoir. I may have forgotten some things and my account of things in this book may not (for those who experienced some of these things with me) be as you remember them. It is, however, an honest account to the best of my recollection.

ISBN: 978-1-48358-603-8

DEDICATION

There are so many people who played integral roles in my life and my music. At the top of that list would have to be my mother, Lucille Liston.

Mom provided a constant flow of music in our house when I was a child. She laid a profound musical base for me. She taught me how to play the guitar and sing harmony. She gave me her guitar as my first guitar. She bought me a very nice Gretsch electric guitar when she felt it was time — which at the time was a great financial burden on her. Mom drove me to gigs when I couldn't drive and then gave me her car to use once I could. She saw to it that I could go to music college at the St. Louis Institute of Music to better understand and hone my craft. When the time came, Mom allowed me to leave home to pursue my music — even though she could have used financial help at home.

Mom was my biggest fan and greatest cheerleader throughout her time here on Earth, and she was also my dearest friend.

We had a bond and could talk about literally anything and everything. She instilled in me a confidence for who I was and what I could accomplish — Mom always felt there was nothing beyond her three boys' capabilities. I hear her voice everyday. I picture her laughing and dancing that silly dance she used to do when my music grabbed her. When I write songs, I always imagine what Mom would think of this one.

So, it is with great pride and honor that I dedicate this book to her.

"I love you, Mom, and miss you every day."

AND TO MY SOULMATE

My mom provided me with that *someone-close-who-believes-in-you* thing throughout most of my life. Almost every successful person I've read about has had that. She instilled a self confidence that I still benefit from, but as they say, "Behind every great man, there's a great woman." I searched most of my life for that one person, and now, I have that great woman in my wife, Dawn.

She believes in me with great fervor. I have accomplished so much in the last eight years. Music is, once again, my life and how I make a living. I'm truly not sure I could have done this (at this stage in my life and with this degree of passion) without Dawn.

She books my performances with unsurpassed confidence. She tirelessly does almost all of the day-to-day business. Dawn is truly my soulmate. She is also, indeed, her own person as well. I'm not sure there is anything that she cannot do or at least give a try. She amazes me on a daily basis. She is one of the strongest women I have ever met.

I regret that Mom could not have met Dawn. Because Mom wasn't a "girly" woman — she was not fragile and spoke her mind — Mom loved strong and determined people, and Dawn embodies those characteristics naturally.

"Dawn, I thank you for the life I've always wanted and only hope that I provide you with the same amount of joy and happiness that you provide me. You were my new beginning. May we have a long and fruitful life together. You understand a *dreamer* because you are, yourself, a dreamer. You challenge us both every day with new ideas. You have taught this old dog some new tricks. You blessed me with our wonderful little boy, Thomas. You've taught me that life isn't just about music or fame. Because of you, I have never written a more honest title to a song than *My Good Old Days Are Now*, because, of course, *You're Easy To Love*."

PREFACE

13 Notes to Life — I know that sounds a bit odd for a title, but let me try to explain.

Back in about 1975 I was sitting in a local bar called the Waterhouse. It was owned by my good friend Billy Waterhouse and I happened to be sitting next to Billy's father, Marion Waterhouse. This particular day Mr. Waterhouse was sitting there quietly in (what looked like) deep thought.

After a time he turned to me and said, "13 notes... it's amazing."

I thought, *Okay, where's he going with this?* So, I asked him what he meant.

He said, "Pat, including the octave, there are 13 notes in a chromatic scale — just 13." I said something like *yea, that's cool,* but in my head I was thinking, *So?*

He continued, "With only 13 notes every song in history has been composed or written — from Beethoven to the Beatles — that's amazing."

I sat there with my mouth agape thinking, *My God. I've played music most of my life. I even went to music college and not once had this amazingly simple fact really dawned on me before.* Here I was, *little Mr. Rockstar,* being humbled by the wisdom and insight of an old union electrician sitting next to me on a bar stool. I never forgot that day of simple wisdom and insight.

My wife, Dawn, knows most of my stories. So she (of course) had heard this one. I had a different book title in my head — *50 Years of Music.*

"You know, I have a problem with that title," Dawn said to me one night. "You told me you didn't want this book to sound like you're wrapping up your musical life — that you have so much more to do."

She continued, "I think that *50 Years of Music* is saying the very thing you want to avoid. Like you've reached this milestone and you're done."

Begrudgingly, I agreed. But the bothersome thing was, *Okay, now what do we call it?*

She saw my worried look and said, "How about *13 Notes To Life* — ya know, from the Mr. Waterhouse story?"

I sometimes have to process things before I like them.

After she went upstairs to bed I started thinking about it... *13 Notes To Life*... Wait! That's a double entendre — it says that there are only 13 notes to life, but it also sounds like a jail sentence! That's great because at times music *is* like a sentence. It's something you can never escape from. I got out of music for several years and always somehow felt incomplete, or disconnected, or something. If you are truly an artist, your art is part of your core. You can never walk away from it. If you do, there will always and forever be a void in your soul or somewhere deep inside of you.

I had to share this with Dawn. *Wait until she hears what I discovered in her title.* I ran upstairs and said, "You know what... that title is actually a double entendre..."

Before I could tell her of my brilliant insight, she said, "Yah, I know, that's what made me think of it."

Well, at least I'd figured out what she'd meant by the title... and we went with it.

From my youth I imagined my life being much different than it is now. I don't think I ever imagined being as big as the Beatles or Elvis. I just imagined being in front of thousands of people doing my songs, and selling millions of records... okay, so that *is* what Elvis and the Beatles did, but I never thought it through in terms of being as famous as they were.

I actually started playing guitar when I was about 10 years old, but I didn't have an active band until I was about 15. I was 65 when I started this book (so, that's where the original *50 Years of Music* title came from). I have told so many of these stories over the years and almost every time I get on a roll, someone says, "You should write a book." But to cover a lifetime of music is a daunting task to say the least.

I must say, the technology of today does make it easier and cheaper to tackle. Also, there are more people out there who can help, so you don't really need a publishing company as you once did. You just need friends who can assist in putting it together in a readable fashion.

The hardest task was putting the stories and events in the proper chronological order. When I talk, I just whip out a story and say it happened in 1978. Sometimes I don't even say when it happened — I just say it happened. In a book there has to be a semblance of order. Things have to be spelled correctly and your grammar should, at least, give the appearance that you've had a modicum of formal education. My *go to* person who helped me create that facade is my good friend, Angela Sebben. She tirelessly waded through the pages and pages of ancient history. She reviewed, literally, hundreds of pictures, suggested phrasing options so that the text might be more palatable to the reader, and gave this book a cohesive appearance. I can not thank her enough for her perseverance and patience.

In addition to Angela doing all she did, another good friend, Chris Moore, helped me seek out and correct grammatical errors. I appreciated his attention to detail and his youthful enthusiasm. Lastly, from the Editing Room came my dear friend, Susan Miller. She gave the book the once over and found small things we'd all missed (some not so small). Susan, along with the others, worked diligently to try to give the impression that I had a reasonable amount of education and made every effort to keep my ADHD at bay.

A large part of this book is the photographs and images. Quite honestly though, I can't remember who took them all or even who provided some of them. This is an attempt to credit all photographers and thank the people who shared their old pictures or images: Ed Beckwith, Jeannine Beckwith, Greg Bishop & The Metro St. Louis Live Music Historical Society, Terry Campbell, Hap Chamberlain, Deej Gausling, John Gellman, Keith Hempen, Indie Image Photography, Sam Kaiser, Dawn Liston, Amelia McCoy, Patti McMahon, Barb Moyer, Pat O'Malley, Natalie J. Pelafos, Joe Pousosa, David Probst, Art Reel, Chuck Sheets, Doug Smith, Keith Tenney, Amy Thorn, Madison Thorn, Claudia Upton, Jim Wilhelm, and Russ Woodmancy. Thank you all.

I tried to include people's names in every stage of my life. I'm sure I've forgotten some, but I really tried to remember all of them. People like to see their name in print.

I start from the beginning of my life to give some background, but the focus is on my music years.

I tell *my* story from *my* perspective, though those I mention may remember things differently than they are described here. It reminds me of a book I once read — *The Lilac Bus* by Maeve Binchy. The novel tells the story of eight people who travel on a lilac-colored bus from Dublin every Friday night to spend the weekend in their hometown, Rathdoon. Each of the seven passengers and the bus driver tell, basically, the same story from their individual viewpoints. The same story can sound very different when you ask multiple people who were present at the time. So, like one of those on *The Lilac Bus,* I'm telling my story from my perspective.

I think I balked at writing a book because (to me) it seemed as though you were wrapping up your life. Like you were saying, "Thanks for the memories, I'm outta here!" I do not plan on being done until I'm not breathing. I'm still writing, recording, performing, and living life to the fullest. I am married to a woman who challenges and stretches my creativity on a regular basis. And we have a little boy who challenges us both. After all, isn't that what life is about... challenge and creating? God said He created us in His image... I believe part of that image is our ability to create and to accept tough times as a challenge, not a burden.

I have done less than many, but more than most. I try to live in the moment. I look at no points in my life as *the best times*. I don't refer to any part of my life as *the good old days*. I am a believer in *carpe diem*... because in my mind, "My good old days are now."

— Pat

Even though the main thrust of this book is to cover my years in music, I should give a little background so it doesn't seem like I just dropped out of the sky.

1553 TAMM AVENUE

I was born on October 15th, 1948. I was premature and was preceded by my older brother Mike of seven years and two miscarriages and two stillborn baby sisters. The doctor promised my mom that she was not going to lose *this* baby. Thank God for optimistic obstetricians!

I was cesarean — always the nonconformist — I had to stay at the hospital quite a while after I was born because of being premature. Years later, people said that those types of things did emotional damage to babies in their later life. I don't know about all that. I fared better than my four predecessors. So, I'm not complaining.

We're all basically screwed-up in some way and it's nice to have something to fall back on when you need to place blame... "Officer, I didn't want to speed but I was in an incubator as an infant!"

My mother was a singer/guitar player and she taught me to play. Mom had had a music career of her own in the 30s. She (Lucille Bennett at the time) and her partner, Hazel Campbell, were on KMOX radio as the Texas Bluebonnets. They were part of "Pappy" Cheshire's Hillbillies. They were one of the most popular KMOX musical units of that time. They still hold the national championship in their field. They won that title in competition with thousands of hillbilly musicians (hillbilly was not considered a derogatory term at the time) at the Municipal Auditorium in St. Louis, Missouri, which was later renamed Kiel Auditorium.

In 1938, "Pappy" Cheshire's Hillbillies withdrew from further contests after having won the title for three consecutive years.

My dad was a handsome Irishman who could charm the scales off of a snake. He had numerous jobs, but for most of his life he was a bartender. He also drank a bit which sadly ended his life far too soon. But he had no enemies. Everybody liked him. I was always amazed at how people lit up when he was around.

At that time we lived in a four-family flat on Tamm Avenue in Dogtown — an Irish-Catholic neighborhood in St. Louis, Missouri. We lived there from the time I was born until I was five.

We lived next door to a Croatian family. Their *whole family* lived in that four-family flat. One of the families had a little girl named Susie. She was my girlfriend. We were inseparable. She makes a cameo appearance in a song I wrote years later called "Hero."

In the fall of 1953, only three days after my own birthday, my younger brother, Danny, was born. I remember staring into the crib when they brought him home and knowing this meant trouble. I'd get less attention now. The fall of '53 was tough on this little five-year-old. My turf had been invaded by a new baby brother, and my little girlfriend, Susie, and her family had moved to California. I was absolutely lost without Susie. I guess, in some way, it didn't really matter because we moved the following year anyway. With a new baby, we needed more room. We only moved five blocks away, but, in those days, that was a great distance for a five-year-old.

Here's one of my most cherished memories of my father. I wrote a song about it some fifty years later — *My Daddy Knew The Cisco Kid.*

I remember I idolized the Cisco Kid in those early days of television and Saturday morning cowboys. One day, Dad told me the Cisco Kid was a friend of his. I had a pretty good B.S. meter, even as a child, but I could tell by his expression that he was serious.

The following Saturday we both jumped into Pop's '47 Plymouth coupe and drove to the Fireman's Rodeo. (In the song I say Chevrolet because I needed three syllables that rhymed with "day"). It was at an outdoor arena at the corner of Oakland and Macklind Avenues in St. Louis. We were walking around a corner in an area that you had to go through before you got to the seats. Dad stopped on a dime and hid behind the corner. I could not imagine why we were doing this. As I was trying to figure it out, I felt this fast tug and... *whoosh!*

My feet left the ground and he ran to this policeman, who was standing in front of a wooden barrier to keep people out of the back area. Dad told him that there was a big fight back where we had been standing. The policeman took off running. I looked back to see where this fight was. How'd I miss a fight? I turned and said, "Dad, where was the fi..."

Whoosh! We were gone again.

We jumped the barrier and ran like hell. Well, Dad did anyway. I just sort of glided through the air as my left arm got longer.

Suddenly we stopped.

All I saw in front of me were two legs. I could see that the pants were very ornate. I looked down and saw the most spectacular pair of cowboy boots I'd ever seen. My eyes slowly looked up as though I was scanning a Sequoia at Yosemite National Park at close range. As I looked straight up, the sun blinded me for a minute. I thought, *Who is this?* Then he stepped in front of the sun to block it so I could see him.

My heart stopped beating and I could barely breathe for fear of the image disappearing. It was him... really him! *The Cisco Kid!*

He was decked out in full regalia: ornate black pants and shirt, fancy boots, a sombrero, and a pearl handled six shooter! I don't know what heaven will be like and I've never seen God in person, but when I do, I can't imagine Him being any grander than *The Cisco Kid* was that day to a five-year-old little boy!

And he was *my dad's* friend.

Dad chatted casually with him... laughing and joking like old friends do. I looked at my dad and thought, *My God, who is my father?*

Dad introduced us and I was barely able to muster the courage to say hi. He tweaked my nose and said, "Howdy, Partner."

Howdy, Partner!? This wasn't TV... he was saying "Howdy, Partner," to me. *In person!*

I felt dizzy.

He said several things... none of which I remember because I was in a trance,

From your good amigo, Duncan Renaldo Cisco Kid

and from me too: Diablo

but he did tell me he'd wave to me when he rode around the arena. And, by golly, he did!

I remember seeing all the kids waving at him excitedly and thinking, *Those poor kids. They actually think he's waving at them. What fools... he's waving to his partner, Pat.*

Dad had his faults, but he came through that day... and no matter what mistakes he may have made in life, this much I can say... "My dad knew The Cisco Kid and he saw to it that I did too!"

Thanks Pop!

6440 WADE AVENUE

We moved to Wade Avenue into a little brown house. It was walking distance from St. James Catholic Church, the Rectory, the Convent, and the grade school. Mom loved this because it meant that God would probably bless you a little more because you were closer to Him. I was glad, too, because we had our *own* house and our *own* yard... something we'd never had before.

I started kindergarten the following year at St. James the Greater Catholic School. I'm not sure why we were *the Greater*. I remember feeling grateful I didn't attend St. James the Lesser Catholic School... if there was such a school. Lord knows there was enough guilt to go around without having to feel you were the lesser of the two Jameses!

Kindergarten in those days was fun. You learned to tie shoes on this big wood shoe. There was also a sandbox on legs. We got the eight count box of crayons and coloring books. So many fun and exciting things! Not like the kindergartens today where you learn advanced math on a calculator, and how Thomas Jefferson was a racist, or if you kissed a girl, it was sexual harassment.

It was simple — very little stress or controversy. The coloring books had food, animals, and people for you to color. I don't know what this taught you exactly, but it was fun. Maybe it let them know if we were colorblind.

I remember I got in trouble once for coloring a girl's hair orange in my book. The nun asked me, quite agitatedly, if I'd ever actually seen a *real girl* with orange hair?

I said, "Yes, I have."

I had to stand in the corner for lying. But I didn't lie. Cindy, the little red haired girl from behind my Tamm Avenue flat had orange hair. Yah, yah, I know they called it red, but it was orange dammit!

Actually I didn't think *dammit* to myself. In those days, you didn't even *think* cuss words when you were my age and Catholic. You'd go straight to hell if you died before making it to confession. And even though we lived close to the church, I hadn't made my first confession yet. So, this would have put me in terrible jeopardy!

My kindergarten nun was a young, sweet, neurotic nun in desperate need of electrolysis! When I would ask her an embarrassing or uncomfortable question, or something that she just didn't want to deal with, she would close her eyes like she was in a trance. I'd stand there watching her, not quite knowing what I should do. This always made me uncomfortable. Do I just go sit down? Was she pondering some answer for me? Had she just fallen asleep? Mom never did this. (If I said something Mom didn't want to deal with she'd tell me to go outside and play.) So I viewed this as being very odd. Sister eventually opened her eyes and acted like I wasn't there. Okay, now I'm afraid to move. What if she really didn't think I was there and I moved and scared the hell out of her? I'd be standing in the corner until I was a teenager!

In time, I learned to just go sit down when she did this. When the class acted up, she did the same thing — closing her eyes or even putting her head down on the desk. We thought she was praying. This is, of course, what she wanted us to think because it might make us feel bad which would be a good launching pad for the life of guilt we were about to embark on as good little Catholics. In reality, I think she was sort of going to her *happy* place... or what we now call severe denial!

Old St. James the Greater Catholic School

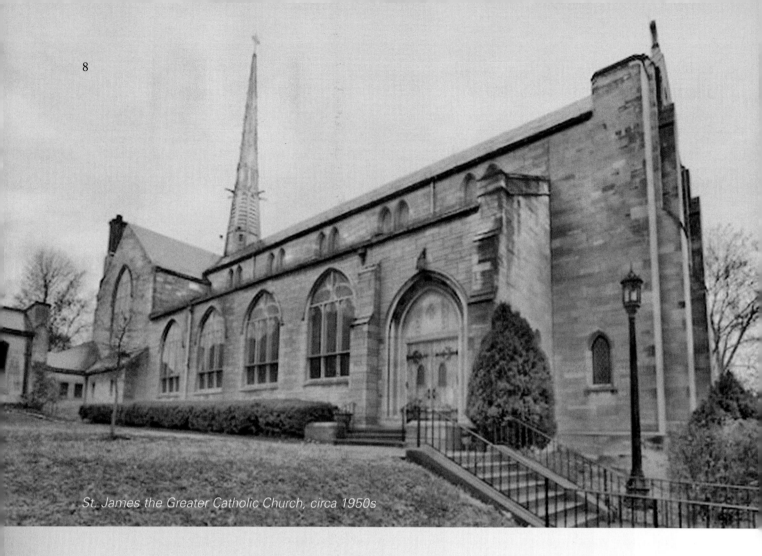

St. James the Greater Catholic Church, circa 1950s

One of my first real shocks in life was the transition between kindergarten and first grade. In my mind, it was like going from Disneyland to a Gulag! No sandbox. No colors (unless they were for charts and graphs). There was also the infusion of the dreaded parochial school *uniform*. There were individual desks all in a row — not the tables full of fun stuff like in kindergarten. We got pencils, rulers, and protractors (whatever the hell they were). We were always given protractors, but nobody ever used them. There were regular chalk boards and we had to listen and not talk. The first time I turned and spoke to Danny Murphy, the first grade nun yelled, "Do you have a problem Mr. Liston?"

What? What happened to the closing of the eyes ritual?

I foolishly said, "No, I was just talking to Danny Mur..."

"Keep quiet!" she yelled, before I could finish my sentence.

Well... Isn't *this* a fine how-do-you-do? I sensed trouble... a foreboding. Where had my mother sent me? Somehow I knew, that just tying my shoes was not going to make things right in *this* classroom? Someone's raised the bar — I don't like this. I don't like this at all!

My father was the janitor at school. In those days it wasn't shameful to be a janitor or a janitor's kid. In fact, it was kind of prestigious to have your dad around all the time... to say, "Hi, Dad," when *Mr. Liston, the janitor,* walked by. He'd always single me out and wink and wave, even if I was in line and not supposed to do that. The nun would scowl at me. Then Dad would wink at her, she'd blush, and all was forgotten.

He was a great janitor... except when kids would vomit. He had a real weak stomach for things like that. He'd throw that red sawdust over it, then run quickly to get Mr. Johnson, the other janitor. Mr. Johnson smoked cigars that smelled like burning rubber, so the vomit smell had no affect on him.

I sometimes would stay after school and just hang out with Dad while he finished up sweeping and everything. He'd do things and I'd just tag along. One day, he casually headed up the stairs of the old school building. Everyone knew that the upstairs was off limits because it was *condemned.* I stopped like my feet had been nailed to the floor!

He turned and said, "Come on, this is where we keep the supplies."

What!? My father, whom I adored, had been going up and down these steps *daily* — risking life and limb for brooms and vomit sawdust!? Is he completely insane!?

He turned a second time and said, "What are you waiting for?"

I slowly said, "Isn't it condemned up there?"

He howled with laughter. "Naw, come on, it's safe."

Before I knew it, *I* was walking up the condemned steps with permission from the janitor — which is almost like permission from the principal, Sister Marcella! This was another thrilling adventure... like The Cisco Kid thing! Dad had his faults, but he was always up for something adventurous.

The second floor was amazing. It was an exact duplicate of the first floor. There were old — very old — desks and school supplies and pictures that looked like they were taken at the time of Christ. Dad took me all around because he saw that look in my eye and he loved it.

Everything seemed so old. It had been built in 1906. It was as though the very spirits of the kids who had been here and gone were watching us. It wasn't scary like I'd thought it would be... it was almost a sort of spiritual experience. I was never again scared of the second floor. Just like with The Cisco Kid, I felt Dad had made me privy to something no one else I knew would experience. I never told anyone I'd been up there. It was *Pop and I's* little adventure and it was no one's business!

I remember that in the Spring of 1956 all hell broke loose because *Elvis* was discovered. My cousin Barb (who was a little older and lived across the street) went from being a fun and sensible person to an absolute loon when it came to Elvis. She had pictures and magazines and *tons* of 45s.... "Hound Dog"... "Don't Be Cruel"... "Love Me Tender"... and on and on and on.

I liked Elvis and I used to listen to the flip sides of the records. He had one called "My Baby Left Me." It was, what was to later be called, "Rock-a-Billy." It was my favorite.

I remember when Elvis was on Ed Sullivan. Barb came over to our house to watch it. She squealed almost the entire time. He did this little dance — a combination of trying to get a spider out of your trousers and putting out a cigarette with your toe. I was impressed and, like most boys my age, I thought I'd like to be like Elvis and be on the Ed Sullivan Show, too. I figured I had a leg up on the other guys in the neighborhood as far as music went because my mom could play guitar and sing and she actually had a guitar. Surely I had *some* of her genes?

That same year my grandfather was killed in an automobile accident, and Grandma eventually announced that she no longer wanted to live alone. Yep... it was time to move again.

Good-bye, Wade Avenue. Good-bye to being closer to God. Good-bye to a normal childhood. Things were about to change... *considerably!*

1507 TAMM AVENUE

We moved to what was always referred to as *The Big White House*. It was back down on Tamm, a block-and-a-half from where my brother, Danny, and I were born. I started playing guitar right after we moved here — when I was about 10 years old.

I remember having a few family gatherings when we lived there. Everyone sang and/or played guitar. It was like having a choir in your backyard. I still remember songs like "Drifting & Dreaming" and "Let the Rest of the World Go By." Mom was always a focal point because she'd been to the *big leagues* from her radio days. Those couple of musical gatherings are some of my fondest memories. All was right with the world when you had a yard full of family members singing. No one could harm you and the sound was heavenly.

My grandma, Louella, also played guitar, five string banjo, and sang. My mom and grandma were raised in Rienzi, Mississippi, where music was a big part of their life. My mom's stepfather — who had been killed in the auto accident — played fiddle and upright bass, too. These days, between Mom and Grandma, there was music in the house most of the time.

Growing up in our house, it was always a challenge learning guitar. Both my mom and grandma occasionally used alternate tunings so, when I picked up a guitar, I never knew what tuning I was going to have to deal with. The very first song I learned on guitar was an instrumental piece called "Silver Strings." It was in a **C** tuning. So I played an alternate tuning before I even learned standard tuning. The first standard tuning song I learned was a song my mom used to sing on the radio called "Hit the Trail and Ride." She said it was my father's favorite song, so I spent countless hours learning how to sing and play it on guitar.

My father would always have me play when anyone came over. The first time my brother brought his future wife, Pat, over to the house, she had to sit and listen to me play and hear my father say, as he always did, "We're gonna put him on television," with his big Irish grin.

My grandfather, Eulos Glover, playing fiddle (far left).

I have a few memories of Dad on Tamm... I remember when my brother, Mike, bought a 1955 Chevy. That was a pretty new car for the time (1959–60). Mike would brag about how fast it was, even though it was only a six cylinder. He kept telling Dad how fast it was until one day Dad said that his 1950 Desoto could outrun Mike's Chevy. Well... the gauntlet had been dropped — Mike challenged dad to a race.

Dad said that they had to race *up* Tamm Avenue and that once they reached the top of the hill it was over. He knew that his old Desoto would never beat Mike in the long run but he could *out-shift* Mike through the gears.

We were so excited we were giddy — Dad was on the *wrong side of the road* — which added to the drama of the whole thing! They took off and you could hear those little six cylinder engines screaming for mercy. Dad beat him out of the hole and with each gear crept a little further ahead. Sure enough, Dad beat Mike up the hill. When they reached the top, Dad backed off. It was over. Mike had lost.

Oh! Mike was mad. Dad teased him endlessly. Dad was a poor winner.

Another short memory I have is my brother, Mike, working nights for MoPac — the Missouri/Pacific railroad. They gave Mike a jeep to drive as a courier. It drove Dad crazy because he wanted to drive that jeep so bad.

Mike slept days because of his night job and one day Dad said to me, "Come on. Let's go." When Dad said, "come on," I always went. We went out to the jeep and Dad messed around with the dash wiring for over an hour. (I realized later in life that he was trying to *hot-wire* that jeep.) He didn't want to take the keys or ask — that took the element of *adventure* out of it.

He was never able to get it started, but it was exciting just seeing him try. He kept giggling under his breath the whole time. Dad was a child trapped in a man's body.

I remember the Christmas of 1960. It was the best one ever.

Dad loved holidays and would decorate extensively for Christmas. He'd have speakers outside playing music and everything. I remember that I'd gotten everything I'd asked for and some I didn't — except a bicycle which I'd just gotten for my previous birthday in October. For Christmas I got a train set, a Fort Apache play set, several box games that I wanted badly, and best of all... they'd gotten Mom's old Martin guitar refurbished and given it to me. Mom had started teaching me guitar that year and I was learning quickly.

I would not remember a Christmas that wonderful again. And it was fitting that it would be so, because, the following March of 1961 life struck us an awful blow. Dad died, March 12th, 1961. He'd just turned 50 years old in February. We'd had a big party for him. I remember I had cut the numbers **5** and **0** out of a piece of thin cardboard and mounted them on his cake. He put a dish towel on his head like a turban because he was Dad and always the life of the party. It was so hard to believe that just 40 days later he would be gone from my life, forever.

For a twelve-year-old, death is very confusing. Hell... I guess it's confusing no matter what your age. My little brother, Danny, was only seven. Pop's wake was two nights and it was virtually packed both nights. I remember thinking, *Who the hell was this guy that all these people knew him?*

There were blue collar and white collar types, dozens of nuns, and priests. To think he'd touched so many lives so profoundly from things they would say. In some ways, I felt like I barely knew him, except for a few special memories. Poor Danny was only seven and really hadn't gotten to know Dad well like I had. I'm sure my older brother, Mike, had an even bigger bond and was devastated at my dad's passing.

Right after Dad died, Grandma went back to Mississippi. She couldn't deal with his death, so she left Mom to deal with it alone. My older brother, Mike, who was almost 20 when Dad died, joined the Marine Corps the following August. I think Dad's death took a deeper toll on him than any of us. He later got married and never lived with us again.

So in a matter of five months, we'd lost Dad, Grandma, and Mike. This truly sealed Danny and I's relationship. We fought, but we stuck together like glue. About a year after Mike left, Mom put the house up for sale, sold it, and rented a house up on Wade, two doors down from where we'd lived previously.

6432 WADE AVENUE

As I said, this was back on Wade. Keep in mind we moved from Tamm to Wade, back down to Tamm, and now back to Wade again.

It was also the end of an era: I'd lost Dad, Mike was gone for good (as far as living with us), and Grandma was in Mississippi. I had a little brother who desperately needed some kind of male role model in his life and a mother who was totally lost and confused.

I suddenly lost my childhood.

I was 13 at the time. I was in seventh grade.

Seventh grade came and went with a whimper... Eighth grade was next. I didn't expect much from eighth grade, even though we were now the *big kids!*

Big kids? Yah, right, I was 4'10" and weighed 75 pounds! Some *big* kid, eh?

THE IMPACTS

In 8th grade I realized that one of my classmates at school, Larry Welsh, played drums. Now, I never played a cheap guitar in my life. Mom had given me the Martin archtop R17. That's what I learned on. (The old Martin is still around. My brother, Mike, has it hanging on his wall at his home. It really isn't playable anymore and is probably better there than sitting in a closet at my house.) But if you're gonna play with a drummer, you need an electric guitar.

Larry Welsh on drums with me on the right playing guitar.

Note the Dixie cup around my microphone — this was my invention to get more gain out of the mic. I spray painted it silver and put glitter on it so it would look cool.

On the Move

Right after we moved to 6432 Wade, my mom decided to become a real estate agent with my uncle who lived in St. Peters, Missouri. She bought a house from my uncle and we moved to O'Fallon, Missouri. We lived in what was then *the suburbs* for about two months. Real estate was not making it for her and Danny and I *hated* it out there.

We moved back to Dogtown to 1123 Louisville... for two months.

Then we moved to 6843 Waldemar because a friend, who lived two doors down from there, talked her into it. Then the friend moved and there we were.

After a brief stint on Waldemar, we finally landed at 1434 Tamm.

Back on Tamm Avenue... *again!*

So from 1961 to 1962, a little more than a year, we moved five times!

The grandfather of my best friend, Ricky Burch, had a Fender Esquire. Rick was able to talk him out of it for a short while. I remember that we dragged all Larry's drums down to St. James schoolyard in Dogtown, along with the Fender Esquire and an amp that Larry's grandfather owned.

We set up and played the only song we knew — an instrumental called "Wild Weekend" that featured a saxophone! We did not, however, have a saxophone player, but we played the background to it and everyone knew what it was. The twinkle in the girls' eyes, the envy on the guys' faces, and my absolute love for music were enough to convince me that I'd found something I wanted to do.

Martin archtop R17

Larry and I would practice constantly over the following year. I lost the use of the Fender Esquire along the way, but by the luck of the Irish, Larry's grandfather had a Gibson L5 with a DeArmond pickup that he let me use. This guitar would be worth a fortune today. I told you, I never played a cheap guitar.

Fender Esquire

When I finally got to high school, Larry said, "Let's start a band!"

Our first attempt was The Impacts. This was comprised of Larry Welsh (drums), Bill Booth (guitar), two saxophones (Tom Zuzenak and a fella I can't remember his name), Ronnie "Maynard" Schwarz (vocals), and myself.

We played parties around our neighborhood. We had a singer because I was too shy to sing, even though I could. Ronnie was not a good singer, but he had the courage, so he got the job. One night, when we were playing at a party, everyone was asking for "Nadine," a Chuck Berry song that was #1. Ronnie didn't know the song, but Larry knew I did. Larry yelled out, "Pat knows how to sing it!"

I wanted to kill him. Ronnie made fun of me and said, laughing, "Yah, let Pat sing it." So I did... the kids went crazy. I ended up singing it four times that night.

Left to right: Me, Larry Welsh (drummer), Ronnie "Maynard" Schwarz (vocalist), unknown tenor sax player, Tom Zuzenak (alto sax), (kneeling) Bill Booth (Guitar).

The Impacts at the Chase Park Plaza's Zodiac Room

Upon realizing I could muster the courage to sing in public and the fact that Ronnie had made fun of me, I fired him and took over singing. At one point we replaced the other guitar for a piano player to get a gig at the Chase Park Plaza in the Zodiac room.

We really thought we'd arrived!

Larry (drummer) and I left and started playing with a different guitar player from Dogtown named John Colletta. John was (for the time) a good guitar player. He also had nice equipment — a Fender Stratocaster and a Fender Super Reverb amp.

I had a good friend in eighth grade named Mike Roggers who wanted to play bass for us. His mom bought him a Fender Bassman amp and a Framus bass. The only problem was, he didn't know how to play it. John Colletta showed him some things and he took some lessons. When we played a party, if Mike didn't know the song, he'd put the amp on stand-by and fake playing. Eventually, through playing and lessons, he got pretty good.

my first song (1965)

A^7-B^7-D^7-E^7

"(HEART OF STONE)"

E^7-G flat-B^7-E^7

Stacotta Tempo

(A^7)   (B^7)   (D^7)
(Well You All Know Her) (But Not By) (Name)

(E^7)   (A^7)   (B^7)   (D^7)
(You Say That You) (Don't) (But Now There All The)(Same)

(E^7)   (A^7)   (B^7)
(I'll Give You A) (Hint At What She's) (Known)

(E^7)   (A^7)
(A HEART OF)STONE)

_____

CHORUS*
(E^7)   (G Flat)
(And If You) (Ever Meet Up With A Girl Like This You Better
(G Flat)   (B^7) -- ----------
Proceed With Caution,Because She'll) (Break Your Heart Break

(E^7)
It In two) (While Your Not Watching)
_____

(A^7)   (B^7)   (D^7)   (E^7)
(I Know Her) (Kind) (They'll Confuse Your) (Mind)

(A^7)   (B^7)   (D^7)
(They'll Make You) (Wish That You Were) (Dead)

(A^7)   (B^7)   (D^7)   (E^7)
(You Know By) (Now) (As What She's) (Known)

(E^7)   (A^7)
(A HEART OF)STONE)
(*)

(A^7)   (B^7)   (D^7)   (E^7)
(Take It From) (Me) (Watch Out For These) (Girls)

(A^7)   (B^7)   (A^7)   (E^7)
(There All The) (Same) (All Round The) (World)

(A^7)   (B^7)   (D^7)   (E^7)
(The Worse You) (Treat Them) (The Better They) (Love You)

(A^7)   (B^7)   (D^7)   (E^7)
(Then They Won't) (Leave You) (Cause They Think Too Much) (Of You)

(A^7)   (B^7)   (E^7)   (A^7)   (B^7)
(Then You Can) (Break) (There Heart of) (Stone For A) (Change)

Larry's parents decided to move to North County that summer and the Gibson L5 went back to his grandfather. Mom realized that I was very serious about music and she took me to Tower Grove Music on Manchester and bought me a used Sunburst Gretsch Anniversary guitar. She paid $200 for it. It did not dawn on me then what an incredible sacrifice that was for her in those days.

Mom did things for people in such a casual manner that you just felt it was no big deal to her. She drove me to all my gigs, no matter how far away, then she would come back and pick me up. I eventually got a license of my own. Then she let me use her car until I, all but, destroyed it. Mom was long suffering and would do whatever it took to get me started. She was the most sacrificial woman on the planet.

I did manage to save enough money for a Fender Concert amp and later sold the Gretsch Anniversary for what Mom paid and bought a used orange 1961 Gretsch Chet Atkins for $200 — an even swap. I still have that guitar and it's worth a wee bit more than what I paid for it.

Sunburst Gretsch Anniversary

THE SKEPTORS

I was afraid, with Larry moving, we might be done, but Larry's parents had bought him a car so we continued to play. We started another band with a new guitar player named Joe Pousosa. Joe lived in Dogtown and was from Cuba (no, not Cuba, Missouri... Cuba the country). He was very good and also sang. He could sing "La Bamba" and actually knew the words. He did instrumentals like "Perfidia," too. It soon became a real band with Joe. We called ourselves The Skeptors. I got the name from the *Sceptor* record label and changed the spelling.

We eventually added a trumpet player named Tom Stallone (from the north side where Larry lived) and a sax player named Paul Kerner. I even took a stab at songwriting and wrote a song called "Heart of Stone." It wasn't exactly "Blue Mist" but I was proud of it. I wrote *stacotta tempo*, on my lyric sheet because I saw that on some sheet music once. I had no clue what it meant... and, of course, I misspelled it.

As with most bands in those days, we all wanted to be Bob Kuban clones. Bob Kuban & The In-Men were a St. Louis staple. They had a national top-10 hit called "The Cheater."

They played all the Teen Towns and colleges around the area. Bands would have the exact same line-up that Bob had. Well... Bob Kuban's band only had one guitar... and The Skeptors had two. I was the leader, so I wasn't leaving. So we let Joe go. To this day I feel bad about that. Joe was, and still is, a very sweet guy, and I cannot hear "La Bamba" without thinking of him.

When Larry moved to the north side it opened up a line to all these great musicians that he went to high school with. This would lead to my first big horn band. We eventually got cards (still The Skeptors) and matching outfits!

The new group consisted of Larry Welsh (drums), Mike Roggers (bass), Bill Noltkamper (keys), Tom Stallone (trumpet), Vince Sala (saxophone), Joe Leppart (trombone), and myself on guitar. We had an off and on front singer, too, whose name was Terry Sparks. He fronted because, yep... Bob Kuban had a front singer. Bands would even buy the exact same PA as Kuban if they could afford it. He used those big outdoor university horns (which sounded awful) and Bogen power amps.

On a side note: We couldn't afford those university speakers and my Dogtown buddies knew that. They told me they'd pitched in and gotten us some. They were used, but worked great. One night I happened to look on the underside of one of the speakers and there, stenciled, was *Property of CBC High School.*

Apparently one of the guys had shimmied up two 40' poles on the football field and *borrowed* them. I painted over it and moved on. They meant well.

Prior to getting Bill Noltkamper on keys, we had tried out several other keyboard players. There was this one guy that came to a try out. I recognized him from seeing him at Teen Towns. He was a wild dancer. He'd do flips and splits, etc. Not in a nutty way — he was really good at it. So here he was trying out for keyboards. He came down the basement with a small case. I thought, *Where's his Farfisa or Vox Continental organ?* Again, thats what Kuban used so there was no room for anything else.

The guy pulls an *accordion* out and starts putting it on. I said, "Whoa, whoa... what the hell is that?"

"An accordion," he says smiling.

I just said "No. We are NOT a polka band. NO accordions!"

He tried pleading his case, but I was firm and wouldn't even let him play it. He left, but it wasn't the last I'd see of him... we would hook up many years from then when he had *real* equipment. His name was Frank Gagliano.

We all had matching royal blue outfits with double-breasted sweaters that were almost identical to Bob Kuban's band. We even had matching Beatle boots. We played all around the St. Louis area... mostly Teen Towns. Bob Kuban wrote a weekly article in the *Post-Dispatch* about the music scene in St. Louis and we got the headline once: *Skeptors on the Rise.*

Skeptors on the Rise

By Bob Kuban

COMING UP in popularity among St. Louis area bands are the Skeptors, a group that plays the American style of music. They have been together for about six months and won two Battle of the Bands for Capitol Records Search '66 on July 30. They were featured at a dance at St. Thomas the Apostle in Florissant yesterday. They will be at St. James Parish Teen-Town Aug. 21. They will also appear in the finals of Search '66 tomorrow.

Bob Kuban

day at St. Peters CYC in Charles.

Tommy James and the S dells, will appear at Chai Rocks Swimming Pool Mon On Tuesday, the Del Rays be featured at a teen danc Collinsville Park.

The Search '66 winners last week were the Malibus the Impacts.

Don't forget, tomorrow is date for the finals for Fam Capitol Search '66. Sp guests will be B. J. Tho Vince Perri, and Steve (mings and the Creels

One of our big thrills came in 1966. Capitol Records was sponsoring an event called "Search '66" — a competition between local bands. Supposedly, the winner was to get a recording contract with Capitol Records or something. The way it went was, four or five bands would compete each week, each doing two songs. This would happen for about four weeks. Then the winners would compete for a playoff. It was extremely hard to even get into the competition.

I was approached by a kid named Mike Diehl. He was a singer, of sorts. What he lacked in vocal ability, he made up for in wild showmanship! He said if we would back him on one song, he'd let us do the other song without him. Well, we jumped at it!

So, he sang "I Feel Good" by James Brown. His approach was so bizarre that the judges actually loved it. Then we did a very good rendition of Bob Kuban's arrangement

OUR FIRST List

SKEPTORS

SONG LIST

1. PRANCIN
2. MONEY
3. SHAKE A TAIL FEATHER
4. LOUIE LOUIE
5. YOU CAN'T JUDGE A BOOK
6. SLEEPWALK
7. SLOOPY
8. HIGH HEEL SNEAKERS
9. DO YOU LOVE ME
10. I FEEL GOOD (I GOT YOU)
11. FEVER
**12. HOLD IT (BREAK)
_____

13. OUT OF SIGHT
14. WHAT'D I SAY
15. TREAT HER RIGHT
16. BOOGALOO
17. THAT BOY
18. MIDNIGHT HOUR
19. ILL NEVER COME BACK
20. LONG TALL TEXAN
21. HITCH HIKE
22. PRETTY BABY
23. HONKY TONK
24. TWIST AND SHOUT
**25. HOLD IT (BREAK)
_____

26. OOH POO PA DOO
27. BIG BOY PETE
28. HEARTS OF STONE
29. BATMAN
30. GOOD GOOD LOVIN
31. THIS POOR HEART
32. I'LL GO CRAZY
33. I GOT A WOMAN
34. TIME IS ON MY SIDE
35. CARAVAN
**36. HOLD IT (BREAK)

JOE--LEAD GUITAR
PAT--RHYTHYM GUITAR
MIKE--BASS GUITAR
LARRY--DRUMS
TOM--TRUMPET
PAUL--SAX
****

of "Theme from Virginia Wolfe" — an instrumental. What we didn't know was Greg Hoeltzel, the keyboard player from Bob Kuban's band, was one of the judges and had had a lot to do with the original arrangement. So between the crazy antics of Mike Diehl and the *perfect* second song.... we won!

Search '66 winners, The Skeptors. Left to right: Joe Leppert (trombone), Vince Sala (saxophone), Tom Stallone (trumpet), Me, Larry Welsh (drums), Mike Roggers (bass), and Bill Noltkamper (keyboards)

One of the other bands that day was a group called Jerry Jay & The Sheratons. They had a lot of pull and got the closing spot. Their stage outfits were amazing for the time and (truth be known) they were probably a lot better than us. One of the singers was a guy named Chuck Sabatino. He later had a group called A Full Moon Consort.

The other male singer was amazing and very young. I had offered him a job with my band just prior to this competition. His response was, "I'd love to, but they already bought me a coat." So, I missed having this kid sing with us because of a coat. The kid's name was Michael McDonald.

Years later we spoke in Los Angeles and I brought up the Search '66 event. He remembered it well and said, "We lost to a band that had this crazy singer." When I said that it was my band he laughed because he had no idea. So, I was bigger than Michael McDonald... for a few minutes.

Jerry Jay & The Sheratons with a young Michael McDonald (far right).

THE MELLA FELLAS

I played throughout high school with the band. We changed the band's name to the Mella Fellas. Not really sure why. Maybe we thought it sounded more soulful. We added a baritone sax. We didn't *need* a baritone sax, but it was cool sounding and the guy we hired, Tim Evans, was a really good friend and funny as hell. We also added a female singer named Michelle Cardillo. She was an absolutely amazing singer.

The bass player, Mike Roggers, left the band to join the Marines and I replaced him with a 15-year-old bass player by the name of Gary Bourgeois. He was fabulous. He could sing background, too. (His brother, John, played excellent guitar and we were friends.)

Left to right: Me, Bill Noltkamper, Michelle Cardillo, Larry Welsh

I used to have to pick Gary up for gigs. Apparently, I had a bad reputation and Gary's mom didn't want her little boy playing in my band. He would leave the house saying he was going to go jam with some friends. He'd put his stage clothes in a bag and I would pick him up at the corner a block away. His mom was sweet and was just being protective. She and I ended up being friends eventually.

Not long after this, I broke the Mella Fellas up.

THE ST. LOUIS INSTITUTE OF MUSIC

I started college at the St. Louis Institute of Music in 1967. The Institute of Music was an artistic epiphany for me. I attended with some of my old bandmates, Bill Noltkamper, Tom Stallone, and Tim Evans. I loved these guys to death.

We basically reeked havoc on the stodgy environment there. We were coined "The Mafia" by one of the students. I'm not sure why — Bill actually tried to be a good student. Tom and Tim were funny as hell.

with Susan Bush

I remember that the four of us found still-in-the-box, authentic, *blue suede shoes* at some shoe warehouse downtown. They were probably left over stock from the 50s. We'd wear our blue suede shoes and what we called *bebop hats*. We'd sneak in to our Music Literature class early in the morning and put Bill Haley & The Comets records on the record player and swing dance. The teacher, Dr. Adams, found little entertainment in this when he would walk in to class in the morning, but the students thought it was great.

There was an annex building that had practice rooms which were very small rooms with upright pianos. We would pack — and I mean *pack* — kids in there and sing Beatle songs. This also was frowned upon which (of course) made it even more fun.

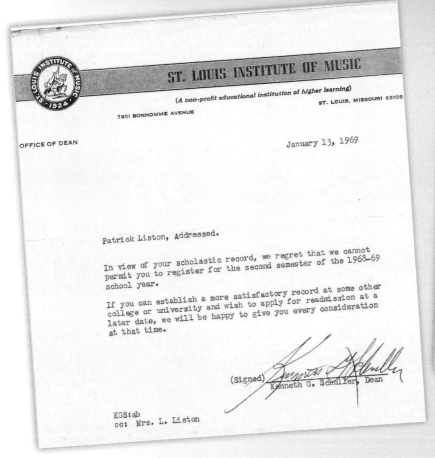

ST. LOUIS INSTITUTE OF MUSIC

(A non-profit educational institution of higher learning)

7801 BONHOMME AVENUE

ST. LOUIS, MISSOURI 63105

OFFICE OF DEAN

January 13, 1969

Patrick Liston, Addressed.

In view of your scholastic record, we regret that we cannot permit you to register for the second semester of the 1968-69 school year.

If you can establish a more satisfactory record at some other college or university and wish to apply for readmission at a later date, we will be happy to give you every consideration at that time.

(Signed) *Kenneth G. Schuller*
Kenneth G. Schuller, Dean

KGS:ab
cc: Mrs. L. Liston

1967-68 School Year
1st Semester

LISTON, PATRICK

	Piano (Hassler)	B✓
ACI	String Class	A
A100C	Chorus	no report
B001A	Pre-College Aural Theory	A
B001W	Pre-College Written Theory	A
B103	Music Lit. and Comparative Arts	F
11-101	English Composition and Rhetoric	no report
9-206	General Psychology	F
	Physical Education	D

Velma T. Honig

I surely hope you will study harder and raise the circled grades by the end of the semester.

Most of the students were from other states. This truly broadened my horizons. One person who stands out above all was a young woman named Susan Bush. She was very funny and very talented. Susan actually taught me to finger pick guitar. She had a beautiful voice, too. I remember her singing one song in particular, "Banks of the Ohio." It was my introduction to folk music.

Susan and I were the best of friends for the two short years I attended. Susan was also the one that suggested I leave St. Louis and go to California. My piano teacher, Miss Hassler, also recommended I leave before the school sterilized my gift for music.

I did quite well at my music classes, but poorly in scholastics, which confused the Principal, Miss Honig. I was going to school and working a 40-hour a week job. At some point I'd saved enough money to do *something*. Susan Bush had left about six months prior and I knew I needed a change.

My decision for change was — eventually — made for me. I basically got *the boot* from school.

While still attending college, I decided to just join a band and loosen some of the *leader* headaches. I joined a band for about a year called the Soulful Illusions. They had horns, a full rhythm section, and four singers up front who would have given the Temptations a run for their money. I got very close to the bass player, Rudy Coleman. When I tried out for the band, Rudy showed me a list of songs and asked if I knew them. I looked them over and said, yes — they were standard R&B favorites. When we started playing he stopped after about 12 bars and said, "I thought you said you knew these?"

THE UNFORGETTABLE SOULFUL ILLUSION

LEON KAPLAN
4323 MARCUS • ST. LOUIS, MO. 63115
AC 314 — 647-1111

I said, "I do... there's a **G** and a **C** and..."

He stopped me and said, "I didn't ask if you knew the chords, I asked if you knew the songs."

I was immediately embarrassed and went on the defense. I was incensed that he would question my ability on songs I had played for years in *my* band! I started packing my gear. He said, "Whoa, whoa... damn, why are white boys so sensitive?"

He managed to calm me down and said he wanted to teach me about feel. He said, "The hell with the chords, Brother, feel it... feel it."

He would call me on a Friday or Saturday night and say he was at "such and such" bar down on Delmar, or somewhere, and to come down and bring my gear. On one occasion, there was this group called the Montclairs. We started off playing and I was lost immediately. I said to Rudy, "Does this drummer ever hit **2** and **4**?!"

He started laughing and said, "You have to hear it in your head... I'll get you started and then you count and see what happens."

As I locked in and was counting, I suddenly heard a groove like nothing I'd ever heard before! It was the most amazing thing I had ever experienced musically. I looked at Rudy with my eyes as wide as saucers. He said, "It's bad ass when it's right, ain't it? I knew you could do it."

Soulful Illusions

Rudy was a brilliant artist. I admired his wisdom — wisdom I had thought came from age. It wasn't until I attended his funeral many, many years later, looked at the funeral card, and realized Rudy was two years younger than I was. Rudy's wisdom came from the streets. I never forgot what Rudy taught me, but more importantly *how* he taught me. He had a patience and a kindness I sorely lacked.

During this time I also did some recording with one of the members of the Soulful Illusions named Morris Vaughn. It was my first recording experience. We recorded at Archway Sound Studios on Natural Bridge in St. Louis. It was owned by Oliver Sain. This was when I first met Oliver.

Oliver Sain

We were recording two sides — "Just One Look" and "Help Me." I recorded with Brenda Foster, a school mate at the St. Louis Institute of Music, on keys and Jimmy Hinds, who played drums and over dubbed bass as well. I (obviously) played guitar.

I remember "Help Me" had what's called *pedal tone chords* which means I played a chord up on the neck and would have a lower string open. In this case it would have been the **A** string — a sort of drone sound. When we started playing the song Oliver stopped the recording and asked, "Who's doing that boom thing?"

Archway Sound Studios

We didn't know what he meant, at first. He said, "It sounds like the guitar."

I played the pedal tone chord and said, "You mean this?"

"Yah!"

"Those are called pedal tone chords," I explained.

While with the Soulful Illusions, we were booked to play a couple of colleges in Oklahoma. The day we were supposed to fly there, the drummer bailed for some reason and couldn't make it. Rudy was in a panic.

My brother, Danny, who was only about 14, had sat in with us once when the drummer was late. Soulful Illusions had a set show, and Danny knew it because he had been listening to the show on a reel-to-reel recorder. A Dogtown friend of ours, Danny Miller, bought my brother a cheap set of drums. He had been practicing so much that I was shocked when he sat in and knew the breaks and everything.

So, Rudy called my mom and asked if he could take Danny. This was her baby and he was 14! Rudy promised he would keep a close eye on him and Mom finally relented. We had no time for anything. Poor Danny went with only the clothes on his back, but he really did a good job. I marvel even more now thinking about it. He was just a kid and learned their entire show lick for lick and pulled it off! I enjoyed playing R&B music, but Danny had a natural passion for it. He still does to this day.

So, 1968 was the first concert that Danny and I did together. Little did we know what would come years later.

"I don't care what they're called. Don't do that," he directed. "It's pinning my needles
in here."

I said, "That's the way we wrote it."

He said, "Well, that ain't the way you're gonna record it, you're red linin' in here."

I was flustered, but acquiesced. Morris released a single. Not much came of it, but it was cool being on a real record.

Also, during this time, I had become friends with Greg Edick. His father, George Edick, owned the Club Imperial at Goodfellow and W. Florissant. There were tons of well-known bands that came in and out of the Club Imperial. Probably the most notable was the Ike & Tina Turner Review. I saw them several times there. Years later when Tina exposed Ike's physical abuse, he denied it, but I saw him hit her one night at Club Imperial on one of the breaks. So Tina was definitely telling the truth.

Club Imperial located at Goodfellow Boulevard and W. Florissant Avenue

Greg took me to Oliver Sain's studio one day to see Ike and Tina record. The musical tracks had already been recorded so the band wasn't there, but Ike was. Tina was laying a vocal track. When we walked in I asked Greg where Tina was. He said, "She's right there," pointing to a woman with really short hair, dressed plainly, and wearing house slippers.

I said, "That's not Tina Turner."

Greg laughed and said, "Man, she doesn't wear her stage outfit or a wig to record."

When she started singing they let us stay in the room she was recording in as long as we were quiet. I was thrilled! She was laying a track of "Ode To Billie Joe." Ike kept making her do it over and over until her voice was getting worn down. Oliver didn't have enough recording tracks to save the previous takes (which I thought were better) so she had to settle for the latter takes.

Ike and Tina Turner

Ike kept yelling at her, saying she could do better. I felt bad for her.

She'd written all the lyrics down and when the session was over, I timidly asked if I could have the lyric sheet. She smiled that sweet Tina smile and said, "Sure, Baby," and handed them to me. Years later I made the mistake of showing them to a bandmate's one-night stand, and she stole them.

I started seriously writing songs in college. Even though I had taken a stab at writing once, I considered this period the genesis of my writing career. I wrote three songs during this time. They were "You Think That There's a Difference," "From That Day On," and "A Love Of The Real Kind." I felt they had a maturity that convinced me I was ready to do something serious.

One of my idols at that time was a guy named Jimmy Webb, one of the most prolific songwriters of the late 60s. I'd read how he'd gone to California and gotten so successful. So, I had Susan Bush from college, Jimmy Webb, and my piano teacher to inspire me to *go west young man...* and I did.

WORDS & MUSIC BY   3/69
PAT LISTON

A Love of the REAL KIND

THE GIRL of MY DREAMS I FIND
ISN'T REALLY THE GIRL THAT SHE SEEMS.
FUNNY, IN DREAMS, WHEN SUN
BRINGS THE DAWN YOU THINK LOVE
IS GONE. BUT YOU'LL FIND AS THE
DAWN SLOWLY BRINGS THE DAY. THAT
GIRL THAT HAS A REAL LOVE FOR YOU.
SHE WILL COME YOUR WAY. SHE MAY
NOT BE THE LOVE THAT YOU THINK
YOUR DREAMIN OF. BUT SHE'S THE
ONE WHO LIVES & DIES FOR YOUR LOVE.
SHE'S THE ONE WHILE YOUR AWAKEN
YOUR THINKIN OF. AND AFTER
ALL, YOU SEE, A ~~——~~ DREAM CAN
ONLY BE A SECOND OF YOUR TIME & WHATS
A SECOND TO A LOVE OF THE REAL KIND!
DON'T YOU CONFUSE & DARE NOT
ABUSE THE LOVE THAT YOU HAVE WHILE
YOUR AWAKE. DON'T BE MISLED
BY THINGS IN YOUR HEAD WHILE YOUR
ASLEEP. IF YOUR LUCKY & HAVE A
LOVE YOU CAN COUNT ON. THEN
DON'T LOOK FOR LOVE FROM THE
GIRL IN YOUR DREAMS. BECAUSE WHEN
DAY BREAKS SHE'LL BE GONE
BECAUSE A LOVE, YOU SEE, IS BASED
ON REALITY. AND REALITY IS
WHAT YOU WANT. A DREAM JUST
LAST TIL DAYBREAK. YOU BETTER
KEEP THE LOVE YOU'VE GOT. I'M SAYING
THIS FOR YOUR ~~SAKE~~. BUT DID

YOU EVER THINK, YOU SEE, YOUR
GIRL IN REALITY COULD POSSIBLY
BE. THE GIRL IN YOUR DREAMS
& THAT YOU ALSO FEEL A LOVE OF
THE REAL KIND.

THE CITY OF ANGELS

On June 15th, 1969, I flew to Los Angeles literally on a wing and a prayer. I really knew no one there. I'd lied to Mom and told her a friend was going to put me up. When I got to LAX, I simply asked a taxi driver to take me to a motel... any motel.

He drove me to downtown Los Angeles to the Kent Motel on Figueroa.

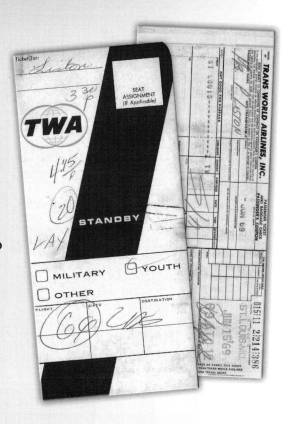

I remember the following day I met a man who said his son was Gary Puckett from Gary Puckett & The Union Gap. I figured I'd done the right thing. I mean, you wouldn't meet a celebrity's father in St. Louis, now, would you?

I obviously had to come clean with Mom about the friend. I still lied though... I said he didn't show at the airport. Mom immediately did what mom's do... she went into action.

She talked to my older brother, Mike. He said that Dave Moharc, one of his Marine buddies, lived in LA. So, she gave me his address and phone number and I promised I would contact him. I knew Dave and his wife, Bev, so I wasn't uncomfortable contacting them. I bought an LA map at the motel. As it turned out, they only lived about six miles from where I was. That may not seem strange, but LA is a huge city. So, with map in hand, I *walked* to their house. I remember Bev being shocked that I'd walked that far.

As fate would have it, there was a carriage house right next to them that was going to be for rent in about a month or less. Bev and Dave offered to let me stay with them for the waiting period — a kind gesture I never forgot.

So my new address was 1647 Golden Gate.

I joined the musicians union and started looking for work. I contacted a friend of my mother's who had lived in St. Louis for a while. Her name was Elaine Rentschler and she managed a singer in LA. She was my first musical contact. She got me a job at this private club called the Standard Club. It sounded glamorous, but all they needed was a dishwasher. I needed money, so... a dishwasher it was.

Elaine did her best to shop my music and help me connect with other musicians. She was very supportive, but couldn't seem to help me much.

I truly loved Elaine for all she tried to do, but I think she was too good-hearted for Los Angeles. So, we discontinued our business relationship. She passed away from lung cancer only about a year or two later. I wrote a song for her simply called "Song For Elaine."

Elaine Rentschler (far left)

Elaine M. Rentschler
TALENT DIVISION

CARLAINE RECORDING CO.
6666 WEBER ROAD
ST. LOUIS, MO. 63123

314 ME 1-8250

12/9/72 SONG FOR ELAINE

BRIGHT LITES & THE MUSIC
BECAME A PART OF YOU
BUT LACK OF UNDERSTANDING
~~THE~~ DISTORTED YOUR POINT
OF VIEW
MANY SAID THEY LOVED YOU
THOUGH I ~~COULDN'T~~ NEVER SAW
THEM TRY THEN WHEN
YOUR ~~LORD CALLED YOU~~ THEIR
WERE THE FIRST TO ~~~~ CRY

IT WOULD BRING ME PAIN
IF I THOUGHT YOU LIVED YOUR LIFE
IN VAIN, CAUSE GOD KNOWS
I WOULD NOT BE THE SAME
IF I HADN'T KNOWN
YOUR NAME, ELAINE.

WHEN I FELT SO EMPTY
YOU FILLED ME WITH A SMILE
WHEN I WAS SO LONELY
YOU STAYED WITH MEA

YOU SAID DON'T ~~~~ YOU
LISTEN TO WHAT THESE
PEOPLE SAY, JUST BEILIEVE
IN GOD, BOY, & HE WILL
GUIDE YOUR WAY!
(——)
NOW THAT YOUR EXISTENCE
SEEMS LIKE A DREAM I HAD
KNOWING THAT YOUR HAPPY
HELPS ME WHEN I'M SAD
SOME MEN CRY FOR PITY
OTHERS CRY FROM PAIN
THIS MAN CRYS FROM SORROW
CAUSE I'VE LOST MY ELAINE

I got another job through one of the members of the Standard Club who owned a chain of surplus stores called D/Jack Frost. They needed help straightening out a warehouse. The warehouse was the biggest mess I'd ever seen and messes of this magnitude always overwhelmed me. I took the bus or hitchhiked to work. The main store was in Santa Monica, a two-hour bus ride with transfers each way. I made $64.27 take home a week.

One day I overheard the boss say they needed a truck driver who knew the LA area. I told him I knew the LA area like the back of my hand. I then went and bought a road atlas for the City of Los Angeles and surrounding areas. I was always good with maps.

I loved driving because I learned the city and I would go to lunch at my house so I didn't have to pay for food.

The store had a variety of odd clothes that were perfect for a hippie's weird taste. I would buy the clothes and put them in the truck so I could drop them off at my house, saving me the trouble of dragging them with me on the bus.

One of D/Jack's friends apparently saw the truck at my house and saw me taking clothes in and told Jack I was stealing. I tried explaining to Jack what happened, but he fired me anyway. This was a blessing because it forced me to try to find music work. I was gone 12 to 13 hours a day working so I never had time.

A week later, two friends from St. Louis came out to stay with me a while — Tom Kaiser and Terry Shaw. They both had money they'd saved and helped me out. Terry asked me one day if I'd already used my unemployment?

I said, "My what?"

He said, "You worked in St. Louis, so you should be collecting unemployment." I went down the following day to the Hollywood unemployment agency and started collecting. I loved going there because all the bit part actors collected there. I remember seeing Larry Storch and Clint Walker.

For a short period I signed a management deal with Billy Ward of Billy Ward & The Dominoes. They were very big in the 50s. They had several top-10 hits. Clyde McPhatter (Platters) and Jackie Wilson were two of the many members of the Dominoes. Billy was very experienced and knowledgeable, but most of his concepts were stuck in the 50s... which was not where I wanted to be. He released me from my contract about a month later when he found out I had a low military draft number. The release said he was doing it so I could pursue a band, but the truth is he didn't want to put a lot of work into a guy who was probably going to get drafted.

8913 W. Olympic Boulevard
Beverly Hills, Calif. 90211
January 26, 1970

Mr. Patrick E. Liston
1647 Golden Gate
Los Angeles, Calif. 90026

Dear Mr. Liston:

Pursuant to our understanding and agreement you are hereby released from the Personal Management Contract between Billy Ward Enterprises, Inc. and yourself, dated November 7, 1969 and the Employment Contract as a member of the Dominoes, between Billy Ward and yourself, dated November 12, 1969. This is done to comply with your wishes and request to form a musical unit of your own, and free youto proceed with your plans as of this date.

In affirmation of the above, please sign where indicated below.

Very truly yours

BILLY WARD, President
Billy Ward Enterprises, Inc.

BILLY WARD, Leader
Billy Ward and his Dominoes

ACCEPTED:

Patrick E. Liston

There is a club in West Hollywood called Doug Weston's Troubadour. It's still there. It was one of the most famous places around at the time. They had amateur night on Mondays. You could come in and put your name on a list. They would pick names and you would get up and sing two original songs.

I went down one Monday, guitar in hand. I took the bus because I didn't have a car. I was so nervous I thought I was going to throw up, but I put my name in. I got picked to be on the list! They'd print it (it was probably hand written) and give you a copy so you knew when you were up next, so as not to slow the process down.

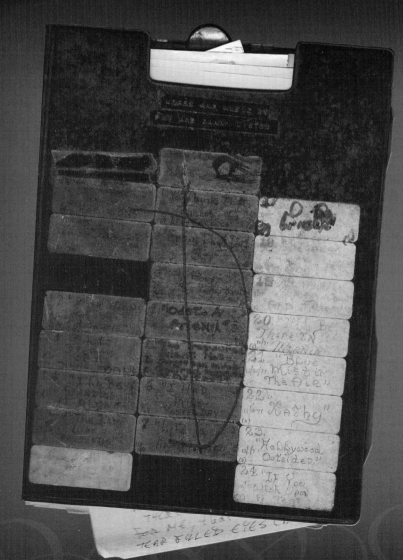

I started writing like crazy.

I had a binder that I would put stickers on with the titles of each song I'd written and the date. I still have that binder, but most of the stickers are pretty hard to read anymore.

I even put a lot of my brother Danny's songs on there. There would be a **D** in parentheses when it was one of his songs.

I was always very proud of all Danny had learned to do with very little help from anybody.

I was only two people away from my big moment when in walks Gordon Lightfoot — who already had songs on the charts. Someone asked him to *sit in*.

Gordon Lightfoot

Really... on amateur night?

He got up onstage and finished the night and I never got to sing at the Troubadour. I've hated his music ever since! Who knows... he may have spared me humiliation because my songs weren't that good at the time. But if I'm going to fail, let me do it on my own time!

I used to beat the streets of Sunset — go to publishers and drop off songs. One of the places I went one day was United Artists on Sunset. I had a song that I thought was a good song... it also had an 11-word title: "The Treasured Silent Not Forgotten Much Desired Memories of My Past." I thought it was a novel idea and would get someone's attention. The guy at UA was a pretty cool guy actually. His name was Eddie Reeves. He loved the concept and the song. He offered to publish the song right on the spot. Then he says, "You know who could do this? Andy Williams."

I thought, *Okay, Andy Williams is a big star... I'm in.*

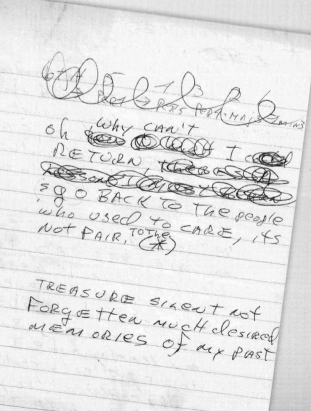

Then he picked up the phone and called Andy right on the spot — I almost choked on my gum. He kept saying what a great song it was. When he got off the phone he said, "Andy is in the studio now and all the songs have been chosen and arranged already. M a y b e   on the next album?"

Well, I learned later in life that this business is about the right place and the right time... everything is about the *moment*. UA published my song, but no one ever recorded it.

This song was my inspiration though. If Eddie Reeves from United Artists liked it and published it — and thought Andy Williams would have liked it — then I needed to write more songs, because somebody notable thought I had worth!

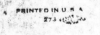

STANDARD SONGWRITERS CONTRACT

Agreement made this   27th   day of   JULY   19 70, between

UNITED ARTISTS MUSIC CO., INC.
(hereinafter called the "Publisher") and

jointly and/or severally (hereinafter called "Writer(s)"):   PATRICK LISTON

Witnesseth:

In consideration of the agreement herein contained and of the sum of One ($1.00) Dollar and other good and valuable consideration in hand paid by the Publisher to the Writer(s), receipt of which is hereby acknowledged, the parties agree as follows:

1. The Writer(s) hereby sells, assigns, transfers and delivers to the Publisher, its successors and assigns, a certain heretofore unpublished original musical composition, written and/or composed by the above named Writer(s), now entitled:

- THE TREASURED SILENT NOT-FORGOTTEN
MUCH-DESIRED MEMORIES OF MY PAST -

including the title, words and music, and all copyrights thereof, including but not limited to the copyright registration thereof No. , and all rights, claims and demands in any way relating thereto, and the exclusive right to secure copyright therein throughout the entire world, and to have and to hold the said copyrights and all rights of whatsoever nature now and hereafter thereunder existing and/or existing under any agreements or licenses relating thereto, for and during the full terms of all of said copyrights. In consideration of the agreement herein contained and the additional sum of One ($1.00) Dollar and other good and valuable consideration in hand paid by the Publisher to the Writer(s), receipt of which is hereby acknowledged, the Writer(s) hereby sells, assigns, transfers and delivers to the Publisher, its successors and assigns, all renewals and extensions of the copyrights of said musical com-

I used to go to San Fernando Valley to see bands at a place called the Rag Doll. There was a band that played there a lot called Chuck Freeman & The Drivers. Chuck, the singer, was a big Irish guy who befriended me because I looked like I was 15 and that just tickled him. One night he asked what I did and I told him I was a singer/guitar player. This amused him and he asked if I'd like to sit in.

Let me backtrack here: I wasn't really known as a singer in St. Louis, but when I moved to LA I would practice for hours on end — singing and playing. I, somehow got hold of a reel to reel tape player and started taping myself.

One day I decided to listen to myself and realized that I *could* actually sing. I had strengthened my voice so much from all the practicing that it surprised even me. So, when Chuck asked me to sing I said, "Okay." He asked what I wanted to sing and I asked if they knew "Try a Little Tenderness" by Otis Redding.

Chuck almost fell off of his stool laughing. That annoyed me some because I wasn't sure what was so funny, but he said, "Sure... go for it."

When the song got to the end section with all the "gotta, gottas" I saw him laughing at the bar. This really pissed me off. The harder he'd laugh the more I would dig in and scream.

When I finished he came over and said, "Holy shit, Kid, where did *that* come from?"

I said, "What the hell were you laughing at?"

He said, "Oh no, no. I wasn't laughing at your performance, I was laughing at Otis Redding's voice coming out of Donny Osmond's face."

I reluctantly took that as a compliment.

He said, "You need to get in a band."

I left feeling energized that night. Our path's would cross again later.

69-2220

RAGDOLL

769-2221

11702 VICTORY BLVD., NO. HOLLYWOOD

(CORNER VICTORY AND LANKERSHIM)

THE MANAGEMENT AND STAFF

proudly present the famous

Chuck Freeman
&
The Drivers

(The Heaviest Sound to Hit The Valley)

SUNDAY — CONTINUOUS JAM, 6:00 A.M. - 2:00 A.M.
LIVE MUSIC & DANCING FREE SPAGHETTI DINNERS
MONDAY — SOUL & TALENT NITE
TUESDAY — DANCE CONTEST, CASH PRIZES
WEDNESDAY — BIG JOE TURNER singing his famous
Corina, Corina — Shake, Rattle & Roll and others.
Plus the famous HARMONICA FATS
THURSDAY — EVERYBODY'S NITE, BAR DRINKS 50¢
FRIDAY & SATURDAY — NO COVER BEFORE 9:30 P.M.

BOBBY & THE INNKEEPERS

My first attempt at getting in a band was something I saw in the paper. When I called, the guy asked if I was good. I said, "Well, yes. I'm pretty good."

He said, "Okay, well, we're looking for someone real good," and hung up.

The next attempt, when asked how good I was, I told them I was great! So, I got the job. The name of the band was Bobby & The Innkeepers.

Bobby Shorter, the leader, was from the Seattle area originally. The band was a real cast of characters. Bobby was African American; the sax player, Dave Cordova, was Native American; the drummer, George Subia, and the trumpet player, Jimmy Loya, were Mexican; the bass player, Laine, was a Colorado flower child type; and me. We rehearsed at Bobby's mom's house in Watts at 98th and Central.

Watts never looked scary to me. I'd rehearsed in inner city neighborhoods in St. Louis and (by comparison) Watts seemed like suburbia. After being with the Soulful Illusions, I felt right at home.

Once we were ready Bobby got this great booking agent in Hollywood — Gail McConkey. Gail was the greatest agent I have ever met. She was an older woman with a gray beehive hairdo, those glasses with the jewels in them, and tons of bead necklaces. She was a piece of work, but could book anybody if they had talent. She booked us everywhere.

❧

Gail booked us all over LA and at the Pussycat a' Go-Go in Las Vegas.

We almost got fired from the Pussy Cat because we did the Sly & The Family Stone song called "Don't Call Me Nigger, Whitey." We loved it because we were a very mixed bag of people. I would sing, "Don't call me nigger, whitey," and Bobby (who was African American) would sing, "Don't call me whitey, nigger."

We loved the ridiculousness of it all, and loved the irony. The Las Vegas club mentality did not, however, share our keen wit. We were told in no uncertain terms that if we did the song again we were fired! I won't go in to it, but the people that ran the place were racists and I think it made them uncomfortable.

Gail even booked us in Anchorage, Alaska! Two things happened in Anchorage that were pivotal for me.

One was, this guy I met that had this weird gizmo he used with his guitar. It became known years later as a *wah-wah tube*. He taught me how to make one and I used it for many many years — long before Peter Frampton popularized them.

Me with my wah-wah tube long before Peter Frampton used one.

The other thing was, the band playing right down the street was my old buddies Chuck Freeman & The Drivers. Their guitar player was leaving them and they wanted to know how to contact me. We exchanged phone numbers before I left Anchorage. They called me when they got back from Alaska and I left Bobby & The Innkeepers.

Left to right: George Subia, Jimmy Loya, Dave Cordova, Bobby Shorter, Me, and Laine in the front middle.

WILD WILD Bobbie & The Innkeepers Will Open THURS JUNE 4

They just closed at the Pussycat in Las Vegas with a smashing success and have just recorded a record on the Hollywood label. They are very versatile—

THEY PLAY IT ALL

- **Hard Rock**
- **Standards**
- **Pop**
- **Country & Western**
- **Jazz**

Bobbie & The Innkeepers are by far the most versatile band ever to hit Alaska

The drummer from Bobby & The Innkeepers, George Subia, used to call me to play guitar with him at the Classic Cat on Sunset Strip. On Sundays and Wednesdays they had what they called *amateur strip night.*

The band would be behind the curtain: George on drums, a bass player, a young woman named Lacy Jones on guitar, and myself. Women would tell you before they went out onstage what song they wanted to *dance* to. We would start playing and they would go out onstage and disrobe.

(I remember that I did this only a couple of times.)

When they were finished they would walk past us completely nude. They advertised it as topless, but it was the full monty when I was there.

One girl asked me for a cigarette and a light because hers were in her clothes. She was comically patting herself down as though she was looking for a light. She stood there talking to me about music. After a minute or two it dawned on me... *she's naked...and it doesn't seem strange!*

I decided not to play there anymore. Noticing that a woman is naked should *not* be an after thought. That is something that one should notice right away!

CHUCK FREEMAN & THE DRIVERS

I rehearsed diligently with The Drivers because they were very polished and somewhat a *show band* — but very good. They also made really good money and played the top show rooms.

I had only played one gig with them when "Uncle Sam" called me. I'd been dodging the draft by transferring my papers to what ever city I was playing. By the time I'd get notice, I was somewhere new. I thought it was a good plan, but they finally caught on and said, "Show up in LA or else."

Fate once again stepped in.

While driving to my induction, I ran a red light at Hollywood and Vine. It was very early and I was a nervous wreck. A taxi broadsided me.

My brother, Danny, was visiting me and he came with me. (I guess to drive the truck back if need be even though he couldn't drive at the time.) My elbow hit Danny's head and chipped in three places. The ambulance took us both to Hollywood Emergency. The doctor had to call the draft board because I knew they wouldn't believe me after all I'd put them through.

My elbow was locked at a 90-degree angle and I was told I would need surgery and that it was very possible I would never be able to play guitar again.

Heartbroken, I moved back to St. Louis.

I went to an older doctor that my mom knew. He said, "Let's see if these chips will work themselves loose — no sense in doing unnecessary surgery." (My how things have changed.) Within two weeks my elbow was about 80 percent straight, I was back playing guitar, and joined a local band.

The draft board wasn't about to let me off the hook though. I was served notice to appear the following week for induction. Vietnam was raging and was *not* part of my career plan. But regardless of *my* plan, I had to go downtown.

Chuck Freeman & The Drivers

I had a doctor's letter that said I wasn't fit, but they ignored it. They said I had 80 percent usage and that was enough... sure, you don't have to be 100 percent to be shot at.

I was sitting on the bench waiting to be bussed to Fort Leonard Wood when a guy walks in with the x-rays they'd taken of my elbow and said that I was 1Y — which meant I was rejected. I have had very few rushes to compare with that one. It was all so strange how it came about. God, obviously, had other plans for me.

Let me mention that while I was back in LA, just prior to this, I was a witness to an accident. I gave the young woman my name and number, but never heard from her again. Somehow — and I've never known how — she tracked me down in St. Louis and wanted me to fly to LA to be her witness in court. She would pay for everything.

"Hell yes!"

I flew to LA and she won her case... for a sizable amount as I remember. After court, she asked if she could do anything for me before I flew back to St. Louis. I said, "Yes. Find out where Chuck Freeman & The Drivers are playing."

She worked in an office and had all her workmates scouring newspapers. Keep in mind this was long, long before the internet. She did manage to find them and, oddly, they were playing within two miles of where she lived. We went to see them and they told me they were getting ready to disband and start another band. The trumpet player, Gilbert Avila, said they had been searching high and low for me, but to no avail. Imagine his shock — and mine — when I walked in just at the right time.

FRIENDS & BROTHERS

I flew back to St. Louis and within a month Gil's brother, Roy Avila, called and said they were ready to start rehearsing. Because he and Gil were brothers they had decided to call the band Friends & Brothers. This would have been sometime in 1970.

Friends & Brothers consisted of Gil Avila (leader, trumpet, keyboards, congas, and vocals), Roy Avila (saxophones, flute, keyboards, congas, and vocals), Al Romero (bass and vocals), Manny Rich (drums, valve trombone, and vocals), and myself.

They were all friends. I knew nobody, really. When I told Manny, the drummer, I was from St. Louis, he asked if I lived on a farm.

A Fun Side Story

When I flew to LA to join Friends & Brothers, I was approached on the plane by a tall African American man in a suit. He asked if I was a musician — I had long hair and was dressed like it, I guess. He said that *the boys* wanted to know if I wanted to join them in first class?

I said, "Who are *the boys*?"

He said, "The Jackson 5."

I almost fell down trying to get out of my seat.

They were indeed *boys* in 1970. They were so nice and outgoing and acted like I was the celebrity. The only one that was different was Michael — who was about 11 at the time, but looked much younger. He shook my hand, but looked at the floor when he did. He seemed painfully shy.

When I got off the plane Roy Avila was there to meet me. In those days you could come right to the plane as people got off. Tito of the Jackson 5 yelled at me as Roy and I were greeting each other. He said, "Hey, Pat, good luck with the new band!" The others waved and said goodbye as well.

I waved and said, "Thanks Tito, nice seeing you." Roy and I then started walking down the concourse together. Nothing was said for a few minutes. He kept looking at me and looking back towards the plane. Finally he said, "Who were those guys that yelled to you?"

In the most casual voice I could muster, I said, "Oh, them... that was the Jackson 5."

Roy said, "You know the Jackson 5?!"

Again, in a cool tone I simply said, "Oh yah."

It wasn't until about a year later — when we'd become very close friends — that I told him the truth.

Friends & Brothers was an excellent band. I enjoyed my time with them and made a few friendships that I still have and cherish. I gained a lot of stage confidence through this band. The bass player, Al Romero, was the most relaxed guy I've ever seen on a stage — a true showman. He rode me hard about my stage presence. He'd say, "Offstage you're funny as hell, but then you get onstage and try to be cool... it doesn't work... be yourself."

We played six nights a week. In those days you would play a club for a minimum of three weeks at a time, six nights a week. We played constantly.

We played Hawaii twice — the first time we won an award for outstanding showmanship. We went into a club that was dying on the vine and in eight weeks turned it around to being packed every night. That's the way they were... workhorses and a fun show/dance band.

Friends & Brothers in Hawaii. Left to right: Roy Avila, Me, Roy (the manager of the club), Manny Rich, Spencecliff Representative, Gil Avila, Al Romero, and another Spencecliff Representative.

Hawaii was fun because you always met celebrities. Of course, as was my way, I rarely took pictures. I did, however, get a picture with Melvin Franklin and Otis Williams of the Temptations on our second trip to Waikiki. They were really good guys.

Left to right: Me, Al Romero, Manny Rich, unknown female, Otis Williams and Melvin Franklin of the Temptations.

When I asked for a picture Melvin stood next to me to pose. The club was very crowded and I said, "No, no... let's get seats and sit down... like we know each other."

He laughed out loud, but was probably grateful for the seats because I had to run a few people off to get seats saying, "Get up, get up, this is the Temptations!"

Friends & Brothers were geared to being a *show band* — which was not my original mission for coming to California. I remember at one point my brother, Danny, came out to spend the summer of '71 with me. He was still in high school at the time. He had a bunch of new songs he'd written. He asked me what new songs I had. I didn't have any new ones at the time. He chided me about settling for bars and parties.

It really shamed me and when he left to go back to St. Louis I started writing again. The first one I wrote after he left was "Young & Free."

I felt that old feeling again — why I came here. Danny was right... I was just playing, drinking, and partying. I had lost my true passion, but it emerged when I started writing again. Although the flip side of that was, I was getting increasingly frustrated with my current musical direction.

WHEN WE WERE YOUNG & FREE

PROLOGUE

YESTERDAY IS what I REMEMBER, IT BEGAN LATE September, WATCHING SNOW FALL ON FOREST PARK. Oh how IT GLISTENED IN THE DARK.

I THINK I FEEL (NOSTALGIA COMIN ON, EVERY YEAR about the SAME TIME it COMES ON STRONG. CAUSE I REMEMBER WHAT LATE SEPTEMBER USE TO BE WHEN I WAS HOME

THE SNOW WAS STRETCHED OUT ON THE CITY WIDE JUST AS FAR AS YOU COULD ROAM

I'M NOT YOUNG ANYMORE AT LEAST NOT AS YOUNG AS BEFORE, But STILL I LONG FOR THE PAST, Oh how I WANTED it to LAST)

THOSE ARE THE things of it ALL, THATS how THINGS USE TO BE

WHAT I RECALL THAT WAS THE THRILL

when WE WERE YOUNG &

YOUNG & FREE

I REMEMBER A little BROWN HAIRED GIRL. YA you would've thought THAT SHE WAS MY whole WORLD. I USE TO GET THE BIGGEST thrill out of HOLDING HER HAND. THE FIRST TIME I KISSED THAT GIRL I FELT like SUCH A MAN. (CHORUS

SOMEDAY I JUST MAY Go BACK TO MY little WORLD, who knows, I may JUST Look up that little BROWN HAIRED GIRL. But I GUARENTEE you, if I EVER Return Go BACK I'M NEVER Gonna LEAVE AGAIN = Buddy THATS A FACT

Friends & Brothers backed up different front people or groups of people. One guy we backed up was a guy by the name of Al Wilson. He had had a marginal hit single in 1968 called "The Snake." He was a great singer and entertainer. We did several dates with him.

During this time Al had signed with another label and was having a big record release. He invited my brother, Danny, and I to the event. These things are basically schmooze-fests while the record plays in the background.

AL WILSON

I remember that a song called "Queen of the Ghetto" came on and Al said to us, "This is going to be the single."

I turned to Danny and said, "What do you think?"

Al looked at me funny and I told him, "Danny is a savant when it comes to picking hits." We were discussing it when the song ended and a song called "Show and Tell" came on. Danny put his hand up and said, "Wait... this is it... this is your hit."

Al called Snuff Garrett (the producer) over and said, "Little Brother here says this is the hit."

Snuff was polite and said something like, "Well, that's cool," and walked away.

Months later, while Danny and I were in a cab, the DJ on the cab's radio says,

"...and here's the new hit single from Al Wilson." Danny and I perked up and to Danny's delight, it was "Show and Tell." They apparently had taken Danny's advice. Danny could have been an A&R man for a record company.

Another guy Friends & Brothers backed was Donnie Brooks. He had a top-10 song in 1960 called "Mission Bell." He'd be the first to admit it was really not a great song, but he used it masterfully to carve a nice career out for himself. We'd back him and he would sing and do light comedy bits.

Some might have considered Donnie's performance corny, but he was a great business man and got us a lot of interesting gigs. Because of Donnie, we were able to back dozens of "oldies" groups. We backed the Drifters, the Coasters, the Platters, the Shirelles, Jewel Akens, the Penguins, Bobby Day, and many more. Rehearsal for these shows comprised of talking to them backstage, getting the key of the song, and going onstage and winging it!

Donnie Brooks with Friends & Brothers

At Twilight Time

Friends and Brothers, a great entertainment group, is appearing nightly, except Monday, at the House of Orlando Restaurant, 556 Thousand Oaks Boulevard, Thousand Oaks.

THE HOUSE OF ORLANDO...A pleasant rendezvous...for cocktails, dinner, and great entertainment. Presenting the dynamic Friends and Brothers Tuesdays through Sundays from 9 p.m.-1:45 a.m. Each and every member of this versatile, exciting, all male group is a singer, dancer and excellent musician...Filling the "generation gap" with modified rock, popular songs and romantic Latin...The kind of music that brings both young and old out onto the ORLANDO dance floor. Also featuring popular individual entertainer and vocalist, Donnie Brooks, every Tuesday. Backed by the scintillating sounds of the Friends and Brothers, Donnie provides one of the Conejo Valley's best reasons for not going to Las Vegas.

ADMISSION $4.00   MONDAY JULY 26

HOUSE OF ORLANDO
PRESENTS
"OLDIES BUT GOODIES NITE"
DONNIE BROOKS - Master of Ceremonies
POPULAR RECORDING ARTIST
FEATURING
THE DRIFTERS
RECORDING GROUP

SPECIAL ADDED ATTRACTIONS

THE SUPERBS

JEWEL AKENS

SURPRISE GUESTS!

FRIENDS AND BROTHERS
AWARD WINNING GROUP
MUSIC FOR DANCING AND ENTERTAINMENT

RESTAURANT OPEN 8:00 PM
MUSIC FOR DANCING 9:00 PM
1ST SHOW 10 PM - 2ND SHOW 12:30 PM

HOUSE OF ORLANDO
556 THOUSAND OAKS BLVD.
THOUSAND OAKS, CALIFORNIA
PHONE (805) 495-2171

I remember one show working with Bobby Lewis who did "Tossin' & Turnin'" — he looked familiar and I couldn't remember why. Then it hit me! So, I walked up to him and said, in a whispered tone, "Weren't you from Don & Juan last week?" Don & Juan did a song called "What's Your Name."

He quickly pulled me aside and said, "Ssshhh. That was me, but white folks don't know the difference, so don't say anything." We both laughed and I never did find out which one he was, or if he was either one.

While my brother, Danny, was visiting we did a show that had Jewel Akens on it. Jewel had a top-10 hit with "The Birds and the Bees" and Danny liked that song — he was thrilled to get to meet him and the others on the show. But Danny got his first taste of the *reality* of this business. At the end of the night Danny saw Jewel go up to the club owner and ask him for the dishwasher job that was advertised in the window. It broke Danny's heart to see Jewel being humbled so.

OAK RECORDS

I was getting more and more restless. I would do songs like "Fire & Rain" by James Taylor and do these long *story intros* ala Isaac Hayes. I did "They Can't Take Away Our Music" by Eric Burdon with an intro that was longer than the song! I think the leader, Gilbert, was getting a little frustrated with me, too, because we were playing clubs and people wanted to dance — not be depressed. I was just trying to find something creative in what I was doing.

One night (unbeknownst to me) a record producer by the name of Ray Ruff came in. I didn't know he was there and he didn't even speak to me that night. Donnie Brooks was involved in a musical project of Ray's and Ray was looking for lead vocalists. Donnie told him he needed to hear me. So, he came in.

Ray Ruff (producer)

It was on one of those nights that I did my long, laborious version of "Fire & Rain." It was good that I didn't know he was there because I probably wouldn't have done it. Ironically, that was the one that blew him away — not the song, but the passion I put in to it.

Donnie Brooks called me the next day and told me what was going on and that Ray wanted to meet me that week. Donnie picked me up and drove me to Oak Records (Ray's record company). I still didn't have a car. Al Romero, the bass player, used to pick me up for gigs, God bless him. In fact, the entire time I was with Friends & Brothers, I didn't have a car or an apartment. I would just rent a weekly place wherever we played.

Anyway, Ray was spearheading a project that was to be a rock opera called *Truth of Truths*. It was the *Old* and *New Testaments* from the Bible in music — a daunting task to say the least. *Jesus Christ Superstar* was released right in the middle of it and he thought of scrapping the project, but he had so much money invested that he just plowed on.

He wanted me to sing three key songs. One was a ballad that, in his opinion, was the best song on the project called "David to Bathsheba." The second song was the closing number for the old testament, "Prophecies of the Coming Messiah." The third song was the closing song of the new testament, "The Prophecies of the Coming of the End of the World."

It was my first real studio experience and I was jazzed! We recorded at the legendary Gold Star Studios. Stan Ross (co-owner) was our engineer.

Here is a list of people who have recorded at Gold Star: Phil Spector, Brian Wilson, Sonny & Cher, Buffalo Springfield, Duane Eddy, Jimi Hendrix, Neil Young, the Ronettes, Dick Dale, the Righteous Brothers, Iron Butterfly, Herb Alpert & The Tijuana Brass, Jan & Dean, Joan Jett, Meat Loaf, Bobby Darin, the Who, the Monkees, the Band, the Go-Go's, the Ramones, the Association, Art Garfunkel, Leonard Cohen, Bob Dylan, John Lennon, Tina Turner, and Maurice Gibb. An impressive line-up to say the least.

The musicians used on the *Truth of Truths* project were equally impressive in the studio world. Sid Sharp, Hal Blaine, Larry Carlton, Dennis Budimir, Joe Osborn, Arthur Maebe, Jerry Cole, and others.

For a kid from St. Louis, this opportunity was like something out of a movie.

My first day in the studio was arguably my greatest musical and performance learning
experience. We started off with the ballad "David to Bathsheba." I really wanted to
do a good job and impress Ray. I got about halfway
through the song and Ray hit the *call button* and
stopped me.

I said, "Were we not recording yet?"

He said, "Yes, but I'm not sure why?"

I thought, *What?*

He came out into the studio and looked me square
in the eyes and said, "Look, Kid, stop trying
to impress me with your voice. If you hadn't
impressed me before, you wouldn't even be here.
The last thing this damn town needs is another
crooner. Stop singing and start feeling. Read the
words... this is a man whose heart is breaking. He's
hurt and ashamed and his child is going to die for
God's sake!"

With Ray Ruff during Truth of Truths *session at Gold Star*

He continued, "When I came to see you in that
bar you reduced me to tears... Do that now!"

I'm not sure I have ever felt so musically humiliated. I was stunned, hurt...
and then pissed!

I thought, *Okay, you wanna cry you SOB? I'll make you wail.*

I did exactly what he told me. I imagined all those things David felt. The shame part
was easy right now, but the sorrow came from deep inside of me.

When I finished he hit the button again and said, "Come in here."

I thought, *My God, what does he want me to do, bleed?*

He told me to sit and listen. He played the first take first. I thought I sounded pretty
good. Then he played the second take. It was like a completely different person.
I almost cried. I looked at Stan Ross and he said, "You made *me* cry and that doesn't
happen often."

I made Stan Ross cry with my performance? Ray turned and looked at me again, but this time he said, "Pat, if I ever hear you sing onstage, in a studio, or in the damn shower any other way but this, I will personally kick your ass. You have a gift... by the look on your face when you were listening, I'm not even sure that you're aware of what a gift it is. Never sing words, Son... tell the story."

I never ever forgot what he'd said. I brought Ray's words with me through every vocal performance I ever did — and I still do. He was a very wise man.

There were a few *singles* pressed from *Truth of Truths*, one of which was my ballad "David to Bathsheba." It was penned by Val Stoecklein — a quirky, but very talented man. I'm really not sure if it ever charted. It seems it did, but if so, it was in the triple digits.

Below: Clipping from Billboard Magazine, November 13, 1971, pg. 66, Spotlight Singles

PAT LISTON—David To Bathsheba (3:02) (Prod: Ray Ruff) (Writer: Stoecklein) (Senor George, ASCAP)—Beautiful ballad from the ambitious "Truth of Truth" LP, features strong performance from soloist Liston and the chorus. Oak 101

After *Truth of Truths* was released we performed it live at a few places. It charted but not very high. The *LA Free Press* butchered it. Donnie Brooks, Lisa Miller (who was about 16), and I were the only ones they liked. It was a wonderful experience though and — except for one incident — it was all positive for me.

Val Stoecklein conducting the choir on Truth of Truths *session.*

Los Angeles Times CALENDAR, SUNDAY, APRIL 2, 1972

MUSIC: POP

TODAY

"TRUTH OF TRUTHS," rock opera in concert version featuring Donnie Brooks, Doug Gibbs, Patti Sterling, Pat Liston. Greek Theater. 6 a.m.

SHA NA NA, rock novelty group, in concert with Crazy Horse and comedian George Carlin. Fox Theater, Long Beach. 8 p.m.

SHIRLEY BASSEY in concert. Dorothy Chandler Pavilion.

OK, the incident: *Truth of Truths* was going to be performed *live* at the Greek Theater in Los Angeles on Easter Sunday morning. It was a *huge* deal. I played the night before with Friends & Brothers. I overslept because we had to be there at 5:30 a.m. I drove like a banshee, hoping somehow, time would stand still. I arrived at the Greek Theater just as everyone was leaving. Donnie Brooks saw me, ran over, and said, "Go home... quick... before Ray sees you! I'll straighten it out and call you tomorrow."

Remember those dreams of going to school in your underwear? Multiply that by about a thousand and you'll be close to how I felt that day.

Ray did get over it and we started work on my solo album with Oak Records. We went back to Gold Star Studios. Most of the amazing musicians on *Truth of Truths* returned for my album. There was another *incident* at this session, too.

Carol Kaye

I arrived at the studio on the first day and saw all the wonderful musicians. I looked around for Joe Osborn, the premiere bass player. Instead there was a woman sitting where he usually was with a bass in her hands and she (to me) looked like someone's mom holding a bass. I turned to Ray and said, "Where's Joe Osborn and who's the chick?"

There were only about five people in the control room, but I knew I'd once again done something wrong because the room went deathly silent. Ray looked at me and said, "The *chick* is Carol Kaye who is doing this as a favor to me."

I wasn't the sharpest pencil in the box, but I damn sure knew who Carol Kaye was.

For those of you who may not be familiar with her, let me just give a list of some of the people she's played bass for: the Beach Boys, Phil Spector, the Doors, Ritchie Valens, Frank Sinatra, Glen Campbell, Leon Russell, Sonny & Cher, Joe Cocker, Barbra Streisand, Ray Charles, Frank Zappa, Ike & Tina Turner, Johnny Mathis, Simon & Garfunkel, the Righteous Brothers, the Buckinghams, Paul Revere & The Raiders, the Monkees, Buffalo Springfield, etc.

If I hadn't had to sing, Ray would've taped my mouth shut.

I grabbed some of the sheet music that had Hal Blaine's stamp on it. He'd stamp the drum charts before he'd leave to go do another gig: *Hal Blaine Strikes Again.*

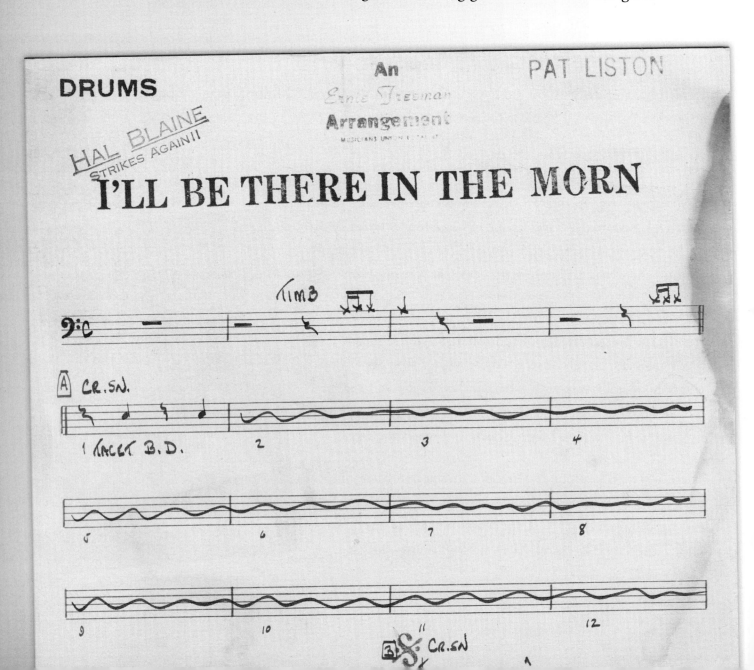

There were to be nine songs on the album. We didn't even have a working title for it when Oak Records went belly-up. For what it's worth, these are the nine song titles:

1. Young & Free (Pat Liston)

2. I'll Be There In The Morning (Pat Liston)

3. Because Of You (Pat Liston)

4. Kathy (Pat Liston)

5. Mobile Blue (Mickey Newbury)

6. Remember The Good (Mickey Newbury)

7. Empty Chairs (Don McLean)

8. Say It's Not Over (Val Stoecklein)

9. I Wonder Who I'll Be Tomorrow (Val Stoecklein)

I had done a photo shoot for the album cover at Will Rogers State Park, but Friends & Brothers got booked in Hawaii around that time and Ray asked me to get some shots over there. I still have a few of the Hawaii film strips.

Even though Oak Records went out of business, I wrote a lot of songs while I was there prior to doing my LP because I had signed with their publishing company as a staff writer. When I signed that deal I really didn't know what it entailed. I just knew that they paid me a working salary to write songs. The guy in charge was another writer named Chuck Tharp.

One day Chuck said, "Pat, we need three songs by next week."

I said, "From where?"

"From you!"

"Oh... I don't write like that. I write when I feel inspired."

Chuck said, "We need three songs by next week or Ray may not be inspired to pay your salary."

"Oh?"

I went home and tried writing and nothing was coming. So, I did my best Charlie Brown impersonation and waited until the day before they wanted three songs. I panicked and started trying to come up with ideas.

I wrote two songs that day, and just could not come up with a third. Neither song was overtly inspired by a present situation. I just drew from what was already inside of me. When I got to Chuck's office I told him I'd only written two songs and expected the worst.

He said, "They better be three songs worth of good."

The first one was a bouncy little number called "Kathy." He really liked it and seemed pleased. He liked the next song — a more down tempo song in a minor key — but not as much as the first one. In fact, Ray felt the same way and even chose "Kathy" to be on my new album.

I thought "Kathy" was a good song, but in my heart of hearts I felt the second song was better. There was just something about it that moved me. Maybe it was the minor key or the melancholy lyric. I've always been a sucker for a sad song.

Anyway, I never recorded that song with Oak Records, but four years later, I finally got to record it. And that song turned out to be a pretty good song for me. That song was "Blue Mist" — the #1, all-time, most requested song on KSHE radio in St. Louis.

11/25/71

BLUE MIST IN THE AIR

STANDING ON A BUS LINE, WAITING FOR THE NUMBER 39. TO TAKE ME HOME FOR THE LAST TIME. HOPING FOR THE MORNING RAIN TO FALL UPON MY FACE SO THAT, IT WITH ERASE, THE TEAR DROPS IN MY EYES!
CAUSE THERE'S A BLUE MIST IN THE AIR & THERE'S A FEELING IN MY HEART THAT I CAN'T SHARE. & THERE'S A TEAR DROP RUNNING DOWN MY CHEEK & I CAN'T EVEN SPEAK WHEN I THINK OF YOU!

— CON'T

WE WERE ONE TOGETHER BECAUSE OF STORMY WEATHER, CAUSE WHEN THE WEATHER GOT BETTER & THE SUN CAME, YOU WERE GONE.
YOU COULD NEVER MAKE IT BECAUSE YOU TRIED TO FAKE IT. THEN LET A STRANGER COME & TAKE IT ALL AWAY.
I CAN LIVE WITHOUT YOU THOUGH I'LL OFTEN THINK ABOUT YOU & WONDER WHAT'D HAPPENED HAD YOU TRIED, & YOU CAN LIVE WITHOUT ME I KNOW THIS TO BE TRUE, SO I'M GIVING THIS SONG TO YOU TO BLOW YOUR MIND

Well, while all this stuff was going on with Oak Records, I was still with Friends & Brothers. We somehow got hooked up with a young woman named Diana Whitman. She was gorgeous and could really sing, but had no clue how to front a show. In her defense she was only about 19 years old. It drove Al Romero completely crazy because he was the quintessential showman.

62   *Friends & Brothers: Left to right: Roy Avila, Manny Rich, Me, (kneeling) Al Romero, and Gil Avila*

She was not only good looking, she was tall and had long legs. She wore these long dresses that looked almost Pentecostal. They covered her completely. We soon realized that her manager also had a thing for her. He was much older and very *protective*.

He booked us at the Sahara in Lake Tahoe. The manager couldn't be there because of one of his bigger artists in Vegas who was demanding his attention. Al Romero took advantage of the situation. He and I went to her room and told her *that this is the Sahara and they want to see skin*. He explained that she didn't have to dress *cheap* but she *did* have to be sexy.

Marquee from The Sahara in Lake Tahoe

We went through her wardrobe and she had some great outfits. Al picked her dress and shoes out and tried (in the brief time we had) to explain being showy. She was a nervous wreck, so Al took her to the bar right before show time and got her half-liquored!

She put on a great show! She was bumping and grinding like Gypsy Rose Lee! At one point Al had to tell her to back it down just a little. She had so much fun and was actually very entertaining. Al was proud of her, but the manager found out — the manager from the Sahara called him to tell him what a great job she'd done, not knowing the *relationship*. We finished the engagement at the Sahara and never heard from him or Diana again. Gilbert (our band leader) was livid.

I used to get off work at the Sahara and head down the road to a place called The Motherlode. It was a *let-yer-hair-down* kind of place. The show musicians (who were usually very, very talented) would go there after work and play real music after doing shows that they'd done hundreds of times over and over — people like Vinnie Cusano (who ended up with a later rendition of KISS as Vinnie Vincent), Neil Stubenhauss (who became one of the most in-demand bass players in LA), and Karen Benson. We'd jam until the wee hours. It was a fun time.

While at the Sahara I also met people like Fats Domino, Karen Carpenter, and "Little Anthony" Gourdine — all three legends in their own right. I played at the blackjack table with Karen Carpenter and engaged her in conversation. She was very nice, but the people with her seemed like chaperons and whisked her away like I was a stalker — very odd.

It was at the Sahara that I used to go down to our huge dressing room and practice bottleneck guitar.

Once, on the way to Hawaii, I had heard Johnny Winter playing a song called "Dallas" and fell in love with the sound. There was a lot of down time in Lake Tahoe so I took advantage of it to learn slide.

My signature scream also had its beginnings there. I was practicing a Rod Stewart song and not wanting to be too loud, I started singing in a raspy falsetto.

Al Romero heard it and said, "I like that sound, you should sing a song like that... it's really different."

I thought he was crazy. He was also the first one to tell me I had two different notes coming out at the same time.

Years later I developed my trademark scream using that same method thanks to Al's insistence that I *give it a try.*

There were so many incredible musicians in Tahoe, but I'd also met some hippie types there that I stayed with off and on and the music that they listened to reminded me of what I was really wanting to do. Mix that with learning slide guitar and it was the death knell for Friends & Brothers and I. The Diana Whitman show was so embarrassingly corny that I just couldn't continue on this career path anymore.

Truth be known, Friends & Brothers may have wanted to be a show band, but they were far too good for a show this bad. Diana's manager/boyfriend wrote the bits we had to do and they were nothing short of moronic!

After returning to Los Angeles I gave my notice. I was really excited about my ideas for a new band, but it was very emotional leaving these guys who — all being older than me and more experienced — taught me so very much about stage presence and music itself... and to never be less than your best! Especially *mi mejor amigo es Alfredo Romero.*

I closed an integral chapter in my life... *Friends & Brothers, los quiero con todo mi corazon!*

MAMA'S PRIDE AND LOS ANGELES

I returned to St. Louis to start a new band. I had been home just a few months before this and went to see the band my brother, Danny, was with — a group called Doc Savage. He started on drums, then went to bass, and now guitar. I was amazed at how good he'd gotten in such a short time. His voice had gotten strong, too. They were a good band and the lead guitar player was exceptional — a 19- year-old kid named Max Baker.

The genesis of Mama's Pride:
(left to right) Me, Max Baker, Danny Liston

The three of us went back to my mom's house and started jamming in her basement that night. His guitar playing had already impressed me, but the vocal blend between the three of us was amazing.

We sang the Beatles, Uriah Heep, Grand Funk, the Temptations, The Impressions, CSN... you name it. Every song sounded stellar, vocally. I was blown away to say the least. Danny and I were siblings, so our blend would have been obvious, but Max's voice was one of those totally different voices that was meant to blend with Danny and I. The *three*

guitar thing was not what drew me — it was those harmonies.

As I said, as soon as I got back to St. Louis I started piecing together my new band. Danny and Max were a no-brainer. As I said, even though we were all guitar players, I didn't care — we would be the core. I sought out two other guys that I had worked with in the past.

Mike Gordon — a drummer who was an old friend I'd worked before. Mike had played with everybody and had a great voice too. At least Mike was old enough to get in a bar even though (like me) he looked about 16!

The other guy was Gary Bourgeois, — an extraordinary bass player who played with me in the Mella Fellas. He was 19 now and more amazing than before. His voice had really gotten fantastic, too. I offered him the job and he accepted on the spot. He was playing with the Jay Barry Band at the time and I remember going to see Gary at his going away to California party. I finally left because this one guy was staring daggers at me. When I asked who he was, Gary said it was the drummer for Jay Barry. I guess when you steal a drummer's bass player they get angry.

I told Gary, "I hope I never see him again." (That drummer's name was Kevin Sanders.)

So, I had my band, but I didn't have a PA system. In order to buy a PA I had to work with another band in town called Clean Dirt at The Red Onion in downtown St. Louis. I worked with them six nights a week for about two months until I saved enough money. They were a good bunch of guys — Jay Marino, Lanny Bowles, Denny Braun, and Brian Clarke.

Once I had my PA purchased, we were ready to go. Max had an old 1965 Ford Econoline van for equipment, Mike and Gary had their own cars, so we had our transportation.

In October of 1972, we were LA bound. I remember I used to have a photo that we took as we were pulling away from my mom's house on Ivanhoe. Everyone was waving and cheering for us. It wasn't until years later — looking at that slightly out of focus photo — I saw that Mom was looking in the other direction as we pulled away. Not until I had children of my own did I realized how hard that must have been to see her last child leave and drive away to California.

Mom was the strongest person I ever knew. She wouldn't have stopped us for anything (even if she could have). She believed in living your dreams and... Mom believed in her boys.

Leaving for California in 1972: (left to right) Danny Liston, Max Baker, Mike Gordon, Gary Bourgeois, "Mama" Lou Liston, and Me.

We drove the southern route to California — Route 66. I knew we needed a name for the band. I told everybody to jot down ideas en route and when we stopped for gas we'd compare notes. We came up with a ton of names... none of which I remember offhand except for *Tumbleweeds* — somebody came up with that because of Danny's hair.

Three cars and five guys meant somebody drove by themself. We'd switch passengers so no one had to be alone the whole time. During one leg of the trip, Max drove with me.

We were trying to come up with names. It was Max who said, "How about *Mother's Pride*? Your mom has always been so supportive and helpful letting us rehearse at her house and hang out."

I thought about it for a minute and (using the vernacular of the time) said, "How about *Mama's Pride*? It sounds a little funkier."

He liked it and wrote it down.

At the next gas stop everyone had more names. I said, "Let Max and I go first. I think we have a good one.

"How about *Mama's Pride*?"

They all looked at each other, smiled, and threw their pieces of paper with names on the ground. We all did that huddle thing where you put your hands on top of one another and said, "We're Mama's Pride!"

Of course, Mom was elated when I told her the name and why — I remember hearing her voice break a little. I know she felt honored.

68

We stopped in San Bernardino and took a picture because it said *Welcome to California*. We were almost there and had a name. When we got to Los Angeles we stayed at a place I had often stayed — Howard's Weekly Apartments. We rented two of them. Each had a living room, a kitchen, and a bedroom. They were clean little places and fairly inexpensive. They were in the heart of Burbank, California. The people who ran it were an older couple named Bill and Esther Pratt. They were very nice and knew me because of how many times I'd stayed there when I was in town.

I knew at some point we needed a house — a place we could rehearse and be together 24/7. I found a house in the center of the *earthquake district* in Sylmar, California. Sylmar was the epicenter of the 1971 earthquake. (I was actually living out there when that earthquake hit. It was very scary!) Sylmar was severally damaged. This was only one year later and *no one* wanted to buy or rent in the area. This worked to our advantage because *no one* in their right mind wanted to rent a house to a rock band either!

Mama Lou visiting the house in Sylmar: (left to right) Max, Danny, Mom, Me, Mike, and Gary

Danny, Mom, and I

The house was on Foothill Boulevard. There were empty lots on either side where houses had once been — both destroyed by the earthquake. We used to like to go up in the foothills and look at the big damage... like Mount Olive Hospital. It was very eerie.

Mama Lou Liston came out to visit while we lived in Sylmar. She felt better knowing that we had a house and were living somewhat normally. She even came to a few gigs.

I started getting us jobs at all the places I used to play with Friends & Brothers. What I had not considered was, we were much heavier in to "rock" than Friends & Brothers. We played House of Orlando in Thousand Oaks, California, where Friends & Brothers had done all the "oldies" shows. Mr. Orlando was a very kind man and I know he felt bad when — at the end of the night — he said, "Pat, you guys are really good, but I don't think you're right for my room. Your music is too heavy."

We wanted to work and get tight so we opted to learn some "pop" songs as opposed to Grand Funk Railroad, etc. With all five of us being lead singers, there was nothing we couldn't do song-wise.

I had an old friend who worked for NBC at the time who used to come and see me with Friends & Brothers. His name was Hap Chamberlain.

I'm fairly sure Hap was instrumental in our first real gig at a place called the Joker Room in Granada Hills. It was a cool gig. We played there several weeks. However, Danny, Max, and Gary were not 21 and would have to sit out in the foyer on breaks according to state law.

Our first gig at the Joker Room in Granada Hills, California.

I really loved Hap and his wife, Kendra. They were so helpful in those early days. Hap took our first promo pictures. He took continuous-type computer paper and spray painted *Mama's Pride* on it for a background.

My old friend, Donnie Brooks, got us some "oldies" shows when we were struggling for work. Donnie was a great guy and always willing to help. He made a commission, but it was a pittance considering what he'd done for us.

I decided to go see my old friend Gail McConkey and see if she was interested in booking us. She came to hear us because she always wanted to know what she was booking. She loved us! I will always have a soft spot in my heart for Gail. You always felt like you were the only act she handled. She made every group feel special. She started booking us around LA. We played the Antique Mirror in Granada Hills a lot.

I'm not sure if it was Hap Chamberlain's idea or whose it was, but we ended up going with the Howard King Agency. Larry Dunlap and Ron Singer ran the agency. Their concept was to make us a *show band*. We cut our hair (some) and got matching outfits. The matching outfits didn't last too long. The whole concept of being a show band was not something I wanted to revisit! They did continue to book us though.

They booked us in Phoenix, Arizona, at Mr. Lucky's. We played downstairs and Conway Twitty played upstairs. They also booked us in Tucson a couple of times. The first time was a big place called Funky's. As I said before, groups back then would play six nights a week, five sets a night, seven on weekends, and you would be there at least four to eight weeks at a time. Funky's was a great place, but it caught fire towards the end of our tenure.

Ron Singer

72

Mama's Pride

We came back to the Antique Mirror in the LA area and played about 12 weeks. We started playing some Allman Brothers stuff one night to just break it up a bit. When the word got out, the bikers showed in large numbers. Not many people were aware of the Allman Brothers out there at that time, but the bikers worshiped them and informed us we were the only band playing their stuff. It was a *dance* club, so the owner freaked a little, but there were so many bikers and they spent a lot of money, so he tolerated it.

Ron and Larry from the Howard King Agency really liked us a lot, but just couldn't figure us out. They actually liked coming to see us play.

We started cutting Gary loose and letting him do some Grand Funk Railroad and Zeppelin, which he excelled on!

We finally started playing some originals which was extremely frowned upon in clubs. We would announce a *new* song by a well known band, then do one of our songs. The first song we worked out was "Blue Mist" — we always would say it was a new song by Three Dog Night.

One night the owner asked where he could buy that new Three Dog Night song "Blue Mist." He loved it. I had to finally tell him the truth. He was very impressed that it was my song, but said, "No more original music." I agreed... but then continued to do more. He never knew.

Max and Danny wrote a song that was a Uriah Heep style song — at least it was the way we first did it — called "In The Morning." It was much slower than the way we later recorded it. Danny and I wrote "Merry-Go-Round" a year earlier when he had come to visit me and the band now took the time to work that out as well.

At some point, the agency booked us in Honolulu, Hawaii, at the Point After in Waikiki — a club I had played previously with Friends & Brothers. The other guys were really stoked because most of them had never been on a plane before. We played there for 16 weeks. A lot happened during that time. We met a lot of big names because they would end their tours in Hawaii, then stay a while.

A big thrill for me was meeting Ricky Nelson. He and his band came in one night and we ended up partying with them later. He was a really nice guy, and I'd grown up watching him on TV, so it was very cool.

Probably a pivotal time for us was the night the Allman Brothers Band came in. The Point After always had two bands play alternately, so there was a lot of equipment onstage — which included two sets of drums. When the Brothers sat-in the sound was perfect with two set drummers. And since Duanne had died the previous year, at this juncture they only had Dickie on guitar so Max sat-in with them, too.

*Above: Mama's Pride
at the Point After in Honolulu, Hawaii*

Below: Gregg Allman

Above: Gregg Allman at the after party

Below: The Allman Brothers band sitting in at the Point After with Max playing with them.

Afterward, we partied with Gregg Allman that night. He was in the middle of mixing his first solo album — *Laid Back*. He played a cassette for me of the rough mixes. (Little did we know that we would be performing some of these songs with him onstage in a few years.) He and I spoke about his new album and music. It was a nice conversation until he said, "You guys are really good. Why are you doing all those bullshit cover songs?"

I said, "Hey, ya gotta make a livin'."

Gregg replied, "I'll see ya in 10 years when you're still *makin' a livin'*."

At the time it really pissed me off, and I tossed and turned all night about it. Then I thought *don't focus on the negative... he said we were real good. Gregg Allman said we were real good.*

We had a band meeting the next day. We had to get our *edge* back.

That night we played "Whippin' Post." The manager (a guy named Bill Walton) almost had a cow! He took me in his office and said, "Pat... what the hell are you doing to me here? 'Whipping Post.' Are you kidding me?"

He continued, "Don't get me wrong, I *love* that song, but it isn't right for here... this is a posh dance club. Play what I hired you to do and when you get back to LA do your thing. I'll be first in line to buy the record."

Bill was a great guy. He treated the bands really, really well. We did so well there that he wanted us to stay another eight weeks.

Because of the jam with the Allman Brothers, Gary suggested we get a second drummer — a friend of his from St. Louis named Kevin Sanders. We thought we could fly him over and use the extra eight weeks to work him in, but suddenly Mike and Gary decided to quit.

I think that Max, Danny, and I were so close that Mike and Gary somehow felt on the outside. Gary was taking voice lessons because he wanted to be a better lead vocalist. This teacher was teaching him to sing *correctly*. I hated it because I thought he'd lose his rock-n-roll edge by what she was teaching him.

We left Hawaii not knowing what was next because Gary and Mike were really good. When we got back to LA the agency had a meeting with us. They talked Gary and Mike in to staying. They also probably wouldn't have suggested a second drummer, but then again probably thought that if it would breath some fresh air into the group, why not?

Also, when we got home I wrote another new song. Again, it was not directly about someone — fans hate to hear that. It was called "Laurie Ann."

We got booked in Tucson, Arizona, again. This time it was a place called the Flying Tiger. Kevin Sanders drove to Tucson and joined us there. The first night I asked if he'd like to set up his drums next to Mike's and just play on the songs he felt comfortable with. He said, "Hell no, I wanna play!"

He started and finished the night playing every song. He just hit the ground running. It was nothing short of amazing!

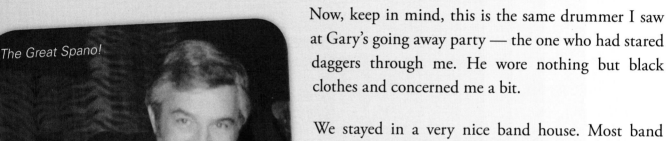

The Great Spano!

Now, keep in mind, this is the same drummer I saw at Gary's going away party — the one who had stared daggers through me. He wore nothing but black clothes and concerned me a bit.

We stayed in a very nice band house. Most band houses were awful. The first night, Kevin and I stayed up talking most of the night. He explained that he hated me for taking Gary, but it was mostly because *he* wanted to go, too. We bonded on some personal issues that I won't go into but, from that night on... we bonded. We didn't realize then that we were going to be lifelong friends.

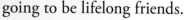

Kevin hypnotized.

At the Flying Tiger we worked with a hypnotist — The Great Spano! He was a lot of fun and could put Kevin under at the snap of a finger. His word for Kevin was *whiskey*. If he said that and snapped his fingers, Kevin was gone. I said *whiskey*

one night to Kevin and snapped my fingers and he almost went out! It scared the hell out of me because I thought, *My God, what if I put him under and don't know how to bring him back?* I never did that again.

After several weeks in Tucson, it became very obvious that Kevin not only fit musically... he was a brother! We headed back to LA and the Antique Mirror again. This time though, we had two drummers and were starting to think *original* music. Kevin introduced us to "southern rock" à la Marshall Tucker, Lynyrd Skynyrd, etc. I never considered the early Allman Brothers southern rock — I considered them a sort of blues/jazz group — so these groups Kevin introduced were a whole new thing to us. He had the first Lynyrd Skynyrd LP and we listened to it. We decided to do "Simple Man." We added a lot of background vocals and sort of made it our own and Kevin sang it.

I have to confess something: I wasn't really that knocked out over "Freebird." I thought "Simple Man" was a better song. I rarely liked the one everybody else did.

Anyway, this was the beginning of a *direction* for us. We had three guitars and they could finally be used to the fullest. Although, right about this time I bought a Hammond B3

Kevin Sanders

Kevin Sanders and Gary Bourgeois

organ and sorta taught myself to play it. I have some old *live* tapes from those days that Gary had recorded and I didn't do too bad for a guy who'd never played organ.

We started doing things like "In Memory of Elizabeth Reed." The two drummer thing was really working for us. Mike and Kevin were great together. We played the Antique Mirror for quite a while and got really tight as a six-piece group.

My infamous "teardrop" guitar

At this time I was playing mostly slide and organ and was starting to play a lot of slide on my Gibson 335, but had to constantly re-tune it because I used open tuning for slide. Kevin had this crazy guitar — it was originally a Gibson Melody Maker and he cut the body down in a teardrop shape. He suggested that I use it for slide because it was so easy to get way up on the neck. It was perfect and I didn't have to re-tune the other guitar anymore.

Kevin, later, gave me the guitar on one of my birthdays. I stripped it to natural wood, designed a chrome pick guard to reflect stage lights back at the audience — there was no such thing as a *chrome* pick guard at that time. I added a stacked Bill Lawrence pickup because the single coil pickups have a tendency to feed back like a microphone at high volume. I put a "Badass" bridge on it (that's actually the name of it), a brass nut, and Schaller tuning keys. It became almost a trademark for me.

I have to mention this: Danny and I moved to an apartment in Burbank, just caddy -corner from Howard's Weekly Apartments. While living there, I had gone out to a bar on an off-night and gotten drunk. I didn't lock the van and it was broken into. They stole one of our guitars... Danny's Gibson 335 that looked exactly like mine.

I didn't give him my guitar (because guitars are personal). At the very least I should have saved towards purchasing him another guitar. But I didn't and we just shared mine. That was very wrong and very selfish. I felt guilty... but not guilty enough, obviously.

The band reached a point where we made the decision to go back to St. Louis.

The agency had booked us in Denver for a few gigs, Kearney, Nebraska, then back in Denver. We decided that would be a good time to go home because we'd be better than halfway there.

Ron and Larry were *not* happy about our decision and futilely tried to talk us out of it. They had invested a lot of time and energy into trying to make us a *show band* or something. It got very ugly, but our minds were made up.

I have to admit that (in the back of my mind) I wasn't sure I wanted to go back. I was afraid it would be like before — with no pressure everyone would end up going their separate ways. I mean there was nothing in St. Louis industry-wise. But everyone was tired of the kinds of places we were playing and felt we could be more creative at home. I wasn't sure I agreed, but I had always been a team player. And for now this was my team. We had moved a bit towards the southern rock style of music, too, and that was closer to St. Louis than it was to LA.

We sold furniture and anything we couldn't take with us and left Los Angeles for good this time. During this time the band decided that they wanted a *real* keyboard player. Sometimes when you're a singer your playing can get overlooked. I was a little reluctant because I liked playing B3, but I wore a lot of hats with Mama's Pride so maybe I wasn't as good as I could have been. But I listen to those old tapes and they sound good to me considering I'd never touched a Hammond B3 in my life and just bought it one day and started playing it at gigs the next. The band probably just wanted someone on keys full time and I wanted to play slide as well. So it was probably for the better.

Regardless of who was right on this, we got a *real* keyboard player — Frank Gagliano. To be fair, Frank was very good and I had known Frank from when he tried out for one of my first bands with his accordion. I still managed to play a little B3 or piano periodically. This also freed me up to play more slide guitar, too. Max was an amazing lead guitarist and Danny was the most rock solid rhythm guitarist I'd ever heard, so slide was something different that I could contribute and own.

Frank's first gig with us was in Denver, Colorado. It was another Mr. Lucky's. It had a huge stage. It was a strange gig because (once again) they wanted a dance band. They also gave us a list of *Do's and Don'ts*. They even had a list of banter phrases we should say to the audience. I had never experienced this and have never experienced it since. I was incensed that someone would give me things to say. Things like: "Even though the lights are bright onstage, we can feel your vibes."

Really? I hated this so much that I would pull the sheet out of my pocket with bravado and read it word-for-word in the lamest voice I could muster! We had a lot of *hippie* types coming to see us and they were very entertained by the intended sarcasm. Even with all that, it was a great venue — it even had a dressing room — but we bucked heads with the owner there for obvious reasons.

Mr. Lucky's in Denver, Colorado

It was at this gig that our drummer, Mike Gordon, announced he was quitting the band. I'm truly not sure of all his reasoning at the time, but he wasn't happy. So, when you're not happy, you move on. I was sorry to see Mike go. I had known Mike longer than any of the guys, except my brother. Mike ran very deep, and I thought (at times) too deep — sometimes *you can't see the forest for the trees* as they say. But be that as it may, things were changing once again.

We left Mr. Lucky's to play in Kearney, Nebraska. The club was called Fireside Inn. We were only there a couple of weeks. They had a huge snow storm while we were there and we couldn't work a couple of the nights and we were bored to death.

Frank Gagliano had been talking about this new place in St. Louis that had opened right before he left town to join us. He said it was different from all the usual dance clubs that St. Louis always had. He said that friends of mine from high school owned it and a friend from Dogtown, Bob Pierce, was booking the bands. Danny and I knew Bob real well.

The band was going back to St. Louis and we had no intention of doing more ridiculous dance type clubs... and Gregg Allman's words were still ringing in my ears. I did *not* want to be doing this stuff in 10 years. Maybe our decision was right — maybe we were ready to go back home and get serious.

Frank had Bob's work number at the bar and I called to see what it was about. When I called, Bob was thrilled to hear we were considering coming back. I shot him the price we *usually* got. I lied — it was way more than what we really were getting and I said we needed more if we were coming all the way back from California. He accepted the price for a four-day gig. I was so jazzed when I got off the phone. Not only were we going home, we were getting paid big money for it! The guys were really happy to be headed home and could hardly wait to leave.

After the celebrating and all, one of the guys said, "Where are we playing? I mean what's the name of this new place?"

I said, "It's kind of a funny name... they call it Rusty Springs."

We did one last Howard King Agency gig at another place back in Denver called My Sweet Lass. It was a difficult gig for Kevin because he'd gotten used to Mike being there and now he was gone. When you have two drummers, they not only concentrate on what to play, but — more often — what not to play. The first couple of nights he felt a bit naked. It was probably a good thing because it gave him a

few weeks of playing without Mike to be ready for St. Louis. But the gig was short, maybe three weeks. I don't even remember a lot about the place. All we could think about was going home!

BACK TO ST. LOUIS

Rusty Springs located in St. Louis at Manchester Avenue and S. Kingshighway Boulevard.

It was 1974. As a band, we had been gone from St. Louis almost two years. I had been gone since 1969. Rusty Springs was comfortable the day we walked in. It was owned by Ed Atwood and Bob Burkhart — two guys I remembered from high school. There was a slew of guys from my alma mater, Southwest High, that worked there. We knew, right from the beginning, that this was going to be a great experience.

The first night we played we knew we had found our audience. Old friends (and some new) showed up. It was packed! People that weren't aware of us were amazed at how tight this *new* band was. They didn't realize that we had been playing almost non-stop every night for two years straight. I think some of the local bands resented how we just drove in and took over.

We started doing more originals and the audience loved it! Even the covers we did — Bloodrock, Ten Years After, Grand Funk, Led Zeppelin, etc. — were things we could have never done in those places we played in California.

People in those days had different receptors than they do now. There were no cell phones or social media. People engaged purely in the music itself. If the youth of today could go back in a time machine and experience the energy that took place there, they'd never want to come back to the present!

There would be over 800 people on a Wednesday. Every nook and cranny was full — downstairs, upstairs, outside, and a line wrapping around the building. Fans had made their own bumper stickers that read: *Mama's Pride... #1 next to none.* We could do no wrong. We responded to this adulation with amazing creative energy.

Rusty Springs eventually put a sign behind the bar that read: *Rusty Springs... home of Mama's Pride.* And that was the truth — it indeed was home.

Rusty Springs staff
Back row left to right: Bob Pierce, Mark Beffa, Kieth Tinney, Bob Bratcher (behind blond girl), Jim Bieler, Ted Whitney, Jack Mahaney (behind Ted), Karen Temper, Rick Turner, Alan Atwood. (In front and on bar) "Fred the Dog," Ed Atwood, Artie Green, Brian Russell, Hershal Williams

Change is always inevitable in any group. The next major change was on bass. Gary Bourgeois was quitting. He wanted to do something on his own. I understood, but was sorry to see such an immense talent leave us — especially now, when things seemed to be going well. I didn't know the St. Louis music scene anymore, so finding someone to fill Gary's shoes was going to be a challenge.

I started going to bars, watching groups. Every time I went in to a bar, the band would always look nervous. We were arguably the most popular band in St. Louis and were looking for a bass player. So, if I walked in, the whole band would turn and look at their bass player to see his reaction. I felt like the grim reaper.

Someone — and I don't remember who — had told me of a guy who was definitely worth seeing. He was playing out at the Marlborough Lounge on Watson with the Terry Toon Band. I knew Terry, and he was a great guy, but all is fair in love and Rock n' Roll. Terry told me later that when I walked in he turned to his bass player and said, "It's been nice working with you."

I was more than impressed with the bass player, as Terry knew I would be. I offered him the job on the spot. His name was Joe Turek. Joe was a great fit and had a good voice as well. Vocals were a must with most anyone who joined Mama's Pride.

(We didn't realize then, of course, that this was to be the line up for our record deal.)

Grandma's House in Pacific, Missouri. Left to right: Stan, Danny, Louise, Kevin, Max, and Joe

We worked Joe in quickly and started expanding our venues. So many places in the area had heard about us and wanted us. One great place was Grandma's House out in Pacific, Missouri. Louise and Stan were the salt of the earth and they loved the band. They let us rehearse there during the day. This is where we originally worked out most of the songs for the first LP.

Grandma Louise had a sign out front that read: *Grandma's House, home of Mama's Pride!* We had a lot of homes back then, but in the early days Rusty Springs and Grandma's were the *go-to* places.

There was a DJ at KSLQ radio named Pete Skye who took an interest in us and offered the station's recording studio to record our original songs. At the time, I was struggling with a hernia that had snapped on me while in LA about a year earlier. I was singing a Chambers Brothers song called "Funky" and felt something odd during a scream. I realized later it was a hernia. So, I was dealing with hernia issues during the KSLQ sessions — the very first recordings of seven of our songs. I saved those recordings along with other reel-to-reel recordings of mine. Thanks to my friend, Eric Aijala, who has since transferred them to a digital format, I will have them for years to come.

Somewhere during this whole deal we had gotten a *real* PA. The little Acoustic columns were just not getting it anymore. Frank Gagliano had PA equipment he was bringing in a little at a time. It was driving me nuts because Frank was diddling with the PA more than he was his keyboards. I was old school and this *big* PA seemed silly to me, but I was to lose the battle, and rightfully so... things were changing. We realized that the only way to get Frank away from the PA constantly was to have the board out front. Mama's Pride was about to have a *road crew*.

We got my cousin Art Reel to run sound. I'm not sure he'd ever done it, but he was a musician himself. He played trombone in some Chicago-type groups. He understood the concept and had good ears. So we had a soundman. At about the same time we added Tim McMahon to the crew for set-up. Tim was a long time Dogtown buddy that Danny went to school with.

We added and subtracted some great roadies through the years. I'll try to mention them all now because I would never be able to do a timeline on when they came and went. There was Art Reel (APRIII), Tim McMahon (TMc), John Venincasa (Vino), "Big" Jim Janis, Jim Wilhelm (Helm), "Grover" Lee Loveless, "Loose Bruce" Sturgil, Jerry Kovac (JK), Ed "Buckie" Burch, Roger Ellmore, Keith King, Steve Otto, Bill (Woodsey) Janis, Jim Egan, Jerry Harvey, and Jack Dedert. They were all very dedicated guys and I still see most of them from time to time.

Well, eventually I had to deal with hernia surgery. It was pretty major in those days. I left the band for a couple of months. Walking is one thing, but screaming and stomping around onstage is another. The band played primarily at a small club on the

St. Charles Rock Road called Club Kapriole while I was convalescing. They needed to work, but couldn't do a lot of the songs because of all the ones I sang.

I eventually healed and got back to work. One of the first clubs I booked when I got back was a new place on Laclede's Landing called the River Rat.

In 1974 there was nothing on the Landing but rats and empty warehouses. A young entrepreneur from Louisville, Kentucky, by the name of Ellis Salem had moved to St. Louis and saw the potential for entertainment on the Landing. He leased a small building at 914 N. 1st Street and dubbed it *The River Rat*. He sprayed the ceiling with vermiculite for acoustics and started having touring bands there. Among the groups back then that played there were: If (the British jazz-rock group), the Outlaws, Grinderswitch, and Heartsfield.

Advertisement for The River Rat — which years later became Mississippi Nights

We played there several times. A pivotal moment for Mama's Pride was the night we played with a newly signed group from Florida called the Outlaws. Their road manager, David Cloud, was present during our soundcheck. The Outlaws had driven a long way the night before and were tired. They were planning on not doing a sound check. David called them at the motel and warned them that they'd better get down there for a sound check because the local band that was opening for them was going to burn their ass if they weren't ready. We all became friends that night.

Ellis Salem had a lot of contacts in the South. He hooked us up with a booking agent out of Louisville, Kentucky, named Steve Cole. Steve booked all the clubs in the South on what is known as the *chittlin' circuit*. We were feeling a bit burned out in St. Louis and were looking to expand our fan base. Steve booked us all over the south. He was a great guy and an honest booking agent (a rarity). We had done numerous gigs through Steve and one night at the Whipping Post in Augusta, Georgia, he had it in mind to ask us to sign an agency/management agreement with him.

Steve Cole with Pat

Steve and I were talking at the bar about this agreement when he looked towards the door and said, "Never mind, I just lost the best band I've ever heard."

I said, "What?"

He pointed to the door and there was David Cloud, the Outlaws road manager, with a blond haired fella. I recognized David right away and asked Steve what he meant by *losing us*.

He said, "Do you know who that is?"

I said, "Yes, that's David Cloud from the Outlaws."

"No, the other guy?"

"No."

Steve explained, "That's Alan Walden — Phil Walden's brother — the Outlaws manager. He also managed Lynyrd Skynyrd and he's here to see you, and when he hears you, he's gonna sign you."

It was time to go back up and play so I told the guys what was happening and that we should burn! We played four hours that night and didn't have near enough original material, so we did a lot of good cover stuff, too. Naturally, if you played the South you had to do "Freebird" (yes, we finally gave in and learned it). I figured if this guy had managed Skynyrd then this would be a good choice for a closing number.

I was right.

Alan had recently lost his management deal with Lynyrd Skynyrd and wanted someone who could replace them. He loved us and wanted to sign us right away.

Looking back, I'm not sure if this was the best thing that ever happened, or the worst. We really didn't like the southern rock label we had because we knew we were different. This defining moment would seal that label.

Alan was looking for a new *Guitar Army* as he called it, but did we really want to be *Skynyrd-light*. If I had had those feelings, they were fleeting because this was as close as I'd ever come to actually moving towards real management and a potential big time record deal. I mean, Alan had done it for Skynyrd and the Outlaws, why not us? And if it meant getting a record deal then, "Yee haw and howdy, Partner!"

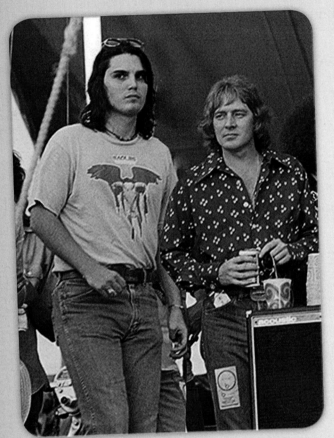

Charlie Brusco and Alan Walden

Alan also had a partner who was out of Pittsburgh by the name of Charlie Brusco. Charlie was actually younger than me (a fact that I was unaware of at the time). Charlie and I bumped heads a little — we were both young go getters and we each had a tendency to be a bit hot-headed. Given that, there's bound to be some friction. At some point Alan decided that Charlie would handle the Outlaws and he would handle us.

In retrospect, the yin and yang might have been a better idea. Charlie and Alan were very different and had very different approaches to things. But *hindsight is 20/20* as they say... so who knows?

Alan was a creature of habit and a definite *if it ain't broke, don't fix it* kind of guy. He took us in to the same studio that he took Skynyrd and the Outlaws — Broadway Sound Studios in Muscle Shoals, Alabama. (Technically, it was Sheffield, Alabama.) He used the same producer/engineer, David Johnson.

We were thrilled. Muscle Shoals was the most famous recording mecca in the South. David was a great guy and loved our band. Those recordings were some of the best we've ever done. It was just raw energy and not overproduced.

Broadway Sound Studios, Muscle Shoals, Alabama.

Alan started shopping the tapes to a lot of labels. I remember Columbia records came to see us in a big club called Doodles Showcase in Atlanta, Georgia. The guy hated us — called us *Allman Brother wannabes.*

ATLANTIC RECORDS

Alan had sent tapes to every label in New York City except for Atlantic because they had turned down both Skynyrd and the Outlaws. So why would they want us, right? The label found out that they'd been left out and then, naturally, they wanted to hear us. Alan got them a tape via his New York lawyer, Eric Kronfeld. They liked what they heard and wanted to come see us.

We were playing all over the South at the time and were in Tampa, Florida, at a club called the P.A.C. (or the Performing Arts Center). Alan called and told us that the Atlantic people were coming to see us. I remember his excitement when he told us that, not only were Atlantic people coming down but *the* Atlantic people — the entire front office: Jerry Greenberg (President), Noreen Woods (Vice President), Jim Delehant (Head of A&R), Anita Wexler (Jerry Wexler's daughter), and the crème de la crème... Ahmet Ertegun, Chairman of Atlantic — the man who signed Ray Charles, Otis Redding, Wilson Pickett, Aretha Franklin, Percy Sledge, Buffalo Springfield, the Rolling Stones, Led Zeppelin, CSN, and so many others. And now he was flying to Tampa, Florida, to see Mama's Pride in a night club!

Alan Walden (who lived in Georgia) flew to Tampa. We had a meeting before starting the gig. We decided we would do cover material until the Atlantic people arrived. Alan would give me a signal when they walked in and we would immediately go in to our original music.

When the Atlantic people walked in we were in the middle of a cover song. I looked at Kevin and mouthed *they're here*. Kevin immediately counted off right in the middle of the cover song and we, seamlessly, went into "In The Morning."

When we took a break we went back in the dressing room with Alan, Charlie Brusco, and Ahmet Ertegun. Unlike the Columbia Records guy from two weeks earlier, Ahmet loved our band. He couldn't say enough. He said, "I know this is gonna cost me but, I want the band... and even if I don't get you, I'm gonna be a fan."

Alan and Charlie let him know that they were up for the deal. Ahmet said, "If I sign you, you will be the first group I've signed personally since Buffalo Springfield and they've got nothing on you!"

It was enough to make your head spin.

Left to right: Me (hidden), Jerry Greenberg (President of Atlantic Records), Max Baker, Kevin Sanders, Kim Balducci, Joe Turek, Trish Turek, Ahmet Ertegun (Atlantic), Tim McMahon, Art Reel, Noreen Woods (Atlantic), Alan Walden, Jim Delehant, Anita Wexler (Atlantic), Charlie Brusco, Frank Gagliano, and Danny Liston.

I truly think Alan and Charlie were, in some ways, more awestruck than we were because they had a better understanding of who this man standing there was. Alan and Charlie believed in us, but to have this giant of the industry fawning over us was truly amazing! Ahmet said that once the deal was worked out we could come to New York to sign. I saw the look on all of our faces and knew what everyone was thinking — because I was thinking the same thing.

So, caught up in the moment, I said, "Can you come to St. Louis to sign us? That's our hometown."

I thought Alan was gonna swallow his tongue. He looked at me, as much as to say *are you insane... this is Ahmet Ertegun!*

Ahmet just laughed and said, "Sure, I haven't been to St. Louie in a while."

92

We went back onstage and finished the night. All the Atlantic people stayed until the end. I remember seeing Ahmet dancing out front to "Ol' St. Lou." It was like something out of some corny movie that you think *that never happens in real life.*

When we finished, we sat around talking to Ahmet. This was not just some record mogul — this man was extremely savvy when it came to music. I remember him saying to us, "Those guitar riffs on "Ol' St. Lou" are old horn riffs." He was the first and only person that ever picked up on that. And he was right, they were horn riffs. Everybody in Mama's Pride had played in horn bands. Actually, Mama's Pride was the first band I had played with since childhood that didn't have horns.

Alan and Charlie went to New York and sealed the deal. It was one of the biggest deals of that time. They gave us $100,000. We were blown away. It was also our first experience with how things work in this business.

Out of that $100,000, Mama's Pride saw $30,000 (or $5,000 each). I'm not exactly sure where the rest went — managers, lawyers, etc., etc. When tax time came (I had never filed taxes, dumb kid), I went to the bank to draw some money out and the IRS had seized almost all of my $5,000. Apparently, we were paying taxes on the entire $100,000 amount!

1st ALBUM AND 461 OCEAN BLVD.

Arif Mardin

Atlantic chose Arif Mardin as our producer for our first LP. Arif, himself, was a legend in the industry. Arif chose Criteria Studios, in Miami, Florida, to record. They rented a house on the beach for us to live in while we were in the studio for the next two months. The house they chose was none other than the famous 461 Ocean Boulevard of Clapton fame.

When we moved in, Stan and Nancy Colbert (owners of the house) had us sign a register. I asked if I could look through the register. This register had everybody from the Eagles to the individual Beatles in it! I was the leader so I got the master bedroom. I barely slept that first night thinking that every Beatle may have slept in this same bed. All their names were in the register. I knew Eric Clapton

461 Ocean Boulevard,
Miami, Florida

stayed here because he named an album *461 Ocean Boulevard*. On occasion, girls would knock at the door wanting to know if Eric was home. Like he'd have put his home address on an album cover!

They assigned us a maid — a sweet lady named Fannie. She would clean and cook for us. In the kitchen was a board that had individual clips with a small light above each clip. You would write down what you wanted for breakfast and put it under the clip.

Above my bed was a button, like a door bell, that was connected to the appropriate light and when I got up, I would press the button lighting the light on the clipboard. Then Fannie would start cooking whatever I had written down.

Again, this was like a fairy tale for me. We usually only ate breakfast there because we were in the studio 12 hours a day, and we ate out or at the studio for the other meals. We didn't go out to clubs or anything because we wanted to be fresh in the studio.

Tom Dowd

We had only been there a couple of days when in walks Ahmet Ertegun with another man. He introduced me to the other man by saying, "Tom, this is Pat Liston… Pat, this is Tom Dowd."

I was speechless.

Tom Dowd was another icon of the music industry. He had produced so many people and was the genius behind "Layla." He was credited with innovating the multi-track recording method.

So, as we were getting ready to record, Ahmet Ertegun, Arif Mardin, and Tom Dowd were arguing over how best to record us. It was surreal. Tom Dowd was in between projects and lived in Miami so he was just there for *fun*, as he put it. Fun!? Tom Dowd was at our recording session for fun!?

Tom didn't come in again until the overdubs — probably professional courtesy to Arif because it was Arif's session. But when he came back during overdubs he stayed out in the lobby where there was a pinball machine. He and I spent hours playing pinball. He was a very genuine guy. He even took us all out to dinner one night.

There were numerous people that came in while we were recording. (They were actually stopping by to see Arif, but we didn't care.) People like Dave Mason, Average White Band, and the Bee Gees.

One day, during overdubs, I saw an attractive petite young woman walk in. She, somehow, looked vaguely familiar. It wasn't until I saw the guy with her that I realized it was Pattie Boyd, George Harrison's ex... and the guy with her was Eric Clapton! Pattie Boyd was *Layla!*

Arif Mardin had just produced the Bee Gees new album, *Main Course.* It was a completely new direction for them. We were invited to their album premier party. It was a huge event. Unfortunately, only a handful of people showed up. The album was such a departure from all their previous hits that industry and radio people basically seemed to just blow it off. We had heard the album and liked it. We considered it "funk" because the term "disco" really wasn't big yet.

I remember sitting with Barry Gibb — both of us tipsy — and him lamenting that maybe they'd made a mistake by going in this direction. Boy, was he wrong!

Criteria Studios had a little fenced in basketball court outside and when things were getting tedious Arif would say (in his Turkish accent), "Let's play basketball." We all sucked at basketball, but it took our minds off the recording and got the blood flowing to the brain.

This one day there were three young guys watching us. They started asking questions about what the studio looked like and said that they were musicians, too. One of us (and I'm pretty sure it was Danny) asked, "Would you like to come in and watch for a while?" This was typical Danny. He has a kind heart.

They freaked and said, "Yes!" We let them stay for an hour, or so, and we never thought much more about it.

In the early 80's a stagehand friend told me that he'd gotten into a conversation with the group he'd worked for the previous night. They were in St. Louis and told him a story of a St. Louis band called Mama's Pride letting them come into Criteria Studios. He talked of how nice we had been to them. The guy was K.C. of K.C. & The Sunshine Band. I guess you just never know.

One day there was going to be this big meeting at 461. There were a bunch of lawyer/accountant people coming down from New York. The meeting was about preparing us for *stardom*. The pitfalls and dilemmas of being rich and famous, basically. They talked about investments, etc.

Looking back, this was the only time during our time with Alan that anything was explained to us with clarity and we were brought into the conversation. Now, we didn't understand half the stuff they were talking about, but at least they made an attempt to treat us with respect and not like we were airheads in a beauty pageant.

When the meeting was over, Eric Kronfeld (our attorney) said to me, "Let's go for a walk on the beach."

I have to tell this story. It is a classic story and classic Danny.

Our manager, Alan Walden, used to talk to us (as my mother called it) like we were *rubes*. This drove my mom crazy because she was very proud of how she raised her boys. She did *not* like Alan at all. She was a mother bear — don't mess with her cubs!

Anyway, Danny rarely wore shoes when he was at the house because it was easy to go out and walk along the beach or in front on the asphalt parking area and shoot the breeze with the limo drivers. The house was clean — Fannie saw to that — but the beach or the parking area in front of the house were not.

When the legal people from New York were coming down to meet with us, Alan started giving Danny a hard time about his feet.

He said, in that Georgia accent, "Danny, ya feet are dirty... you need to wash ya feet."

Danny ignored him saying, "This is my house, we're paying for it, I don't have to do anything."

Alan would not let up. He kept on and on.

Danny finally said, "*Fine!* I'll wash my damn feet. Come watch me."

461 had these fancy low-profile toilets. Danny walked into the bathroom with Alan and I right on his heals. I came because I knew my brother — he was not giving in this easily.

Danny casually stepped into the toilet with both feet and flushed it. Alan turned to me — and I have never seen a more blank look on a man's face — and said, "Yo brother is hopeless."

I literally dropped to my knees laughing. Alan rarely said anything *helpful* to Danny again.

Danny also called Ahmet Ertegun "Abdul" once when he'd come to see us. Alan was mortified and corrected Danny right in front of Ahmet.

Danny felt bad because he didn't want to offend Ahmet.

Ahmet just laughed and said, "That's ok, Danny, Otis Redding used to call me "Omelet.""

Danny felt he was in good company! Ahmet was a class act.

As we walked he said, "So, whadda ya think Paddy?" Eric was the first one to ever call me Paddy — an Irish derivative of Pat.

I said, "Ya know, Eric, bein' rich sounds like a major pain in the ass."

Eric laughed and said, "You're a wise young man, Paddy."

By the time we were finished recording we felt like big stars. It was time to go on the road — a tour maybe?

"Not so fast, Boys."

We went from 461 Ocean Boulevard to the Goats Head Bar in Raleigh, North Carolina, and stayed in a band house that I wouldn't let a dog live in. Talk about taking the wind out of your sails.

This brings me to a sore subject: We signed to Paragon Booking Agency — basically owned by Phil Walden (Alan's brother) and was part of the Capricorn dynasty. Even our lawyers and accountants were from

Macon, Georgia. (I'm not sure what became of all the New York people that came to 461.) We may have been doing southern rock, but we were yankees and we felt it.

I was told by an Atlantic insider that Ahmet wanted us to go with Premier Booking out of New York, but Alan insisted on Paragon. Alan says that that is not true.

I was also told by a reputable concert promoter I knew, that when he tried to book Mama's Pride, he was told we weren't available, but that they could have Wet Willie.

Our concerts were few and far between — and when we got concerts they were always 300 to 800 miles apart with all different headliners. We were only making (on average) $500 a concert and that had to take care of gas, rooms, and food for six band members and three or four roadies.

We would go back home and play Rusty Springs (periodically) because there we could make $2,000 to $3,000 a night. Alan would get mad when we would go back home instead of staying on the road, but we were literally starving.

If all the road gigs were concerts, we might have stayed out there, but most of the road gigs were bars that didn't pay anything and had minimal exposure to promote our record.

Alan would constantly say, "You have to pay your dues."

We had been together three years prior to Alan and had paid plenty of dues. We wanted to prove ourselves with real concerts. When Skynyrd did their first album they toured with the Who — they got famous. The Outlaws got a Doobie Brothers tour after their first album — they got famous.

After our first album we played scattered concerts, two or three at a time. Then back into several whiskey bars, each for several weeks. Then a few more small concerts. Then back in the bars. Instead of famous, we just got lost.

People don't buy albums by bands that they've never heard. And the only way you get heard is concerts with thousands of people, not bars with 30 or 40 people (on a good night). The first album was not selling anywhere but St. Louis and quite honestly we created that market single handedly.

Full-page promotion is Billboard *Magazine, October 18, 1975, pg. 7.*

KSHE radio and Shelley Grafman took care of us with airplay. My relationship with Shelley and his love for the band got us tons of airplay. This had nothing to do with management or record label — it was because he liked us. I was at KSHE as often as possible doing any interview they wanted and nurturing relations between us.

Shelley Grafman was a great guy and he is the reason KSHE is what it is today.

I remember being in Shelley's office once and seeing all the gold and platinum LPs on his wall. These were given to him by bands he'd broken in the Midwest. I remember feeling bad that we had nothing to give for all he'd done for us. So, I composed a *thank you* and then I went to a leather shop and had it burned in to a piece of leather with a ring on it for hanging. A little embarrassed, I took it to Shelley and told him that hopefully someday I could replace it with a gold album like all the others on his wall.

The next time I was at KSHE I went to see him just to say "hi" as I usually did. There on the wall — dead center behind his desk — was the leather piece I had given him.

I said, "I can't believe you gave that such a prominent place among all this gold and platinum."

"Pat," he said, "all these were given to me by record companies. They give them out like candy. But you had this made with your own words on it and brought it here yourself. To me... that means more than all this gold and platinum. Yours is truly personal."

That was Shelley. He was the real deal.

Shelley Grafman

Left to right: (standing) Shelley Grafman, Me, and Danny; (seated) Ted Habeck (on air personality), Sam Kaiser (local St. Louis rep for Atlantic Records), and Max Baker

Mama's Pride
Atco SD36-122

by Wayne Robins

Mama's Pride is a "Southern" band with a twist: They're from St. Louis, a fact they brag about repeatedly in songs like "Ole St. Lou" and "Missouri Skyline."

This routine regionalism is one of the few hackneyed elements of an otherwise appealing debut album. More hard-rock oriented than the Allman Brothers and yet not quite so rugged as Lynyrd Skynyrd, Mama's Pride goes with a standard instrumental lineup for bands of this sort: Lead guitarist Max Baker shares the attack with slide guitarist Pat Liston. And while the vocals occasionally slip into conforming Rebel-band hoots ("whoa," "lawd," etc.), Liston's hoarse improvisations on "Where Would You Be" show some real passion.

This band eschews lengthy jams in favor of shorter songs. They show at least a familiarity with R&B on songs like "Ole St. Lou" and "Young and Free," while "In the Morning" has an aggressive snap reminiscent of Skynyrd. "Blue Mist" is an ethereal, Moody Blues-type song without the saccharine, and "Kind Lovin' Woman" touches amiably on country rock. What's best about Mama's Pride is that they explore this diversity of material without relying on the most obvious clichés, excepting their tedious home town jingoism.

Our very first concert was in Jackson, Tennessee, with the Charlie Daniels Band. We were nervous as cats. We had rehearsed a lot for this, but had not taken into consideration *time-frame*.

The second from last song was "In The Morning" and then we were gonna do a big finish with "Where Would You Be." About midway through "In The Morning," Charlie's guitar roadie caught my attention and — with gestures to his watch — let me know that we'd gone over and this was to be the last song.

I freaked! I got everyone's attention and gestured this was it — everyone except Danny. (I swear I thought he saw me.)

When we finished the song we all ran off the stage. Danny, however, walks up to the microphone and says, "Thank you, thank you. Right now we'd like to..."

It was at this point he looked around and realized he was onstage alone. So he finished his sentence by saying, "Right now we'd like to... say good-night!"

He came back to the dressing room and wanted to kill me. I said, "Danny, friends honor," (this was an honor code we had that you could *not* lie to if someone called it), "I thought you saw me." I guess it was the bewildered look on his face, but suddenly the room erupted with laughter. Danny even laughed. The guys always had the ability to laugh at themselves. It was part of what made us a real team and a family.

We did get a favorable review in *Rolling Stone* that December. The worst they could say was we seemed too patriotic to St. Louis. We considered that a compliment. They referred to it as *tedious home town* [sic] *jingoism*. The journalist, obviously, had their thesaurus opened to the **J**s that day.

I do remember, right around this time, playing in Louisville, Kentucky. We played a placed called Beggars Banquet. We had played there before — for a week or two at a time. We had a lot of fans there. Sometime they'd even bring in an additional act like a comedian or something on weekends. It was a great concert-style night club.

One night we went back to the motel where two of our rooms were adjoining, and we had a party. We had some fans from St. Louis come down, too. The male fans all got along great, but the female fans from St. Louis and Louisville... not so much.

Colossal Man!

Kevin Sanders felt it was time to lighten the moment. He said, "I'll be back in a minute," and left the room. We had about four rooms there and roadies were coming in to the party rooms grabbing pillows and giggling. Try as I may, I could not figure out what they were up to with all those pillows. They took at least eight from the two party rooms.

Well, about 15 minutes later in walks our roadie, Tim McMahon, laughing so hard he could hardly speak, but still managing to choke out, "Ladies and gentlemen...Colossal Man!"

Kevin had bought a huge — and I mean *huge* — pair of long underwear a while back as a joke. The roadies had stuffed all those pillows (around 18) along with Kevin inside that long underwear! He put on a cowboy hat, cowboy boots, sun glasses, and came in as Colossal Man!

The band and road crew were losing their minds laughing. It was a sight to behold because the band, roadies, and male fans were dying laughing. The females — *all* of them — just stood there. Kevin had accomplished his goal. The two groups of women were finally talking and getting along... they all agreed that there was something wrong with us and left! Oh well, it was sure as hell funny.

The first weekend on this trip they brought in a comedian. Then about midway through the following week the club owner said, "I'm gonna bring in a group to headline Saturday. I'll pay you the same. This group is touring with Bachman-Turner Overdrive and they have an off night Saturday."

I said, "Sure, as long as we make the same." We liked stuff like this because we never got to see local bands anywhere. I asked who they were.

"They're not from here, they're from Michigan. They're called Bob Seger and the Silver Bullet Band." I had no clue who that was so the owner played "Ramblin Gamblin' Man" from an album he owned.

Quite honestly, I wasn't knocked out by the recording, but was glad to be getting some paid down time for the weekend. They came in Saturday and played. They may not have knocked me out on record, but they sure as hell did live!

Bob Seger was a real friendly guy. He and I and the club owner stayed after, drinking beer and playing pinball. Bob kept telling me *get out of this business while you can.*

After several beers I said, "You know, I have to tell you something. I heard your recording of "Ramblin' Gamblin' Man" and it left me flat, but when you did it live, you blew my doors off."

"That's what everybody says," Bob responded. "It's getting frustrating. We've actually talked about breaking up. We're going to try a *live* album and see if that makes a difference."

I said, "Well, I'd sure buy it". Then we went back to beer and pinball. He was one of the nicest most down to earth people I'd ever met. And that *live* album — it did okay.

One of our bookings was in Denver, Colorado at a place called Ebbets Field. It was named after the famed Brooklyn Dodgers ballpark. It was a small club that in the 70s had big name acts. They would have two full turn-overs a night. We worked there with Spirit as well as J.J. Cale.

I loved J.J. Cale's music and told him that I'd love to play dobro-type slide on his song "Magnolia." He brought me up on stage one night to do it. It was his third song.

He was so laid back he said, "I like what you're doing, just stay up here". I ended up doing the entire set with him.

When we worked with Spirit, Randy California wanted to arm wrestle one of our roadies, John Venincasa. I'm not sure why. John beat him easily. John was extremely strong. They actually laid on the floor to arm wrestle, right in the middle of the club. John was laughing the whole time, because it seemed such an odd request. When Randy lost, he jumped up, then dropped and did 20 push-ups real fast. He was a peculiar guy.

After their set, our bass player, Joe Turek, went up to the drummer, Ed Cassidy, and said "Great set."

Joe was just trying to be nice, but apparently they'd had a bad set because Cassidy got up in Joe's face and said, "You must be an idiot! That was a horrible set!"

Poor Joe was just being nice. I felt bad for him. Spirit was a strange cast of characters.

2nd ALBUM, MUSCLE SHOALS, AND CHANGES

So, time for a second album.

The band was not real thrilled with the first LP. Sure, it sounded slick to us, but we didn't think it captured who we really were. Arif was a genius — but maybe not the guy for us. Alan suggested we go back to Muscle Shoals and Broadway Sound Studios with David Johnson producing and try to capture that raw energy that we had had there. We felt that was a good idea, too.

Keep the fancy house and limos, let's do some music.

Just prior to this we were having a little trouble with Frank, our keyboard player. He seemed very bored. We were trying to work on the new material and I couldn't get him to play the same thing twice or even get engaged in what we were trying to do. In a group environment there has to be some consistency. Kevin Sanders was an integral part of arranging the songs and he was getting very frustrated with Frank being all over the place. He came to me and said that we had to do something because it just wasn't working.

Kevin and I met with Frank and told him that we felt he should pursue some other style of music. It was very, very difficult to let someone go who is a friend, but I was under a lot of pressure from the band to do something and in my heart I knew they were right. It had nothing to do with Frank as a person or even as a musician. He just wasn't into what we were doing. So, I had the difficult task of letting Frank go.

Paul Willett, second from left.

Once again, we had to find a new member. We tried out several people, and the job went to Paul Willett. Paul had a lot of talent, but his greatest asset was his passion for music. When he tried out, he was very animated when he played, it was like he embraced every note. I loved that about him and he was a shoe-in for the job.

We rehearsed intently for the new LP and getting Paul familiar with the older material as well. Danny had a couple of songs that he'd written in California that we were revisiting.

One was a bluesy shuffley song. He and Kevin worked some on a re-arrangement of it — speeding up the tempo and driving it more. Danny also had a slow front tag to the song that really set the mood for when the whole band came in. The front was just Danny singing and Paul on the piano (almost jazzy), then the snare drum gave a driving roll and... "Can I Call You A Cab." It was one of the most fun songs we'd ever worked out.

The other song was a slow ballad he'd also written in California. I actually liked it just the way it was — very mournful. One day Jim Delehant, the head of A&R at Atlantic flew to St. Louis to see how things were going. He asked if we had anything like "Freebird" — a ballad that could crank up at the end. We took Danny's song and did just that. Once again, I felt we were getting away from the music and trying to *be* something. The song was "Long Time." The jam at the end was a fan favorite, but again, I worried about us being something we weren't, and deep down I think the band felt the same way. I always liked "Long Time" — so mournful and deep. If you ask a fan about "Long Time," the first thing they'll say is, "Yah, the big jam!" — a damn shame because I don't think anybody listens to the song itself.

We went back into Broadway Sound Studios with David Johnson for the second LP. We felt good about these recordings and were waiting to hear back about mix, release date, etc.

David Johnson

We were in Roslyn, Long Island, New York, playing at My Father's Place with Commander Cody. To our surprise, our attorney, Eric Kronfeld, came in and told me we were going to LA to re-record the second LP. Someone at the top at Atlantic didn't like the way it sounded. This was not what I wanted to hear.

We rehearsed for quite a while. We had all the songs chosen already because we'd already done the album once at Broadway Sound Studios. We had a few dates to do before going in to the studio again. One was a club in Mundelein, Illinois.

I had just been through a rough relational-thing and was doing a lot of writing. While in Mundelein, I was sitting by the pool (which was closed for the season) at the motel where we were staying. A song started coming to me. You always know if a song is special or not. I finished two verses and the chorus

While at My Father's Place in Long Island, we were getting ready to go onstage to open for Commander Cody and we were going over vocal harmonies. I looked up and saw this young girl standing at the door listening.

She sort of blushed at being spotted and softly said, "You sound like angels... may I just listen?"

Hell, a cute young girl with hair almost to her calves wants to listen... absolutely.

We sang every song we'd ever written!

We only played one night there and I never saw her again... that is until I was watching "Saturday Night Live" one night a year or so later and there she was!

"Oh, my God! There's the girl from Long Island!"

She still had that long, long hair and she wasn't singing background with Commander Cody. She was singing her own song — "Lotta Love."

She was Nicolette Larson.

BIG HORN

Route 176 & 60-83

Mundelein ● 949-5551

| BEER GARDEN SPECIALS 25¢ BEER Friday and Saturday nights only - In the beer garden only 8-10 p.m. | WEEKDAY SPECIALS WEDNESDAY MONDAY - THURSDAY 25¢ BEER 8-11 p.m. ALL THE MEISTER BRAU OR MILLER YOU CAN DRINK 8-10 p.m. $2* 9-10 $1* *plus admission for bands | WEEKEND SPECIALS FRIDAY & SATURDAY Weekly drink specials. Different drink each week. 8-9:30 p.m. |

IN CONCERT!
JULY 2-3

MAMA'S PRIDE

Toured with the Allman Brothers

and couldn't wait to play it for someone. Most often, my go-to guy for songs was our drummer, Kevin Sanders.

I played it for him and he said, "Dude, finish that. We'll bump a song if we have to, but that has *got* to go on the album."

I went back and finished the third verse and added it to the list. Kevin knew how to approach it also. If the song had had a backbeat it would have sounded silly (like a country song), but Kevin knew what I wanted. The song was called "She's a Stranger To Me Now."

2nd ALBUM (again) IN LOS ANGELES

After the few dates we had scheduled, we flew to Los Angeles. It was better than the last trip there, driving. They had us record at a studio called Davlen in North Hollywood.

As our producer they hired Jim Mason who had produced Poco and had just finished producing a new group's first LP — *Firefall*.

Davlen Studio, North Hollywood

Atlantic asked where we'd like to stay — we chose Howard's Weekly Apartments. Hey, it was a great little place.

While recording, Timothy B. Schmidt came in to see Jim. This was prior to his joining the Eagles. What many people don't know is, Timothy sang some background on that album. I gave the information to our manager when the project was done, but because he'd never heard of him, he failed to add his name to the credits.

It was thrilling for my brother and I to see all the strings playing on our two songs. They played "She's A Stranger To Me Now" first, but when they did the opening to "Can I Call You A Cab," it sounded like a Gershwin song! We loved the reaction that the string players had when the snare drum went *rat ta ta ta ta... Can I call you a Cab.*

You have to understand, these were the best string players in LA and they never see the charts until they're in the studio. They didn't have a clue what the song was going to be like. The beginning was so orchestral that they figured the song was, too.

Surprise!

There were always musicians hanging around in the studio. We got really tight with two guys who were there a lot — David Paich and Jeff Porcaro. They were there late at night (after we'd leave) rehearsing with this new band they were putting together. When we were finished recording I told David we'd keep an eye out for the new band and I wished him well. Unbeknownst to me, they wouldn't need my blessing. The following year Toto's first album was released.

About a year or so later, they played at the Checkerdome in St. Louis. David Paich contacted us. My brother Danny, David Cloud, and I went down to see them. We couldn't stay because we were playing at a club that night. I remember the guitarist, Steve Lukather, and the singer, Joe Williams, had heard our LP and went on and on about how great we were.

Joe Williams said, "We should get Mama's Pride to open for us on tour."

My eyes lit up, but David Paich said, "No way, when Mama's Pride plays, you wouldn't want to go on after them."

It was an incredible compliment, but I'd have rather heard him agree and take us on the road!

2nd ALBUM CONTINUES AND MORE CHANGES

I worried a lot about this LP — there was way too much partying. Not as much the band, but the producer and the engineer. (The mixing board actually had a beveled mirror built in to the console.)

After we were finished recording everything we went back to St. Louis. While we were there, Joe Turek, our bass player quit. He had some family issues going on. He was married and they'd just had their little girl, Heather. This life style can take a toll on a family and Joe took the high road and walked away. I respected his choice, but here we are again.

What made it even worse was, Joe had written a song called "Wandering Man" that was going to be on the album. He also sang it. Well, we could hardly have him on the album and singing if he wasn't even in the band. Now we not only had to replace the bass player, but we were short one song.

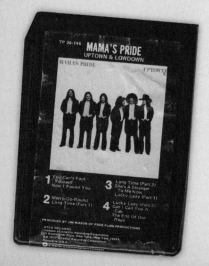

But first, the dilemma of finding a new bass player.

When I flew back to St. Louis, I went out for three nights running and never saw a bass player that I would even consider. Danny and I lived at our mom's house when we were off the road and I was sitting at her kitchen table one morning, fretting over our bass player dilemma. Someone knocked at the front door and I went to answer it.

When I opened the door, there was a girl named Susie who was one of our Louisville,
Kentucky, fans. She had a crush on one of the guys in the band, but I knew she wasn't a stalker or anything. Susie was a real sweet girl, but to this day, I don't know how she knew where my mom lived. I was somewhat stunned.

I invited her in and offered her a cup of coffee. We sat and talked and she asked about the guys. At one point she asked, "How's Joe doing?"

"Well, oddly enough, Joe just quit and we're looking for a bass player."

She jumped out of that chair like a Pentecostal and said, "Oh, my God, I came to St. Louis because my new boyfriend is playing here — he's a bass player. He's the best bass player in the world!"

I hadn't been up real long so this came at me way too fast. I thought, *Great, I've seen nothing but bad bass players for three days and now this.* She was out of her mind with excitement and insisted I come see him. That was an easy sell — I was desperate at this point and figured it couldn't hurt. She said he played in a show band at the Red Carpet Lounge in Cahokia, Illinois. I went to see him that night. *Get it over with,* I thought.

Susie came and sat at my table, which was uncomfortable because if her boyfriend sucked as a bass player, what do I say to her? The band played before the main guy came out. I sat there in disbelief. The bass player was great, just like Susie said. I mean he was incredible! Then they introduced him to sing some song. They called him Dickie Silver — and he had a great voice! Oh, my God, pinch me!

On the break he came to the table and I talked to him. Susie had already told him we were looking for a bass player. Ironically, he was from Louisville, Kentucky, and was a fan. I told him I wanted him in the band, ASAP! I asked him if his name was really Dickie Silver?

"I had to make it showy for the band. My real name is Dickie Steltenpohl."

Dickie was then, and is now, one of the most amazing bass players I've ever known. Susie eventually broke up with Dickie, but it was an amazing story, and the way it happened was nothing short of providential.

Kevin, Danny, and I flew back to LA leaving Max in St. Louis to teach Dickie the songs. I love Max, but he isn't the most patient person in the world. I knew if Dickie survived Max, we had a true talent!

Kevin, Danny, and I flew to LA because our producer had an idea for a song. We had recorded a song called "When Will You Learn" and decided not to use it because there wasn't enough room on the album. When Joe quit, we figured we'd just use that. Apparently, someone at Atlantic felt we needed a cover song. Why? I never knew. Jim Mason decided on "End of Our Road" — an old Motown song. I think he just wanted to play bass. He had been a bass player before his producing career. We had no bass player, so he was it. I considered this an odd decision. Jim played bass just fine. I just didn't know why we were doing this song. In my opinion, this was far and away the weakest song on the LP.

Another thing that bothered me a lot was the vocals on "She's a Stranger To Me Now." Kevin Sanders had arranged these wonderful five-part harmonies. I tried explaining to Jim Mason the difference between harmony and background vocals. Background vocals are *ooohs* and *aaahs* behind the lead vocal, mixed below the lead. Harmonies, on the other hand, are vocals singing *with* the lead singer. They should be mixed almost even with the lead like Crosby, Stills, and Nash style. Jim said he understood, but then mixed them in the background. The haunting synthesizer needed to be more out front and it was not.

On the first album I was clueless — as were most of the guys in the band. But on the second album I was starting to get an understanding of the recording process, how it worked, and what I wanted to hear. I sensed we were in even bigger trouble with this album. I was right. This one didn't even do as well as the first album.

Things were looking bleak for us. Also, it seemed like Atlantic Records had suddenly become disinterested. Our manager never truly understood who we were. He just wanted another Lynyrd Skynyrd and we were not them.

We went right back into little crappy bars. We did a few concert dates, but very few. I knew the album wasn't right and this was a lousy way to promote it. We hit rock bottom one night when we played Iron City, Tennessee, on Christmas Eve. There was virtually no one in the bar. The heat had gone out and we could see our breath when we sang. The owner said if we didn't finish, he wouldn't pay us, so we played with our coats on. Merry Christmas!

We were so fed up. We always seemed to get the bottom of the barrel for gigs and it seemed like no one at Atlantic cared anymore. They had just hired a guy named Michael Klefner from Arista Records. He loved the Outlaws, but absolutely hated us... and now he's with Atlantic.

We knew our days were numbered.

RONNIE VAN ZANT (A New Beginning Ends Too Quickly)

One great thing that happened during this period was David Cloud left the Outlaws and became our road manager.

I was doing most of the regional booking of the band. I was the leader, sang most of the songs, wrote most of the songs, and did all of the day-to-day business. The band was not in favor of hiring David at the time. It was not that they had anything against David — they liked him. It was because, to them, he was another mouth to feed.

David (to me) was much needed help. The band never realized how much I actually did while still making the same money as the other members. I never took extra. I cannot begin to express the pressure relief David supplied for me.

The band accepted David because he was a great guy. I don't think they knew what he did anymore than what I had done for years. Most musicians are clueless to the business aspect of music. When they show up and everything is done — they think it all just magically happened or that I made one phone call and everything fell in place. David did way more than road manage. He co-booked with me and eventually took over booking completely. He and I would brainstorm over lunch on how we could make the band more money.

David mostly booked the clubs — or as we called them *the money gigs*. Paragon was still holding the concert strings and any concerts we got were very small ones and very little money.

...but then a glimmer of sunshine came.

As I said before, Alan Walden had managed Lynyrd Skynyrd at one time. They had had a bad falling out. Ronnie Van Zant wrote "Cry For the Bad Man" about him. It was brutal. At the time, I actually felt kind of bad for Alan.

They seemed to sort of make up at one point. It was during that time that Ronnie Van Zant heard our music. He loved us! He'd been wanting to segue into producing. Lynyrd Skynyrd had one hit after another — they were arguably the biggest band in the world at that time. The fact that the leader liked us was nice to hear. Then he announced that he'd like to produce us. Atlantic was going to drop us and Ronnie saved our sinking ship.

On July 8th, 1977, we opened for Lynyrd Skynyrd in Springfield, Missouri.

I talked with Ronnie at length after the show. We sat on a freight case together cross-legged while he graciously signed dozens of autographs for fans. He was really excited about producing us.

Ronnie told me, "I want you with me 24/7. You're the leader and principal writer." He said he didn't feel we were southern rock. He thought we had incredible vocals and harmonies, and that should be the emphasis.

Hell, I knew that the first time Max, Danny, and I sang. That's why I put the band together in the first place. Finally, someone with clout got it, too.

We went back to the dressing room where the rest of the band was. Ronnie said he wanted us to open for their world tour. I kiddingly said, "Can we start tomorrow?"

Ronnie Van Zant

He was a stand up guy. He said there were already groups slotted to open shows through October. He didn't want to bump anyone off these shows and put them out of work. He said, "I'm sure you have plenty of work until then." I was thinking to myself *yah, down in Bull's Ass, Alabama, somewhere.* But it was okay. We were gonna tour with Lynyrd Skynyrd!

I saw Billy Powell when we were leaving and he told me he was really looking forward to working with us. Ronnie walked up and said, "Here. It isn't released yet. Give it a listen." He handed me the album *Street Survivors*. In my opinion it was their best album yet!

Finally, we caught a break. This was going to be huge!

Left to Right: Danny Liston, Kevin Sanders, Art Reel (sound tech), Grover Lee Loveless (road crew), Jim Wilhelm (road crew), Dickie Steltenpohl, Max Baker, Paul Willett, and Me.

We went out on the road again. While we were out this time, Paul Willett decided to leave. This was a tough loss for me. Paul, at that time, was my best buddy. We were very close. We were the closest in age and had a lot in common. I was almost angry with him, even though I understood. He was newly married and his wife was pregnant.

I was getting so tired of finding new people and losing old friends. I actually put an ad in the paper. I knew that was opening me up to every hack in the world, but I just didn't have the energy to hit the clubs again.

We did get a lot of strange responses. I was sorry I hadn't just gone looking like before. This may sound strange, but we were having four guys try out one day and I prayed that the right one would be wearing a red shirt. That sounds crazy, I know, but I was desperate.

The first three guys were not very good. The last guy walked in wearing an orangish/red tank top. I thought, *close enough!*

He had obviously gone over some of the material because he requested certain songs. Danny asked him if he knew any blues songs. He looked a little flustered and said, "You mean like Moody Blues?"

Danny looked at me like *oh, my God.*

I chalked it up to him being nervous. I was a little unsure of this guy, but it was obvious how hard he'd worked on the songs, so I went with him. This was Jeff Schmidt and he was a great guy.

Jeff worked very hard. He was very different from a bunch of South Side guys like us. There were times he looked at us in (what seemed) utter amazement. We approached life differently than a more rural type guy like Jeff — he was pretty laid back and we were very *in your face* type people at times.

We got a call from our booking agency one day: Alice Cooper was touring and The Tubes were opening for him. They had a sold out show in Nashville, Tennessee, on August 6th, 1977. The Tubes had to cancel at the last minute and I'm guessing they couldn't find anybody to fill the slot so we got the nod.

It made us a bit nervous because this wasn't exactly our type of show.

I told the guys, "I know this is Alice Cooper, and I know the first six rows are people with face makeup just like Alice, but... *this is Nashville.* We may not be as far out of the realm as we think."

We actually had a great show and afterwards I was walking around backstage — the "backstage" of the Nashville Municipal Auditorium being a beehive of rooms and spaces — and I saw a curtain by this one room and peeked in.

It was a big concrete room that appeared to be empty until I saw a soccer ball come flying by and hit the wall. I looked at the other end of the room and there he was... Vincent Furnier... a.k.a. Alice Cooper!

He was all dressed up and ready to go on stage. I said, "Oh, I'm sorry, I thought this room was empty."

"That's cool," he said, and kicked the ball to me.

I side-footed it to the wall and back to him. He said, "You've played soccer."

"Yah," I replied, "I was raised in an Irish-Catholic neighborhood, ya had to play soccer... but I was lousy."

"Where are you from?" he asked.

I told him St. Louis and he yelled, "Budweiser!!"

We chatted about St. Louis for a few minutes. He told me it was one of his favorite cities. Then he heard his intro music. "That's my cue... gotta go."

He tipped his top hat with his cane and off he went like something out of *Alice in Wonderland*. If not for the make-up, he was just a regular guy.

As I turned to walked back to our dressing room, I thought, *Wow! That was Alice Cooper. I kicked soccer with Alice Cooper. Cool!*

It was Thursday, October 20, 1977. We were in a bar called the Waterhouse celebrating our soon-to-be fame and fortune when it came on the news... *Lynyrd Skynyrd's plane had crashed.*

Among the dead: assistant road manager, Dean Kilpatrick; pilot, Walter McCreary and co-pilot William Gray; guitarist/vocalist, Steve Gaines; backing vocalist, Cassie Gaines (Steve's older sister); and lead singer, Ronnie Van Zant.

We just sat there. Stunned.

Not only had one of the greatest bands *ever* come to an end, so had our recording career with Atlantic records.

Yep, Michael Klefner had gotten his way after all. He said that his first line of duty with Atlantic was to drop Mama's Pride from the label — and he did, two days later.

Michael Klefner was the guy at the end of the *Blues Brothers* movie that signed them to a label — his presence ruined that movie for me. I'm not a hater, but the closest I ever came was what I felt for Michael Klefner.

HAYS DAILY NEWS

er killed

pilot, co- were ...ded and ...mer ...eon ...ayer ...ton, ...e in ...Pyle ...as ...ler- ...t of

gas and plowed nose first into a thick forest only 200 yards from a open field which the pilot apparently was trying to reach.

The plane, en route from Greenville, S.C., to Baton Rouge, La., for a concert Friday night, went down two miles northeast of Gillsburg near the Louisiana-Mississippi line.

A spokesman for Sir Productions, which manages the group, said all occupants

RONNIE VAN ZANT

of the plane except the crew were connected with Lynyrd Skynyrd or its members.

Find give wa

WASH Compro provide workers wage cleared Preside

The final a increa wage s An e worker increa

Sunbacker™

Right after this we went to Hartford, Connecticut, to play with Sea Level. It was an outdoor show during the day. We had a great time. Chuck Leavell even sat in on "Ol' St. Lou."

We went back to the motel after the show. It was still daylight and the guys were all talking. I decided to go out to the motor home and just be alone and quiet. The whole thing with Ronnie Van Zant was still weighing heavy on me.

I started playing guitar with a drop **D** tuning. I was getting some lyrics in my head and started looking for writing materials. I found a pen, but no paper. I was so frustrated because lyrical ideas were coming fast and furious.

I looked over on the table where we played cards and there was an empty pizza box. I tore the lid off and used it for paper and penned "Sail On" — inspired for Ronnie Van Zant's passing.

We had befriended a guy named Kent Kesterson. He and his wife, Marilyn, had opened a beautiful new recording studio in Earth City just outside St. Louis. For the time, it was state-of-the-art. We told our Manager, Alan Walden, about the studio. We told him we could get great rates, too.

Alan was not only our manager, he was also our publisher. According to our publishing contract, he was supposed to pay for studio time. He refused to pay for the time. His reasoning was: he would only pay for studio time if we came to Muscle Shoals, Alabama. We knew he had a deal worked out down there and that's why he said that. But that was not how the contract read. It, technically, was a breach of the publishing agreement.

Plus, if we recorded in Muscle Shoals, we had to drive 800 miles round trip and get rooms. This would entail the cost of gas and accommodations which we were expected to pay for ourselves.

So, we started recording at KBK because it was cheaper for us to pay for studio time ourselves than all the travel and motel costs. Kent was a great guy and eventually ended up almost giving us studio time. We did favors to buffer this.

We would record for his classes that he gave there at the studio. He taught recording and the students got to learn *and* have Mama's Pride as their aid. They would also get the recordings they mixed. This means there is a ton of Mama's Pride songs out there that are all mixed differently. I wasn't crazy about that, but it afforded us free studio time so it was a trade off.

NO MORE MANAGEMENT

Our manager, Alan Walden, kept pushing for more Skynyrd-type songs. I was writing some good music, but he wanted no part of it. He literally hated my new songs. This, in part, brought about our leaving Alan. Also, I had embraced Christianity.

The whole rock scene and lifestyle was weighing on me. I wanted some semblance of normalcy. I was getting sick and tired of touring considering we were only playing small clubs that paid less than we could make in St. Louis.

Alan had run out of ideas and really had nothing left to offer us. We were sick of hearing about paying dues and doing these terrible gigs out on the *chittlin' circuit*.

And we just kept going into KBK Studios and recording more demos that *we* had to pay for.

We had come to an impasse with Alan. We wanted out. He wouldn't let us go until we all signed these promissory notes that said we *owed* him $20,000. We wanted out so bad we'd have signed anything. We never got any breakdown on what this money we owed was for. I never received a dime of writers royalties, but somehow I owed him a ton of money in the form of a promissory note?

I have to say that, during our entire tenure with Alan and Atlantic Records we rarely knew what was going on. I mean, we signed contracts, but what 20-something musician reads all that crap? Or, understands it if he does read it?

No one ever broke things down. We didn't know that everything spent (and I mean everything) came out of our small percentage. It seemed like all our lawyers or accounting people were either affiliated with Alan or Atlantic somehow. I'm sure that it's just the way things were done back then.

Writers royalties were mere pennies for each song and artist royalties were about a dollar per record. Atlantic spent a lot of money, so we never saw artist royalties. This was mainly because the two albums simply didn't sell enough. Record companies rarely, if ever, take writers royalties in a group situation because it's an uneven breakdown. In our case, I wrote or co-wrote most of the songs, so if they took writers royalties, I would stand to lose more than the other guys. Given that, it just wasn't done. However, someone not only took some of the writers royalties... they took them all, because we never saw a penny in writers royalties. It wasn't a huge amount, but it wasn't chump change either.

LIFE CHANGES AND GREGG ALLMAN

Early in 1978, I got married. Shortly there after my wife got pregnant.

Mama's Pride was playing in- and out-of-town. I was trying to stay in town as much as possible because I wanted to be in town when the baby was born. But there was one out-of-town job that had already been booked — to play at a place in Daytona, Florida, where we always did well — the Wreck Bar.

The owner was a woman that we called "Ringo." I'm not sure we ever knew her real name, but Ringo loved Mama's Pride and Mama's Pride loved Ringo! She was a class act and treated us like gold when we were there. We would play there six nights a week for several weeks at a time.

Me and Danny with Ringo at the Wreck Bar, Daytona, Florida.

On this particular occasion, she called and said she wanted us to come a day early for the gig so we could see the band playing there. Had it been anybody else but Ringo I'd have made an excuse and blown it off. But she was insistent so we went down a day earlier.

When we pulled up to the Wreck Bar we saw her little lighted marquee. It read: *Tonight, Gregg Allman.*

At first I thought she was just playing a trick on me. Then we walked in... and there he was onstage, Gregg Allman. He was playing with some god-awful band, but he sounded great.

I had heard about his divorce from Cher and that he'd moved back to Florida, but here he was in the Wreck Bar. I also knew that Ringo and he were friends — it was common knowledge. I was glad we were there to see it, but it still seemed a little over the top to ask me to drive down a day early for this.

She had a gathering afterwards in her apartment upstairs. This was unusual because no one *ever* went upstairs. We all spoke to Gregg and I asked if he remembered Hawaii. He, of course, did not. I didn't expect him to remember. The road can become a blur sometimes. Ringo chimed in and said, "They're playing here tomorrow night, you really need to come see them."

Gregg said, "I'll do that."

I'm thinking, *ri-i-i-ight, sure you will.*

Mama's Pride at the Wreck Bar.

The next night, he actually came in. He walked in and sat at the bar. In a split second our road manager, David Cloud, ran over and sat next to him. David told me later that while I was singing and doing one of my elongated screams, Gregg said, "Who the hell is that singing?"

David said, "That's Pat Liston, the leader of the band."

"Holy shit, he's amazing!"

Well, naturally, between David and Ringo, Gregg was coerced into sitting in with us. We played for about an hour together. When we were done Gregg said, "I can't believe how well you guys just fell into these songs." What he didn't know was, we'd probably played these songs more times than he had back in our early days.

At the end of the night we were all chatting and saying we should do some dates together... but I knew that was just musician banter. Again, things don't just *happen* because we all get together partying in a room and say, "Dude, you know what'd be cool..."

Jeff Schmidt, Gregg Allman, and Me

David and I made arrangements with Gregg to come by his house the following day and talk... sober.

We told Gregg that we had our own PA and lights, a great road crew, the perfect musician line-up, and David Cloud could book it. A total *in-house* deal. We'd split it 50/50. He thought that sounded great and gave David permission to move forward on it.

This wasn't the whole Lynyrd Skynyrd thing, but it was Gregg Allman. He was happy with the deal and David and I would figure out the whole scenario: the money (much more than we'd been making), the tour, routing, everything. All the band had to do was learn a few songs and we were good to go.

David booked a few small dates to get our feet wet and get a feel for working together. We'd open as Mama's Pride so as not to lose our own identity again. Then we would come out as the Gregg Allman Band. Those first few shows were probably only about 75-minute shows. We needed to learn more of his material.

David and I asked him what songs we should work out for the next leg of shows. He didn't really care. He said, "You pick 'em, I trust you." We got together with the band and we chose our favorite Gregg songs — some Allman Brothers Band, some from *Laid Back,* and some from *Playin' Up A Storm.*

Gregg came to St. Louis to practice with us in Danny's basement. Nobody in St. Louis knew he was there. We had been practicing for a week or so when he arrived. When we started rehearsal with him we opened with "Good Thing" — the old Oliver Sain song off of his *Laid Back* album. He stopped the song halfway in. We thought something was wrong. We had worked out all these additional background vocals and I thought maybe he didn't like the changes we'd made.

He said, "My God, the vocals are great! My last solo tour had three black women that didn't sound this good!"

He was very pleased with everything we were doing.

David Cloud booked a small tour and we went out with Gregg. Towards the end we came back to St. Louis and did several local shows with him. One of the places we played was the old Collinsville Park Ballroom. The guy apparently thought that — because it was Gregg Allman — he didn't have to promote or advertise. There were only about a hundred people there by show time. When I found out that the man had done no advertising of any kind, I went to Gregg and told him, "Gregg, there's only about a hundred people here because the guy didn't promote the show. We've already been paid, you don't have to do this if you don't want to."

Gregg looked me square in the eye and said, "Pat, never punish the ones that came."

He put on one of the best performances he'd done with us. He seemed to really enjoy the intimacy. People just rushed the stage and sat on the floor in front. It ended up being a great night.

We had a lot of fun with Gregg on the road. Kevin Sanders was very into Hollywood monster make-up. He had his own make-up kit and everything. One night he made Gregg up to look like he'd been beaten up. He used an egg shell to make his eye look swollen and everything. He was very good at it. I'm not sure how he talked Gregg into it, but Gregg was lovin' it.

We called Gregg's road manager, Paul Burke, and told him Gregg had been beat up in the parking lot. Paul came to the room in a rage, waving a chrome .45 pistol and threatening a person that didn't even exist! It was so convincing that Paul never knew it wasn't real until we finally let him in on the joke. He was extremely angry with us, until we told him that Jimbo (Jim Essery), the harmonica player, hadn't seen it yet. Then Paul was into fooling Jim and we pulled the same prank on him!

Gregg didn't like doing interviews — particularly TV interviews. Unlike radio interviews, television is quick and condensed and always just fluff.

He was slotted to do an interview in (I believe) Youngstown, Ohio. He required them to come to the theater after sound check. They got all set up and were waiting for Gregg to come and get seated because it was for the 5:00 p.m. news and *live*.

Gregg insisted, as he always did, that Danny and I be there, flanking him. We knew what he didn't want to talk about. If there was that type question, Danny and I would crack a joke or interrupt it with some silliness. Gregg actually enjoyed interviews with us there because we drove the interviewer crazy.

Anyway, the interviewer was a young woman who was the quintessential TV talking head. She had her little paper with her notes. They were counting down the *live* interview, "Ten... Nine... Eight..."

At that very moment Gregg turned to her and said, "Don't ask me anything about drugs or Cher."

She went pale.

It was obvious that that was all she had written down. She frantically said, "What can we talk about!?"

"You could try talking about my music."

Needless to say, it had to be the worst interview on record. She knew *nothing* about Gregg's music. She did have one question that Danny and I liked because of Gregg's answer. She asked, "Who are your favorite contemporary blues singers?"

Gregg turned to Danny and I and said, "They're right here with me."

It was not the answer she wanted. She wanted to hear B.B. King or someone more notable. It was cool for Danny and I though. We were giving each other *fingertips* behind Gregg's back.

More often than not, we would get together in the motel room after the show with acoustic guitars and sing. Sometimes, Gregg would sing something. He did a great rendition of the Beatle song "Rain." We always told him he needed to record that. (I think he finally did record it on a demo, or something.)

Most of the time, all Gregg wanted to do was harmonize with us. He thought our vocals were stellar and he rarely got to just harmonize. We would sing old Beatles or old R&B. He liked the simple stuff like the old Don & Juan song "What's Your Name."

He and I had a time together one night — just the two of us. He reached in his pocket and pulled out a joint and said, "You want to do this?"

I said, "Oh hell, Gregg, I don't smoke weed anymore."

"Neither do I," he said.

"Then why do you want to smoke it?"

He smiled and said, "What, do you have an appointment in the morning?"

I laughed and said, "Well, no..."

We talked for a long time. He was pretty tight lipped about his personal life, but we covered a lot of ground that night. He told me a lot of things that I've never spoken to anyone about, but he did tell me an interesting story that I don't mind sharing.

When he was married to Cher, she called him at their house one day while she was rehearsing for her weekly show. Her guest that week was going to be Ray Charles. She told Gregg that she was having trouble understanding what Ray wanted and would he (Gregg) drive down to the studio and help her. Gregg said he was thrilled because Ray was one of his idols. He went down and it all went well.

What seemed odd about the story was that Gregg seemed shocked to discover that Ray was familiar with his music and glad to meet him. Gregg recalled that he'd probably sounded like an idiot talking to Ray because he had so much admiration for Ray's music and was so honored to finally meet him. I laughed about Gregg being surprised that Ray knew who he was and said, "Well, good Lord, son, you're Gregg Allman. We're friends, but I'm honored to work with you." For some reason, that made him uncomfortable. Gregg didn't seem to have a handle on his importance in the music scene.

Gregg always got uncomfortable around people that would fawn over him too much. It could get embarrassing for us because it would seem like he was being a jerk when, in fact, he didn't feel worthy of the adulation.

There was one incident we had in Orlando where we were playing a small concert theater. We were getting ready to go onstage. Gregg was running his hands through his hair and noticed a young woman standing there with a brush in her hand. He asked if he could use it. She handed it to him, obviously thrilled. When he was finished brushing his hair he handed it back to her. She said with a smile, "I'll never wash this again." He gave her a disgusted look and walked out onstage.

I could tell she was crushed. I said nothing to Gregg until later in the dressing room. I told him that he'd probably hurt her feelings by reacting so negatively to her response. He said, "I just hate that crap — like it's a big deal that I used her brush."

I said, "You're Gregg Allman for God's sake."

"So what?"

"Gregg… you're her Ray Charles."

I'll never forget the look on his face. "You think she's still here?"

I laughed. "No, she's already at a party telling everybody what a jerk you are."

He said, "Gee thanks."

I read an article recently where he said he has finally come to grips with the fact that he's famous and that he'd never really *gotten it* before. Maybe our talk made him think about that?

We had a couple of days off and we were scheduled to play in Atlanta, Georgia, in a few days. Gregg called David and I one afternoon and asked us to come to his room. When we got there he showed us a telegram he'd gotten from Phil Walden and Phil Hodges of Capricorn Records. The telegram read, *Gregg… we strongly urge you not to play Atlanta with Mama's Pride.*

He asked me what I wanted to do. I said, "Let's send them a telegram and strongly urge them to kiss our collective asses!"

"Pat, they are powerful people down there, they're no one to mess with."

"Well, we're playin' Atlanta," I said. "I don't care what they say."

I went and told the guys so they'd know what was going on. They were in total agreement. So it was on to the Agora Theater in Atlanta.

Gregg and I had talked about him getting new management — possibly in New York — and that we could do some writing with him and back him up on a new solo project. He was seriously thinking about it. I'm sure the Georgia overlords had heard about this. I assumed this was why they were threatening us not to play in their backyard. There was so much irony in us recently cutting ties with Alan Walden and Gregg looking to do the same with Alan's brother, Phil Walden — irony that Phil wasn't going to take laying down.

The day we set up for sound check, Paul Burke (Gregg's road manager) said that we shouldn't drink anything but beer that night and only if he opened it while we were standing there. I thought, *my God, are they going to poison us?* Paul was nervous, and that made me nervous, so we agreed to his suggestion.

We were standing in the back of the theater when two Mercedes limos pulled up. I saw them getting out of the limos — Alan Walden, Phil Walden, Alex Hodges, Jerry Womack, and others. All the Capricorn Records and Paragon Booking Agency people. I thought, *they just live in Macon and they brought Mercedes limos?*

They were trying to make a statement. They did.

We went inside and waited in a dressing room that was *not* big enough for this gathering. I'm not sure the Astrodome would have been big enough given the collection of people. They came in, everyone did their mandatory pleasantries. Gregg said hi to Phil. We greeted Alan Walden and Jerry Womack. The others ignored us as though we were invisible. Thank God we were getting ready to go onstage.

We rocked!

The place was packed. The Agora Theater was a very big concert-type nightclub and it was packed! To say the crowd was enthusiastic was an understatement. Gregg grabbed the microphone and said, "It's good to be back home..." and the crowd erupted. We went right in to "Sweet Feelin'" from his *Playin' Up A Storm* album.

After playing for about an hour and a half we got a very, very enthusiastic encore. We came back out and did "Statesboro Blues" and the crowd exploded with applause!

On a side note: Our soundman, Art Reel, used to record these concerts on a really nice cassette deck that he always brought. I will be eternally grateful that he did, because I still have these recordings and they definitely capture the energy of the Agora concert.

When we came offstage we felt akin to David slaying Goliath. The "Macon Mafia" — as Gregg called them — could not deny their eyes and ears. They knew they were in trouble and something had to be done about it.

To make matters even more strained than they already were, Robert Nix and Dean Daughtry from the Atlanta Rhythm Section were there. They'd come to see us and Gregg. We'd done a few shows together. They were both half drunk. Dean Daughtry, the drummer from ARS, was a really big country boy. He went over to Alan Walden (who is a very small man) and hovered over him, laughing and tauntingly said, "These guys sounded great! ...and you lost 'em... and now your brother's gonna lose Gregg!"

I immediately went over and put my arm around Dean and said, "Hey, Dean what 'cha drinkin', I'm buyin'," and hustled him away.

We played a second night there, minus the Macon crowd. It was every bit as enthusiastic as the previous night. After this gig, we went back to St. Louis.

Before leaving, David and I met with Gregg. David was already booking a second tour — with bigger concerts, more dates, and more money. Gregg was thrilled and said to call him when David finished and he'd fly to St. Louis for rehearsals. He wanted to work out a few more songs.

One of the songs he wanted to work out was "Midnight Rider" because, while we were playing in Cleveland once, we'd planned on working the song out. We were at the sound check to go over it. While waiting for Gregg to arrive we ran through it several times. After about two hours we got tired of waiting and shut everything down and the crew started putting guitars back in the dressing room. Everyone wanted to eat and rest some before the show.

As we were coming off the stage, in walks Gregg and Jim Essery, the harmonica player. Gregg walked up and apologized for being late.

I said, "Twenty minutes is late... we're done. See ya' back at the hotel."

He apologized profusely and I was gracious about it. We all just went to eat and dropped it.

Mudbone and Tyrone Shoelaces

One night, during one of the motel sessions, we were all talking about the Cheech & Chong album *Los Cochinos* and the Richard Pryor album *Is It Something I Said?*.

Two characters came up that tickled Gregg, one was "Mudbone" from Richard Pryor's album and the other was "Tyrone Shoelaces" from the Cheech & Chong album.

For some reason, after that night, I started calling Gregg "Mudbone" and he would call me "Tyrone Shoelaces."

Years later a friend of mine was getting an autograph from Gregg in Las Vegas and told Gregg that he was a friend of mine.

Gregg reared back laughing and said, "Tyrone Shoelaces," then signed the autograph and got on the bus.

The friend called me and said, "Who, the hell, is Tyrone Shoelaces?"

I started laughing and said, "You ran into Mudbone?"

My friend either assumed we were both crazy or it was something way too esoteric and didn't ask me to explain.

That night at the concert, after the last song, we left the stage waiting for the usual encore applause. The crowd, as was usually the case, was very enthusiastic. Gregg and I had gone behind the amp stacks instead of offstage, knowing we'd get an encore. Suddenly we heard this chanting coming from the first five or six rows... "Midnight Rider! Midnight Rider!"

He looked at me very sheepishly and said, "I'm sorry, man, I screwed things up."

I smiled and said, "We'll do it next time, Mudbone... let's do 'Statesboro.' They'll love it." And, of course, they did.

ADIOS GREGG

We got back to St. Louis and started rehearsing. David started booking like a man possessed. It seemed like no time before he had over 20 dates booked! That's when he got the phone call. Gregg called and said he couldn't do the dates. Phil Walden had figured out how to get Gregg back — reunite the Allman Brothers Band.

Gregg Allman and Dickie Betts had had a falling out when the Brothers disbanded. Phil called Gregg and told him that Dickie Betts wanted to put the band back together. (With very little research, David Cloud discovered that Phil had told Dickie that Gregg wanted to put the band back together.)

This was the Allman Brothers Band, they had legend status. Mama's Pride was good, but we couldn't compete with that.

David had booked over 20 dates starting in November. It was September now. We not only lost a great tour and the potential for another record deal... we were out of work.

We only did one of the gigs from the tour — in Celina, Ohio. We did it, naturally, without Gregg. The guy was a fan and wanted us anyway, but for a lot less money considering they weren't getting Gregg Allman. This was the only out-of-town gig we did before my daughter, Elisha, was born.

David managed to get some local bookings so we wouldn't starve. I was worried that we'd have to go out on the road to make money. I was having a new baby, but the rest of the guys weren't, and I had to consider their livelihood as well.

A NEW BABY GIRL AND A.B.B.

On November 14, 1978, at Deaconess Hospital in St. Louis, my sweet little Elisha was born. Most babies look like, well, babies when they're born. Smooshed little faces and wrinkled. I have to say, Elisha was beautiful. She even gave a little smile in her birth picture. I loved her the moment I saw her. Losing a Gregg Allman tour suddenly had very little relevance.

The following spring, Gregg did call me, when the Allman Brothers played in the area. I couldn't go to the concert because Mama's Pride was gigging, but Danny, David, and I went the following day and hung out with him. He played some of the new *Enlightened Rogues* album for us. He was drawing my attention to his vocals and saying, "See what I'm doing there?" I really didn't know what he meant at first and then he said, "I copied your scream." I thought to myself, *wow, what a great compliment... a compliment I can't tell anyone because they'd just say, 'yah right'* — but I swear, he really did say it.

Gregg called David Cloud a month or so later and asked if we wanted to open for the Allman Brothers in Elkhorn, Wisconsin, at the big 37,000-seat outdoor facility, Alpine Valley Music Theater. Naturally we were thrilled to do anything with the Allman Brothers.

The day we got there, the crew was unloading equipment. The Allman Brothers had already done their sound check. One of our road crew, Eddie Burch, asked their crew if we could just use Gregg's Hammond B3, so we didn't have to pull ours out. They quickly told him, "No one uses Gregg's organ."

Ed laughed and said, "Why not? He used ours on about 20 dates."

The crew guy actually called, just to check. When he got off the phone he said, "I'll be damned, Gregg said Mama's Pride can use any damn thing they want to... that's a first, Brother."

After the check, we went to our dressing room downstairs. We hadn't seen Gregg yet and we didn't really know the other guys in the band. Bonnie Bramlett was touring with them, too, but we didn't know her either. Danny said, "If I knew which dressing room he was in, I'd just knock, but I don't know any of the other guys."

I told one of the crew to go to the dressing room and get an acoustic guitar. There was a long hall with a lot of doors. Instead of us going to him, we were gonna get him to come to us. I told Max to play "What's Your Name," the old 60s Don & Juan classic.

He started playing and we started harmonizing in the hall. The acoustics in that hallway carried the sound very well..."*What's your name, is it Mary or Sue, what's your name, do I stand a chance with you...*"

It was about at this point in the song that we heard two doors slam at the other end of the hall and saw two people running down the hall at full speed. They ran up to us and finished the song with us, harmonizing. It was Gregg Allman and Bonnie Bramlett.

When we did the vocal tag and ended it, Bonnie turned to Gregg and said, "Who, the hell, are these guys?!"

Gregg answered, "This is the band I told you about."

Bonnie said, "You guys are some bad-ass singers!"

There were over 30,000 people there and we had a pretty good set. After the show we all went to the Playboy Club in Lake Geneva. Some of the Allman Brothers were there, but Gregg sat with us. There was a black man trying to talk to Gregg. He seemed like a fan and it was annoying Gregg. This was his down time and he was wanting to talk to us. It took me a minute, but I suddenly realized who the guy was — it was Chubby Checker.

I leaned over and told Gregg. He started laughing and then spoke with him briefly. We stayed there for a while, but people were realizing Gregg was in the house and started to come over to him. He said, "Let's get some beer and go."

We bought a case of beer, which cost us about $75 because we had to pay the bar price for each bottle. I don't think they'd have even sold it to us if it wasn't for Gregg. We went back to the hotel and sang a while. One-by-one everybody started going to their rooms to go to bed.

When Gregg left he said to me, "Tyrone, you guys are as good or better than any band I've ever played with, and that includes the Allman Brothers, but I have to tell you, I have never had that much fun on the road. You guys are some crazy sons 'a bitches. You were like traveling with a rock-n-roll Marx Brothers. And I made more money with you than I do with the Allman Brothers, too. It was a great time. Thanks."

I spoke to Gregg one other time after that, at Stages Nightclub in the St. Louis area. I later wrote a song for him, well, it was more *about* him than *for* him. It was called "In Time." Maybe someday he'll hear it.

HELPIN' HENRY AND **MORE CHANGES**

Around this time, we also came to the aid of an old friend. Henry Paul had been let go by the Outlaws. (He was an integral part of the band, but it happens.) We were in Daytona, Florida, at the time and Henry approached us and asked if we would help him lay some tracks for a few demos. He was wanting to start his own band and get a record deal, but he didn't have the band yet.

We went into a studio in Tampa, Florida, and recorded about three songs for him. He landed a deal with Atlantic Records — what bitter irony that Atlantic would like Henry's recordings not knowing we were the band backing him on the project. He did not thank us on the album when it was released. This is an oversight that can very easily happen. I've done it. As it turned out, it was almost better because it has given me years of pleasure teasing him about it.

Henry and I are still very close friends. He later went on to form the country band Blackhawk. Their first album — *Strong Enough* — went platinum and was in the Billboard top ten on the country charts. They were also nominated for a Grammy as Best New Country Band.

After we got back to St. Louis, we just started playing clubs. We played Stages Nightclub every Wednesday. It was a cool place with a concert vibe. The owner, Bill Benjamin, was a great guy. He was always trying to come up with ideas.

There were these big double doors right next to the stage for load-in because they got a lot of well known groups there. One night he hired a Marcella Cab to come there. We all got in the cab. They opened the double doors and the cab pulled right into the club. We got out and played "Can I call You A Cab." It was fun stuff.

Performance at Six Flags St. Louis circa 1980.

Around late 1980 Jeff Schmidt gave his notice. I guess we were hard on keyboard players. We replaced him with a young guy named Jim Vogts. Jimmy had a lot of chops, but not a lot of experience — but he was young and had a ton of energy. Watching Jim's energy level somehow made me aware that I was running out of steam. I was staying out late after gigs and drinking too much. I was married and had a little girl at home. We were still recording, but it wasn't meaning much.

We met a guy named Eddie Kritzer who managed us for a brief time. He loved the song "Maybe." He briefly got us with Tapestry Records (Bobby Vinton's record label)and we released a single with "Maybe" on one side, produced by LA engineer/producer Tom Knox, and another song I'd written about addiction called "Monkey's Gun" — which I produced. This was my first attempt at producing as well. I was very flattered when I went to LA to do the mix and Tom Knox said my producing was very good.

Eddie Kritzer did his damnedest to get someone interested in us, but it just fell flat. I flew to LA a couple of times to meet with people, but I knew it wasn't going to happen. Also, Eddie had taken "Maybe" in to a studio and had Mike Miller (Gino Vanelli's guitarist) overdub a bunch of guitar harmonies. I figured Eddie had told him we were southern rock, so he laid down a slick California studio musician's rendition of *southern* guitar harmonies. He filled every hole there was with this.

I absolutely hated the finished product. All these distractive guitar riffs sucked the beauty out of the song, as far as I was concerned. The band, however, liked it and we spent countless hours working it out for our live performances. Eventually, we stopped doing the guitar parts because my opinion of them played out in a live situation. It was too busy.

I was getting more and more frustrated. I was real involved in my church and doing music there periodically. I was writing Christian-type songs and the band wasn't really diggin' it much. They were good songs. "Rapture" was almost like a Kansas-type song, while "Let's All Go To Heaven Together" was a more gospel style song. I kept bringing songs to the band and they kept — in the nicest way they knew how — rejecting them.

I wrote one called "All In The Game" it was a song that lamented the whole business of music and the emptiness of the road. It wasn't a Christian song in its core, but I did a long vocal jam at the end that was nothing short of a Sunday sermon. This part of the song used to really annoy some of the guys. The new songs were good songs, but the lyrics were making them uncomfortable. Max heard a guy, who was waiting to get in at Stages say one night, "I don't want to see these guys, I heard they're a Jesus band."

It really freaked Max out. Looking back, I see why they were uncomfortable. All my new stuff had some type of spiritual overtone and they didn't share my enthusiasm at that time. Also, with the heavy drinking, occasional drugs, and staying out half the night, I was not practicing what I was preaching... and I knew it.

ARTIE KORNFELD, MY FAREWELL SONG,
AND A "MAN CHILD"

The last contact we made was Artie Kornfeld — one of the key people who put on Woodstock. I always felt bad that I'd missed Woodstock, but here was the guy who spearheaded it! Like Eddie, Artie loved the song "Maybe." It's funny... I almost didn't even bother bringing this song to the band because (to me) it was just another melancholy *Pat ballad*. Artie, like Eddie, tried his best to stimulate interest in "Maybe." Artie also loved "Monkey's Gun." He had lost a loved one to drugs and, at the time, struggled a bit himself, so he related to the message.

Artie was a hippie in a suit — he was funny. Half the time I didn't know what the hell he was talking about, but the guy was so damn lovable and had a passion for music which was refreshing in the business world. He is the only business person who I am good friends with to this day. I have come to cherish who he is and our friendship. I think Artie *got* what I was doing more than any other person I'd known in this crazy business... and he still loves "Maybe" and "Monkey's Gun."

In the second half of 1981 we were playing a place called Night Moves on St. Charles Rock Road. It was a big concert-style club. Jim Vogts would annoy me at times because he was like a young cocker spaniel... way too much energy for me. I felt like an old Bassett hound sometimes (even though I was only 33 at the time).

Jim lit my fuse that night and I came completely uncorked. I could not tell you what brought it on... too many years have passed. I tore into him like a banshee. My brother then started yelling at me. It was like that slow motion accident. I heard myself say "I quit, I've had it, I can't do this anymore!"

We had already finished playing. David Cloud grabbed me and got me out of there. He took me outside and said, "Go home. Get some sleep. If you still feel this way in the morning, call me."

Well, I still felt that way in the morning. It was almost as though a huge burden had been lifted off of me. No one, except David Cloud, ever knew how hard I worked. I never stopped — morning, noon, and night it was Mama's Pride. I never made extra money, though I'm sure the guys thought I did sometimes.

Mama's Pride, as a creative force, was over and I knew it.

4B St. Louis Globe-Democrat   Fri., Jan. 22, 1982

Sounds Around Town

Mama's Pride makes change

Mama's Pride, one of St. Louis' most durably popular rock 'n' roll bands, will give what is being billed as the group's "farewell performances" Friday and Saturday at Fourth and Pine, 401 Pine St.

But in many ways, the farewell actually is a new beginning for these rock veterans who have been making music for 10 years, playing in St. Louis clubs as well as touring with big names like Gregg Allman, the Charlie Daniels Band and Kansas.

Group founder Pat Liston is leaving the group, but the remaining five musicians — Danny Liston, Max Baker, Kevin Sanders, Dickie Steltenpohl and Jim Vogts — will continue to perform.

The elder Liston brother, 33, says his exit from the band was "the hardest decision I ever made in my life."

"But I am a born-again Christian, and lately I've felt my affectiveness in that area starting to diminish," he said. "I needed to make a change."

According to Sanders, the group plans to "freshen up" its sound, perhaps turning to harder rock. They have no plans to add a new member and will continue as "The Pride."

"Since Pat is leaving, we decided to retire the name (Mama's Pride) with him," Sanders said. "It wouldn't seem right to be Mama's Pride without him."

The group will perform from 10 p.m. to 2 a.m. Admission is $3.

Mama's Pride

I called a band meeting and told the guys I was done. We did a series of *final* concerts at different places. It became a joke: *Mama's Pride's last concert... again.* But so many places felt a personal connection with us and when we'd play their places for the last time, they would promote it as such because — for them — it was the last time.

Our last St. Louis show was at 4th and Pine. It was *very* emotional. People hung banners from the upper balconies that they'd made themselves. We did the last song, then an encore. The crowd was still stomping. The band was off to the side of the stage.

Danny said, "What should we do?"

I said, "Nothing... just listen."

I walked onstage alone and went and sat at the piano. I had written a song for the occasion. I had to practice it dozens of times to harden myself to be able to sing it without choking up. The band had no idea what I was going to sing. The song was called "Farewell Song."

It was almost a love song to the fans. It was a poetic explanation of why I was leaving and a thank you for all they'd meant to me, personally. The only one without tears was me, by the grace of God. At home, I cried every time I sang it. It was one of the most moving experiences of my life.

Our very last two shows were at Fat Cat's in Edwardsville, Illinois. (That was the old Grainery.) Lou Biggs was the owner. They were January 29th and 30th, 1982.

On the second night Lou Biggs rented two limos to pick us up. He had a bottle of Dom Perignon in each limo. He took us to Charlie's — a fine dining restaurant in Granite City. He ordered every appetizer on the menu. There were a lot of things on the appetizer list: Oyster Rockefeller, Hearts of Palm, Escargot, etc., etc.

After that we went to the club and played. At one point, as a joke, he brought a large bag of White Castle hamburgers onstage for us. The dichotomy between Charlie's and White Castle was a hoot.

Musically, it was a great night. It didn't really have the emotional ending of the 4th and Pine show. But it had its own unique ending.

They were predicting *some* snow. They were predicting 6–8 inches, maybe. We were getting reports on the last set that it was looking like we might get more than that. We ended the night and thanked the audience. Every one went out side to what was going to be the worst snow since 1912.

There was 24 inches of snow on the ground in Edwardsville! This was so unexpected and the limos were basically buried. We couldn't leave Fat Cats.

I was a video game junkie. I loved a game they had there called Frogger. Lou Biggs walked up and said, "Here's two rolls of quarters... have fun."

I said, "Where is that bag of White Castles?"

There was some wild party nearby that people were going to... I was invited, of course, but this was one of the very reasons I was quitting. So, I played Frogger and ate White Castles.

I slept at the club. I actually fell asleep on the stage. When I woke up, I noticed right in front of me, on the stage floor, a strange bit of irony. There was an empty Oyster Rockefeller shell laying right next to an empty White Castle box. I thought to myself, in those waking moments, *there is my career.... one day Oysters Rockefeller, one day White Castles... and they're both empty.*

We eventually dug the limos out and got home. What a fitting end — the biggest snow storm in 70 years!

Now what?

There were some nice posts in the *Riverfront Times* about missing me — it was comforting.

I knew I was doing the right thing in walking away, but you must understand, I wanted to be a star from as early as I can remember. I would stand in front of the mirror and perform as a small boy. Yes, I knew I was doing the right thing — to focus on my family and my faith. But now it seemed like my musical dream had ended. I remember looking at my wife, tearfully, and saying, "I'm nothing now."

I got a very blank stare back. She just didn't understand.

I remember I was reading the Bible, feeling empty and needing to feel something positive. I prayed for a verse of some kind. I read the Bible a lot, but I didn't believe in just opening it and pointing, but that's what I did. My eyes fell on this verse — Isaiah 43:18,19:

> ¹⁸ Forget the former things;
>   do not dwell on the past.
> ¹⁹ See, I am doing a new thing!
>   Now it springs up; do you not perceive it?
>   I am making a way in the wilderness
>   and streams in the wasteland.

There was my comfort. I was going to be alright. The thing is, I am, by nature, a doer and a control freak. I figured this verse was telling me I was ready for the next leg of my musical career. I know at the time I felt like I was going to get something musically *better* right away. But God says, "Your ways are not my ways." He wasn't kiddin'.

(I hated reading that Moses was in the wilderness for 40 years.)

I went to Clayton Community Church at the time and was pretty involved in the music, so I did continue to be creative. I wrote a song not long after my "being nothing" comment — called "Dreamer." It was a good song.

On Sunday, August 1st, 1982, I had a wonderful trade off for leaving the band. My beautiful son, Eugene, was born. This was in the days when you were not told gender before birth. I had my sweet baby girl. I wanted a son.

He was born cesarean. An African American nurse lifted him out and lifted him into the air like Kunta Kinte and said, "It's a man child." I broke down and cried. It was so beautifully announced.

A QUICK SIDE TRIP THROUGH MY SPIRITUAL JOURNEY

This book is about my music and my life and I don't want to turn it in to a sermon, but the spiritual aspect of my life was, and is, an integral part of my musical self.

I was *saved* in 1977. That term has become almost caustic to some. A big part of the blame for that is Christians who use their faith more like a weapon than an olive branch towards those who are not like-minded.

My spiritual journey is deeply embedded in my personal life, but I've chosen to tell this *story* in a separate chapter. I do this so, if you don't want to hear it, you can merely skip this chapter — although you may, in so doing, miss an integral part of who I am.

So, let me go through my spiritual journey: In 1977 I was at a low point in my career. Mama's Pride had been dropped by Atlantic Records. I had just gotten out of a very painful relationship. I felt like I was going to snap. We were getting ready to go back out on the road.

I used to buy paperbacks for the motor home we toured in. We often spent an inordinate amount of time in *the box* (as Gregg Allman used to call it). A lot of the boys and roadies liked to read. So I tried to buy things that might interest them.

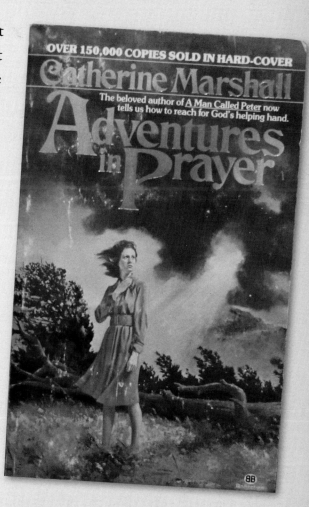

I was at a book store one day and noticed a book that had a really cool cover. I was very drawn to it and didn't really even noticed the title at first. I finally looked to see the title — *Adventures in Prayer* by Catherine Marshall. I just threw it in the stack of books I was buying and checked out. The book sat on the *library shelf* in the motor home for months. Periodically, someone would say while looking for something to read, "What, the hell, is this?!"

I finally picked it up during some down time. I had to agree with the guys — *what, the hell, is this and why did I buy it?* I didn't have a clue who Catherine Marshall was. I learned later that her late husband, Peter Marshall, had twice been appointed as Chaplain of the United States Senate and that she had written a book about him called *A Man Called Peter*. The book was made into a movie in 1955 and had been nominated for an Academy Award. If she was a nut, she was a nut with credentials.

The book (as I remember) was simply a book on different ways of praying. Being raised Irish Catholic, our prayers were written down and you prayed them verbatim — no ad libbing! So, the concept seemed rebellious, at first.

I liked it. But the more I read, the more she drew me in. Her faith seemed different from mine. She had a joy and a peace that I'd never heard in any of my religious experiences.

Every denomination seems to have its chink in the armor. I was raised Catholic. Almost everything could doom you to hell. If you died suddenly and didn't have the good fortune of being within shouting distance of a priest, hell was your fate. There was no *two minute warning*. Also, guilt was a Catholic staple. You were encouraged to abstain from anything that could bring about any semblance of physical pleasure. God loved when you suffered — the more you suffered, the better He liked it. And, if ya' weren't Catholic... you were going to hell.

My mom was raised Baptist and they thought everything was a sin. Although, unlike Catholics, some physical pleasure was okay. They had to have the males taken care of when the wife wasn't *in the mood*... as long as it didn't involve dancing. And if ya' weren't Baptist... you were going to hell.

As a kid I once went to a Pentecostal church. Pentecostals believed you had to pray in a heavenly language and if you didn't, you would lose out on 1/3 of the trinity. Which made you a lopsided Christian, I guess, and kept you in the dark about any *deeper* truths. And if you were Catholic... you were going to hell.

Growing up, it seemed a lot of people were going to be in hell. It felt my only hope for salvation hinged on the potential for overcrowding.

Catherine Marshall was a Presbyterian. I'd never met a Presbyterian, so I had no preconceived notions about anything she might have to say. She had a *clean slate* so to speak. She did not seem judgmental. She sounded like God wanted us to be happy. She seemed happy, even though she'd lost a husband who she obviously loved dearly. One of her first statements was,

> I believe that old cliché, "God helps those who help themselves," is not only misleading, but often dead wrong. My most spectacular answers to prayers have come when I was so helpless, so out of control as to be able to do nothing at all for myself.

"Okay, that's me right now."

She had my attention. I went through the book quickly, like your favorite dessert.

After I finished it, I bought the book she wrote about her husband — *A Man Called Peter*. He seemed to have the same rock-solid faith. He approached God as someone who was loved by Him... as a father loves his children. Really? She also referenced and quoted from a book called *The Christian's Secret of a Happy Life* by Hannah Whitall Smith. She quoted from it so frequently that this was my third book to read.

Hannah seemed to have an even deeper concept of God and who He was. I devoured the book not realizing, at the time, that this book was written in 1875 by a Quaker.

What?

Hannah Whitall Smith

You mean this wasn't a new concept? I wanted this deeper relationship. They talked of accepting Christ as your savior. If this was the fruits of that decision, I had no problem accepting that.

The guys in the band were getting mildly concerned with the books I was reading and the way I was talking. Keep in mind, this was all taking place while we were touring on the road.

My fourth book was the one the other books all referenced — the Bible.

We were in Florida. Where does one go to purchase a bible? Are there different kinds? I happened to see a Christian book store one day while I was out driving and the guys were at the motel. I went in and said I wanted to buy a bible and asked for suggestions on a good one, sounding like I was asking for an appetizer at a restaurant.

142

I remember the sales lady was very sweet and very patient. She said that the newest version was called the *New International Version* and that it was being translated from the *Dead Sea Scrolls*.

"Really? I'll have one of those."

She said, "At this point, they only have the *New Testament*. The *Old Testament* hasn't been fully translated yet in that version."

"Good, I don't think I could handle the *Old Testament* right now anyway."

So I bought a leather bound *New International Version New Testament* with a snap-button cover. I thought it looked rather spiffy. She asked if I wanted my name added to the cover in gold. I'm thinking, *I'm a rock-n-roll musician, of course I want my name emblazoned across the front in gold!*

When I got back the guys were awake. I walked in with my new leather bound snap-button Bible with my name emblazoned across the front in gold and said, "Check it out. Cool, huh?"

The look on their faces was priceless. I think I was so excited at all the new found peace and joy I was reading about in all these books that I, somehow, thought it would spill over or something.

Not so much.

I had tried to read the Gideon's Bible a few times while having an insomnia attack at some random motel. (It never worked spiritually, but it did, however, always cure my insomnia.) But this one was different. It wasn't just because it was in the present vernacular — I could not get enough of it. I would read all day. I would go out to the motor home on breaks and read (that really spooked the guys in the band). I was not trying to impress anyone with my new found *spirituality*. I think it was actually scaring the guys. I'm sure they just wanted their old leader back to the way he was before.

I wasn't even drinking alcohol anymore, mostly because I'd decided to quit smoking and not drinking helped. I was not doing this for any *religious* reasons — I simply

---

* The Dead Sea Scrolls *were discovered between 1946 and 1956 in eleven caves from the immediate vicinity of the* ancient settlement at Khirbet Qumran in the West Bank. Among other writings, the scrolls comprised all of the Hebrew Torah *with the exception of two books. The Hebrew* Torah *is also the foundation of the Christian* Old Testament.

A Christian Bible *typically contains both the* Old *and* New Testaments. *In 1977, the New International Version (NIV) — a Bible written in a more present-day vernacular — only had the* New Testament *available (published in 1973). The* Old Testament *written in the NIV vernacular from the* Dead Sea Scrolls *translations wouldn't be published until 1978.*

felt smoking was a bad habit. Again, I wasn't trying to impress anyone with my *good behavior*. It was a spiritual journey and — like being present when your child is born — unless you've experienced it... it is not going to make sense.

The funny thing was, I felt closer to God than I'd ever felt in my life and I didn't know one other person who shared this experience except two authors: one a Presbyterian I'd never met, and the other a Quaker who died in 1912.

I've often said, "The Bible spoke to me so sweetly because I didn't know any well-meaning Christians to screw it up for me." I know that sounds a bit harsh, but (for me) my experience with tangible Christians and my *re-introduction* to the Bible was, at times, not as sweet.

A pastor, named Wayne Carson, once told me that the ideal way of reading the Bible would be to be on a deserted island with no preconceived notions and with only God as your navigator. Basically, that's what I did. I was most definitely on an island alone, because the band wanted no part of it and I, again, knew no other Christians, personally.

We went back to St. Louis and I told my mom what had happened. To my surprise, she was thrilled because she was having almost the same experience at the same time.

Mom always had a strong faith. As a child during Lent, Mom and I would go to Mass every day. Mass was always an uninteresting ritual for me. Getting up with Mom and walking up Tamm Avenue together was the part I liked best.

At the beginning of Lent there were no flowers or greenery. Very often it was still cold weather. As time would go on during these six weeks before Easter she would have me take note of the flowers as they started peeking through the soil. They were often in full bloom by Easter. She would marvel at God's beauty and creation. Mom grew up without a real father and had a lot of hellish experiences as a child, so God was really her only reference to a loving father.

Christianity was, in part, how I met my wife in 1977. I wanted to have a family. As I said, I did not know any other Christians. She was a new Christian, too. We started dating and it seemed logical. (I believe opposites attract, but if you're polar opposites it can create a problem.)

We had our first child, Elisha, on November 14th, 1978. She was a beautiful child. Most newborn photos are not that endearing to anyone but the parents and grandparents.

Her new born picture was beautiful. She remained a beautiful child both inside and out. We had our second child, Eugene, on August 1st, 1982. He was a cesarean just like his non-conformist father had been.

I loved my children. They brought a meaning to life that I had never known. There were challenges (as with all children), but I would not change it for the world. As with so many married couples, children are what get you through a (sometimes) rocky relationship.

We attended Clayton Community Church — a non-denominational church from 1977 to about 1990. I had a lot of biblical growth there. I was very involved in the music program — it allowed me to keep my hand in music and kept me playing. I led Bible studies out of my home in Dogtown for different people I knew in the neighborhood who were so-inclined to come.

At one point, I even had a Catholic priest coming — Father Murphy. He was an older priest. I really loved Father Murphy. He had a seekers heart. When he was dying, I remember going to his hospital bed and reading scripture to him and speaking words of encouragement the day before he died.

I was also involved in these church plays they used to have at Clayton Community Church. They were Purim plays — plays based on the *Book of Esther* from the *Old Testament*. They were meant to be humorous and spiritually enlightening. They were always done as musicals. We would take the *Book of Esther* and meld it into some current play or movie. We did a take off on *Play It Again, Sam* by Woody Allen, *It's a Wonderful Life*, Garrison Keiller's *Prairie Home Companion*, *West Side Story,* and *The Wizard of Oz*. It was very challenging to make the two selected stories work together.

By professional standards they were probably not that good, but people loved the silliness and it fed my creative side. I wrote 50 percent of the scripts and a friend named Charlie Bethel wrote the other half. I was the director as well... and, of course, one of the actors. It wasn't rock-n-roll, but it was fun.

As my kids went through school there were always challenges. My son, Eugene, always had a hard time with school. It was (sometimes) hard to discipline him knowing how much I had hated school as a child. We changed schools a few times, but when he was going into fourth grade we sent him to Central Presbyterian School. For the short time he was there (through sixth grade) it was an excellent fit. The church had a great children's ministry, too, so we decided to change churches after, roughly, 12 years at Clayton Community Church.

We spent about five or six years at Central Presbyterian Church. I laughingly call it my *Presbyterian years* because I cut my hair short, shaved my facial hair, and wore suits and ties to church.

I longed for another non-denominational church because I did very little music at Central Presbyterian Church. I played in a small church band there that had Randy Mayfield in it. He was very well known in the national Christian music circles. He was a lot of fun. He had a razor wit. I still see him and his wife, Sharon, from time-to-time. Also, in this *church band* was Ken Hensley — the former keyboard player for the British super group Uriah Heep.

Ken Hensley & Visible Faith

Around 1997, I visited a church at the prodding of an old friend. I liked the church. They met in a YMCA building.

Like most fledgling churches, there was a sweet spirit about them in those early days. A successful church grows, and with that growth comes the thinning out of friendships. It's similar to a small business growing and becoming a corporation. Though their message is the same, large corporations tend to lose their intimacy — that certain bond that got them there. Everything is done differently... and for the dreamer, it seems to lose something.

It was at this church that I experienced my separation and divorce in 2006.

As I alluded before, if you don't have a bond to begin with, and if there is no commonality and no real joy, it will come to a head when the kids are grown. This happened to me.

I began to feel alienated at the church. They (to me) had gone the way of most megachurches. At one time I had felt more connected to this church than any I'd attended. But as churches get bigger and bigger people can feel pushed aside — they don't want to hear about peoples problems, they want new members.

I believe my church life is what kept my marriage together for as long as it was. Once I felt alienated from one, it was only a matter of time.

I met someone else. There was no *affair*. I just fell quietly in love. I was then summarily asked to leave the church.

My whole spiritual journey has been different since then. My core beliefs have not changed, but my approach and interpretation of some things has.

Mama's Pride, for all practical purpose, was over. I could deal with that because my musical journey did not start with Mama's Pride, it was just one of the many paths. I was up for a new adventure, but what was it?

I continued to write songs at first. I felt disconnected from my musical path. Towards the end of Mama's Pride, and after I left, I wrote songs about hope (usually spiritual), but also songs about disillusionment (usually relational). I had been married about four years now and we had a little girl, Elisha. Within months we also had a little boy, Eugene. I took to the roles of father and husband. They were roles I wanted. I loved my kids and felt they were the best thing that had ever happened to me.

I also got very involved in church and church activities. I played music at church on Sundays, but there wasn't much of a musical challenge there. I did a solo concert once down in Cape Girardeau, Missouri, that was Christian-geared. I have seen people since who attended and said it was great — I hated it. I was not used to being solo and it was a huge adjustment. I was so bored with my performance, I was literally daydreaming while I was singing.

During this time I was approached by a guy named Russ Kirkland. I knew Russ, having done a project at KBK studios with he and his Contemporary Christian Music group — September. They were in dire need of a sound man for some small- to mid-sized concerts. I told Russ I was not a sound man, but had good ears for level balance. He said that he would set up all the EQs and all I had to do was mix the volume levels. I was so desperate to do something — anything having to do with music — that I agreed and went out on the road with September.

These were all *Christian* concerts and that was a whole new experience for me. I was a fairly new Christian and was looking forward to this. I experienced a lot of really cool things and a lot of not-so-cool things. It was, however, a growing experience for me.

We had a lot of fun on the road. I wasn't in charge, like with Mama's Pride, and I reverted back to the *class clown* of my youth. I kept them all laughing with stories and characters. I did the soundman thing for several months off and on.

Towards the end of the Mama's Pride era, I had befriended a young man named Pat Schunk, who wanted me to teach him slide guitar. I never gave lessons, but he was so likable that I agreed. In mentoring him, he asked what I thought about him going to California to GIT — the Guitar Institute of Technology. I told him he was young and single (although he had a girlfriend) so do it now, while he had the chance. He and his girlfriend, Sandy, moved to LA. He was a definite *do-er* type.

The following year, my wife and I went out to visit them. I was probably testing the waters, but while out there I contacted David Paich from Toto. He encouraged me to come out — he said I'd probably get all the work I wanted.

In September 1985, Mexico City was devastated by four earthquakes, the worst being an 8.1 that killed over 10,000 people. My church wanted to help and asked if Mama's Pride might get back together for a benefit concert. I asked the guys and they agreed to do it. We also garnered the help of Billy Peek (who had done a stint with Rod Stewart) and Dan Peek from the group America.

We put on a three-day concert series with each respective act headlining, at the Westport Playhouse in Westport Plaza in St. Louis. They sold out immediately. We even had former members of Mama's Pride join us from the very first band.

On the upside, it was a rousing success and brought in a lot of money. On the downside, the man who owned the place took all the money and skipped town. (I would hate to have had his karma.) It was rumored that we had gotten back together, but it was just the one charity gig.

Even though I had no desire to reform Mama's Pride, I struggled with a lack of a musical career. Church life filled my time in those days. I did remodeling, some light carpentry, and even laborer work when I could get it. I wanted someone home with our children and since my wife had a good job and no intentions of staying home, it fell to me. Whenever I got work, Mom would come down and watch the kids when they were small. I felt, at least it was family and not a stranger.

Musically, I was writing, but frustrated. I had a greater responsibility now, being married with children and couldn't just run off and try something new. My wife, getting increasingly annoyed at my moods, suggested we move to California. Her company had a branch in LA and it would be simple to transfer. I was reluctant because I knew, from experience, that just going to LA was not all there was to it. Music had changed, I had few contacts, and I was 37... but it did stir something in me.

We had paid our house off because we bought it very cheap. I had completely remodeled it, so when we sold it, we got four times what we paid. So, we had plenty of cash.

Now it was 1985 and I was on my way back to the City of Angels.

BACK TO LOS ANGELES: MOVIES AND A DOSE OF REALITY

We moved in to a humble three-bedroom apartment in North Hollywood that was three times the rent it would be in St. Louis. I contacted everyone I'd ever met there. I found out Chuck Sabatino, from St. Louis, was playing with another St. Louis friend, Warren Hartman, as a duo in Pasadena every Thursday. I went every week to reconnect. I knew *networking* was the best method of accomplishing my goal.

My wife — who knew nothing about how it all worked — insisted I put ads in papers and magazines and follow up on the recipients. This was a bad idea (as I knew it would be). Because my credentials were so good every LA *wanna-be* called me, in hopes of me advancing *their* careers. I spent countless weeks of ridiculous follow-ups because of this.

Chuck Sabatino invited me to one of Michael McDonald's rehearsals and we got to talk. As it turned out he lived within a few blocks of us in Studio City. Unfortunately, he was in the process of moving to Santa Barbara. He had invited us to dinner, but was unable to follow up because of the move.

I ran into Steve Lukather, from Toto, in a park one day. We talked and he remembered nothing about the encounter five years earlier at the Arena in St. Louis. I asked Steve if he had a number for David Paich who I had talked to just a year earlier. Steve said he didn't (which I knew was not true). But, if he truly didn't remember me, then he wasn't going to give a stranger David's number. I gave Steve my number and told him to have David call me... he never did.

Pat Schunk called me one day and wanted me to come to a try out that his band was having for some record execs. I agreed and it was at that time I realized that the industry was changing.

I was not a big name, but I carried myself like I was, and all these record people were asking me *my* thoughts of the band etc., etc. It's like they didn't have a clue what they were listening to. Pat and his band got a deal eventually. They were called Britton.

On another occasion, Pat Schunk called and said that he had someone come into his music store and ask if they had a Hammond B3 or knew someone who did for a one day rental. Pat was a salesman at a music store. He thought of me because I had a B3. He called to ask permission to give them my number. I agreed.

When the woman called, she said they needed it for a movie. That they would come pick it up and bring it back and give me $200. *Two hundred bucks and I didn't have to move it myself? Hell yes!*

I asked her what the movie was. She said the B3 was going to be in a scene to replicate Woodstock. The conversation went like this:

                    ME:
          Really... who's playing the organ?

                    MOVIE REP:
          An actor... we haven't gotten him yet.

                    ME:
          Well, obviously, I play.

                    MOVIE REP:
          They have to be in character.

                    ME:
          Like at Woodstock, right?

                    MOVIE REP:
          Yes.

                    ME:
I have long hair.

                    MOVIE REP:
How old are you?

                    ME:
I look younger than I am.
  (Which was the truth.)

                    MOVIE REP:
How old are you?

                    ME:
Young enough for a scene in Woodstock.

                    MOVIE REP:
If you get here and you don't fit, I'm not
obligated to use you... and we still use the
Hammond.

                    ME:
Fair enough... what's the name of the movie?

                    MOVIE REP:
Return of Bruno.

                    ME:
Who's Bruno?
  (With a slight chuckle, because I know she
  needs this Hammond bad and is trying to be
  somewhat cordial. I'm guessing they'd been
  looking high and low because she was being
  uncharacteristically nice for a Hollywood
  type.)

                    MOVIE REP:
Bruce Willis.

                    ME:
Who?!

```
              MOVIE REP:
      You have heard of Bruce Willis?


              ME:
      Oh, hell yes! Whoa! What time do I have to
      be there?


              MOVIE REP:
      This Saturday at 6:00 a.m. Sharp!


              ME:
      What?


              MOVIE REP:
      This is the movie business, not rock-n-roll...
      we need the right lighting... and if you're
      finished with Q&A, I have things I have to do.


              ME:
      See ya' Saturday at 6:00 a.m. Sharp!
```

Holy crap. Bruce Willis! My creative juices started flowing and imagining myself being a movie star. *That's it! I'll make it in movies first, then music... me and Bruce... like Butch Cassidy and the Sundance Kid.*

My child-like imagination was still intact.

I went out that day to a second hand clothing store and bought a pair of vintage bell bottom jeans. I had a shirt to wear from back-in-the-day (tie-dyed). I got out all my old turquoise and coral rings and my round sunglasses, too.

The morning of the shoot I got up early and dressed. When I arrived the stage was set up and it was a misty morning... it actually did look a little like Woodstock. Everyone had to report to wardrobe when they got there. When I walked in, she looked at me and said, "Have you been here already?"

"No, I just got here... I bought my own wardrobe."

She looked at me and said, "Hmm... good job. Okay, report to the stage area."

I went onstage and there was a grand piano right next to my B3. Some guy was sitting behind my B3. I said, "Who are you?"

He said, "I'm playing the keyboard player."

I said, "Really?"

I went looking for the person in charge that I had talked to on the phone. When I found her I said, "I own the B3 and you told me I could be in the movie as the keyboard player."

She said, "...and?"

"There's a guy onstage that says he's the keyboard player."

She said, "Whose organ is it?"

"Mine."

"...and who told you that you had the part if you fit?"

"You."

She said, "You fit... I don't see a problem. Send him to me."

I figured he was my back up, just in case I looked like Walter Brennan.

I went to the stage and someone on a bullhorn said, "Have all the musicians gone over the song?"

I yelled, "What song?"

He said, "You didn't get a recording of the song?"

I said, "They just contacted me yesterday."

He pointed to a tent and said, "Go down there and listen to the song." I thought, *crap, I have to learn a song now?*

I went to the tent and they were playing the song. Oh, hell yah... it was "Young Blood" by the Coasters. This was gonna be simple.

I turned to a guy holding a guitar and asked, "What key is this in?"

He said, "I don't know, I'm just an actor."

I turned to a guy holding a bass guitar and asked the same question, getting the same response. I yelled, "Is anyone in here a musician?!" All I got was blank stares.

So, I listened to the song, hummed the tonic note to myself, and ran to the stage as fast as I could before I forgot. I hit the piano a couple of times — key of **A**. I started playing it on the piano just to refresh my memory. Someone sat down next to me on the piano bench, but I ignored them figuring they were just resting. I was focused, because I wanted to do a good job.

The person next to me said, "Cool... you're actually a real musician."

I turned and said, "I know, nobody here can actually play."

It was at that moment I realized that the person I was talking to — who had sat down next to me and engaged me in conversation was — Bruce Willis!

I said something like, "Oh, hi, Bruce."

Someone had told me he was a jerk, but he couldn't have been nicer. He asked where I was from and we talked a little about St. Louis. He sang a little of the song as I was playing.

He spotted the necklace I was wearing — a bear claw and turquoise nugget necklace that had been given to me years earlier by my friend, Ringo from the Wreck Bar, in Daytona. He asked if he could wear it for the scene. I told him he could, as long as I got it back because it was a gift. He assured me that I'd get it back. I had a choker type necklace in my pocket from 1969 just in case, so I wore that one.

When they began shooting I tried to be very animated because I knew they wanted action. It worked! I had cameras all over me during the scene. Unfortunately, when I saw the movie, the necklace I loaned Bruce got more screen time than I did in the final cut.

When it was over and I was gathering up my things, I saw Bruce's Mercedes driving away. "Damn... he took my necklace."

At that moment, a prop person walked up and said, "Here. Bruce said to give you this and to say, 'thank you'."

"Cool. A class act."

The movie was not one of his best and, as I said, if you sneeze you'll miss me. For some reason the only people they forgot to credit were the folks in the Woodstock scene. This was also my last movie experience.

Oh, well. At least I can say I played at Woodstock... sort of.

I considered putting together another band and playing at some of the old places I'd played years before. I went to the old Antique Mirror in Granada Hills. The old bartender, Sam, had bought the place. He was thrilled to see me. When Mama's Pride was out there in 1976, we had taken him and his wife out to dinner in a limo. I told him I was considering putting a band together to play out. He looked at me and said, "Pat, things have changed. I pay bands about half of what you made back in 1972-73 — there are so many bands out here now that I can get them dirt cheap."

That was not what I wanted to hear. The cost of living was outrageous and bands were making *chump change*. My wife was starting to complain about nothing happening.

I had tried everything I knew to do. It just wasn't happening quickly and we were running out of money. I felt pressured from all sides. I finally thought, *this is not going to happen fast*. (I knew that prior to coming out.)

Everything had changed. My style of music wasn't the music de jour. I had to admit defeat for the sake of my family. I moved back to St. Louis with my tail between my legs after less than a year in LA. I did know, however, that I could make better money back home. There just wasn't the *opportunity* back there. But when you know your music isn't what record labels are looking for anyway, what difference does it make.

We moved into a little one bedroom apartment next to my mom in Dogtown. The kids got the bedroom and we got a pull-out couch — for 14 months! We had to save towards a house because we'd already spent most of what we'd had from the sale of the old house.

BACK TO ST. LOUIS, A REUNION, AND **THE PHLAMING PHLEGMATICS**

During this time I was contacted by Mark Klose, a former KSHE on-air personality. He and several key people left KSHE and went to a new station.

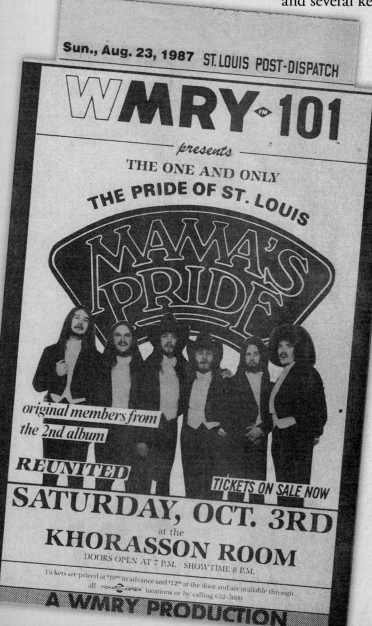

Sun., Aug. 23, 1987 ST. LOUIS POST-DISPATCH

WMRY · 101

presents

THE ONE AND ONLY

THE PRIDE OF ST. LOUIS

MAMA'S PRIDE

original members from the 2nd album

REUNITED

TICKETS ON SALE NOW

SATURDAY, OCT. 3RD

at the

KHORASSON ROOM

DOORS OPEN AT 7 P.M.   SHOWTIME 8 P.M.

Tickets are priced at $10⁰⁰ in advance and $12⁰⁰ at the door and are available through all ticketmaster locations or by calling 652-5000

A WMRY PRODUCTION

Mark was now a program director at the new station WMRY. He asked if Mama's Pride would be interested in doing a one-time reunion concert at the Khorassan Room at the Chase Park Plaza. The band had a meeting and decided it would be fun and the money was very good.

So, on Saturday, October 3rd, 1987, Mama's Pride did yet another show. It sold out faster than any concert WMRY had done to date, including the Allman Brothers Band. It sold over 2,000 seats, 400 standing room only, and turned away several hundred.

It was an amazing night. The fans were on fire and so was the band. The St. Louis Cardinals were about to begin another postseason and St. Louis was in a party atmosphere. Mama's Pride added to that by being the *rock-n-roll Boys of October*!

When the concert was over, I remember sitting with Kevin Sanders in the dressing room. The fans were gone and the rest of the guys had left — it was just he and I. We sat there for the longest time, saying nothing. It's like we didn't want it to end.

Finally, I remember saying, "Well. Now what?"

Kevin said, "I guess we go back to our day jobs. We were kings for a day."

It wasn't like when I left the band in '82 and felt there was something better ahead. This seemed almost cruel and very, very depressing. It wasn't like I wanted to put Mama's Pride back together… Mama's Pride was like an ill-fated marriage that took a ton of work. You had moments of greatness, but in the end, it went nowhere. And the final days were painful. Once you divorce — amicably — you have no desire to go back to that treadmill, even though when you get together, it still sparks those elusive moments of greatness.

The following year I decided to do a musical project. I wanted to do a big R&B band. I wanted a full rhythm section, a four- or five-piece horn section, and three background singers. A real show! I was going to call it the Phlaming Phlegmatics!

In putting together a solid rhythm section, I went to the best drummer I knew — my buddy, Kevin Sanders. I'd been working with a bass player at church who was really good and had become a close friend — Vince Corkery. On keyboards I got a new friend — Rob Bernstein. I met Rob when I was doing door-to-door evangelizing (yep, I'm serious). I also recruited premier St. Louis jazz guitarist, Dave Black. My background singers were Thayne Bradford, Fred Lang, and Wayne Givens

The Phlaming Phlegmatics

Now, if you're wondering, the word *phlegmatic,* according to the Webster's Dictionary, means: *a person having an unemotional and stolidly calm disposition.*

There was a term my pastor used in reference to one of the other pastors who fit this description. He called him a "flaming phlegmatic" because he was *really* laid back.

I was always uncomfortable around people with this personality trait because I talk so much. They say very little and this made me uncomfortable… so I would talk even more.

I tried avoiding these types because I didn't like feeling awkward. Ironically, most of the musicians I chose for that project ended up being this personality type.

I felt like God was having fun with me. So I leaned into it… I changed the spelling to make it clever and came up with the Phlaming Phlegmatics!

— who were also accomplished musicians. The horn section was Gerald DeClue on alto sax, Marla Feeney on baritone, Dan Smith on trumpet, Cary Sheley on trombone, and Mike Karpowicz on tenor sax.

I put a ton of money into this project. I rented matching tuxes for the rhythm section and the singers, paid Cary Sheley to do charts, and (of course) paid everyone for their performance. We played at Mississippi Nights and packed the place. I'd spent so much money that I barely made any profit. But what a great night! I did a mixture of my songs and old R&B.

I did another rendition of the Phlaming Phlegmatics a year or so later. This time my rhythm section was the band Street Corner: Billy Barnett, John Coatney, Bill Montgomery, and Jeff "Doc" Taylor. We did it at the Casa Loma Ballroom down on Cherokee Street.

It was a great show, but it didn't seem to work as well (attendance-wise) as Mississippi Nights and I lost money. This did not make my home life too cheery. The guys in the band took less money to help me out. I appreciated it, but my wife was so angry that I never did that project again.

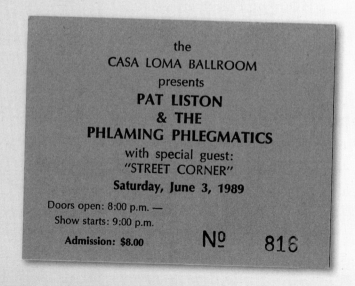

the
CASA LOMA BALLROOM
presents
**PAT LISTON
& THE
PHLAMING PHLEGMATICS**
with special guest:
"STREET CORNER"
Saturday, June 3, 1989
Doors open: 8:00 p.m. —
Show starts: 9:00 p.m.
Admission: $8.00   N̲o̲   816

A NEW HOUSE, THE OLD BAND, A NEW CD, AND RINGO

We bought a house in Dogtown in 1989. It was a great 100-year-old house on Kraft Street with a big back yard. I absolutely loved it. My wife did not, but it's what we could afford. It needed a lot of work, but I could do most anything and was excited to give it some character. This would be the house I would raise my two children in for the next 15 years.

The year after buying the house on Kraft, I was approached by a guy named Gene Ackman who had an oldies band called Butch Wax & The Hollywoods. They had a full rhythm section, a couple of horns, and two female singers. Gene was a big Mama's Pride fan and just called out of the blue asking if I would join them.

I spent a couple years doing this. Gene was the leader and keyboard player. We had Bob Hammett on guitar, Mike Tate on bass, Mark Kersten on drums, Tom O'Brian on tenor sax, Kevin Rauscher on trumpet and two female singers, Carol Rowley and Brenda King. I truly enjoyed working with them. I got to choose the old R&B songs that I wanted to sing. I liked all the guys in the band, but my favorites were Carol and Brenda. Carol was the only one who lived in the city and her (then) husband was tired of coming to the gigs and was thrilled when I offered to come pick Carol up. Those were fun times. Carol was a real hoot.

During this time I decided to try to contact Ahmet Ertegun at Atlantic Records. He liked me once, why not again?

I sent a letter to Atlantic Records. It was a casual letter, telling him that I was writing again and wanted him to hear me.

About a week later I got a response from him that, basically, said that the next time I had a gig, he would send someone from the A&R department to see me.

I was blown away that he took the time to dictate a letter. I, then, decided to call him. What the hell, he wrote, maybe he'd take my call?

He took the call and we chatted for some time. He gave me some fatherly advice about being careful with my money and cautious about overspending for CDs. He was very kind. I asked if I could send him some songs. He said, "By all means." I sent him what I had.

About a week later I got a call from him. It was very polite, but he wasn't interested in what I was writing at this time. He almost seemed like he didn't know who he was talking to. He said I had a nice voice. He seemed detached. I thanked him and hung up.

AHMET M. ERTEGUN
CHAIRMAN

August 28, 1990

Mr. Pat Liston
1203 Kraft
St. Louis, MO 63139

Dear Pat:

Thank you for your letter. Please let me know if there's anything I can hear at this time.

I don't get to St. Louis very often, but next time you have a gig, I'll try to send someone from our A&R department.

With all good wishes.

Sincerely,

Ahmet M. Ertegun

AME:vva
Dictated but not read

ATLANTIC RECORDING CORPORATION, 75 ROCKEFELLER PLAZA, NEW YORK, N.Y. 10019 (212) 484-8133

The first thought I had was, *he's from the old guard... look forward. Don't let this deter you from your goal.*

Because I am a *look forward* type guy, it didn't upset me — I was flattered he took the time to respond.

I learned many years ago that just because someone doesn't like your music doesn't mean it isn't good. It just means that *they* don't like it.

So, "Get up, dust off, and keep moving forward." After all, the main person you have to please is you.

When I'd pick Carol up, we always brought a six-pack cooler and had a couple on the way to the gig and back. (I know — you shouldn't be drinking while driving.) There was this one particular gig I remember in Washington, Missouri.

Washington was pretty far, and on the way home I got something in my left eye. We always talked a lot, but we were tired on this particular occasion and it was a rare quiet moment. While I was trying to rub whatever it was out of my left eye I closed my right eye out of reflex. Well, it looked to Carol like my eyes were closed. She freaked out and slapped me upside the head and said, "Hey, wake up!"

I almost ran off the road. I said, "Are you out of your mind!?"

She said, "You fell asleep at the wheel!"

"The hell I did. I was getting something out of my left eye!"

Carol said, with a grin, "Oh. Sorry."

Carol always made me laugh. She was a free spirit and I was somewhat uptight. By this time in my life I had gotten a little conservative and needed a friend like Carol. She may have been the first one to wake the sleeping giant inside... or at the very least, she gave him a nudge.

I had been with Butch Wax & The Hollywoods about a year and it was 1992. My brother, Danny, came to me with an idea. It was more than an idea, really. He wanted to put the band back together and do a CD. CDs had come about during this time and they were much cheaper to do than vinyl had been.

I was a hard sell because I am not a *look back* guy. Once I'm done with a project I look forward. I really didn't want to do it for a number of reasons. In the past, I had always had a ton of songs to pick from, but I hadn't really been writing much and felt I didn't have much to bring to the table.

I reluctantly conceded.

The other guys were a pretty easy sell — hell, they may have already agreed and were just waiting on me. Danny recruited keyboard player and long time friend, Tom Denman, from the group Macks Creek. He was a really good keyboard player and had an amazing voice.

Another question I had was, who was going to finance this project?

Danny also recruited some local management to help. They were Rich Dryer and Joe Rumbolo. This helped because I didn't want to end up doing everything again. They suggested that the band go out and perform and use the earnings for the project. It would also give us the opportunity to get the band tight. We mainly did our older stuff because that's what the fans wanted, but mixed a few new ones in. The band got tight, but holding the earnings back for the project was an abysmal failure. The guys kept asking for draws and eventually just wanted pay.

So, now we had no money again.

Jim Gaines (right)

There was a producer in town who was working with the group PM. Rich and Joe got in touch with him and brought him to see us at a club called Off Broadway — a great little place on Lemp Avenue owned by the Camarata's. The producer's name was Jim Gaines. Jim had produced or mixed tons of groups — Santana, Steve Miller, Stevie Ray Vaughan, Journey, Tower of Power, etc., etc. Jim really liked us and was interested in producing us. This was great news, but it was going to elevate the costs as well.

Rich and Joe convinced us we could pull it off. The band talked and Danny wanted to bring in investors. I was reluctant, but saw no other feasible way of pulling this CD off.

It took us a while, but we found enough investors for the project.

Danny had a lot of new songs. Most of them were partial, so he called Paul Willett to help him out. He and Paul finished all the songs that he wanted to use on the new CD. Danny also collaborated with Frank Gagliano on one of the songs.

Because of Paul and Frank's input, the songs were very keyboard driven. This eliminated the need for a third guitar. And because Paul *and* Tom Denman were going to be on the CD, there was no need for my keyboards skills either. So, in my mind, my role was losing definition.

Rich Dryer and Joe Rumbolo convinced Danny to let me sing his songs. They said I was the voice of Mama's Pride. Danny didn't take offense to this — I think he also knew that I might not do the project if I didn't have a larger role than where it was headed.

I had no desire to sing three songs and sit out for the rest of the CD. I had started this band and was not going to be stuck in the background. I'd have rather just not been a part of it at all. They could have still called it Mama's Pride and I'd have been fine with it. Being able to sing all the songs, to some degree, gave me a little more purpose, but I still was not thrilled with the *singer only* role.

The band chose the songs — there would be ten songs in all. They chose seven of Danny's songs. They were, indeed, great songs. They decided we should do two of my old songs that were never released on an album — "Sail On" and "Maybe." These were fan favorites when we played them out live.

We had recorded both of these songs several times back in the early 80s at KBK Studios in Earth City, Missouri. We had released "Maybe" on that single through Tapestry Records, but it had not been on an album project. I wasn't really crazy about doing older songs when I felt I had not only newer songs, but an entire catalog of unreleased songs from the KBK days.

I think Danny's new songs were so involved that the band just wanted some songs they could work out more comfortably. (Although, both songs were hard to record because we had recorded and played them out live so many times, we were tired of them.) This left one slot. I had a few songs I'd written in California in 1985. We were performing a couple of them live, but the band didn't show much interest in them as far as recording them back then.

I was able to get one recorded, a song called "Que Linda" — a Latin song I had written in 1985. Everyone thought I had written it about my wife because her name was Linda. That wasn't the case. In Spanish, the term *que linda* is not a proper name — it simply means *so pretty*. I wrote it about a young man who would see a young Mexican girl at a bus stop every morning. He was completely smitten by her, as were all the other boys, but he was too shy to tell her.

I really loved everything about the song, but talking to Paul Willett one day, he said he felt the song needed a bridge and played some chords for me. I didn't want to change it or add a bridge, but after hearing his chords, it did seem to fit and make sense. I agreed and added words and melody to the chords. Paul was right — it worked perfectly.

I had wanted to do an a cappella vocal at the beginning of the song. The words were as follows:

> *I see you passin' each morning, and I long to catch your eye*
> *I want to call your name out, but I can't bring myself to try*
> *I guess until that time, girl, I'll remain your loving unknown*
> *But someday I'll tell you, "Que yo Te quiero con todo mi corazón"*

I wanted to layer lots of cool harmonies. The guys were fabulous singers, but horrible with accents! The Spanish phrase at the end had to have somewhat of an accent.

We went over it several times to no avail. They sounded ridiculous and they knew it. They would end up laughing hysterically. Consequently, I went in the studio one morning and did all the vocals myself. My time in LA playing with Friends & Brothers had taught me how to not only speak Spanish, but speak it with an accent.

Danny's songs were incredible. I was so glad that they'd decided to let me sing them. However, there was one song of Danny's that I refused to sing — a song called "Who Gave You The Right." It was a song about the *troubles* in Northern Ireland.

Danny was very involved in an organization called Irish Northern Aid. All of Danny's songs were personal, but this song seemed personal to him on a whole different level.

I just could not see myself delivering this song with the same fire that he did. It seemed ludicrous, so I went to Jim Gaines with my argument ready.

165

I said, "Danny has to sing this song!"

In his slow Memphis drawl Jim said, "Okay."

Jim would argue some things, but he didn't even flinch on this. I was almost disappointed... I had a great argument ready.

As I said, Danny's songs were great. They were also very moving. Two in particular that were very hard for me to sing both in the studio and live were "Guard Your Heart" and the medley "Song of Hope/Love Can." The lyrical content and haunting melodies often would literally choke me up when I sang them.

We brought in several additional people for this project. I'd like to mention:

Tenor Saxophone: Pete Deluca
Trumpet: Elliot "Doc" Simpson
Baritone sax: Ed Savoldi
Soprano sax: Mark Biehl
Percussion: Rusty Parker

On Danny's song "Who Gave You The Right" we used a lot of Irish instrumentation because of the lyrical content. All of the Irish instruments were played by Niall Gannon. We recorded my older brother, Mike, doing a *newscast* over the solo section. This was not a stretch for my brother because he had been program director and on-air personality for years at KEZK radio.

The last song was the medley "Song of Hope/Love Can." In between the two songs we decided to have the "Love Verses" from *I Corinthians 13:4-8* recited by children. We used our families' children, some friends' children, and some inner- city children from my church.

I produced this three ring circus... there were 15 kids running around the studio! I would take each child into the vocal booth and help them. I had each child read the entire section. That way I could decide who would say which phrase later in a mixing session. For the ones who couldn't read, I would read each line to them first and have them say it back to me, then just eliminate my voice later.

I made a cassette recording of all the voices and brought it home. I had a small four-track recording unit at home and I spent countless hours listening to all the voices and choosing which child would say which phrase. Once I knew the order they would be in, I notated it and brought it back to the studio and mixed them accordingly.

The children involved were as follows:

Elisha Liston	Richard Steltenpohl, Jr.
Erin Lang	Jessica Lang
Natasha Johnson	Eugene Liston
Rachel Baker	Sarah Reel
Allison Finn	Sean Liston
Lauren Willett	Josh Lang
Jasmine Parker	Dorothy Johnson

We mixed part of it in St. Louis and part in Memphis at Kiva Studios where Stevie Ray Vaughan did some recordings.

I put together the artwork and the booklet for the CD. We had a friend — Tom Corbett — who had a print shop in Dogtown and I went down everyday for about two weeks and used his computers. I'd bring down photos to scan. I would also type all the information, credits, lyrics, dedications, etc., and then Tom would work with me for placement. Tom was a godsend because, at that time, having someone do this would have cost a lot of money.

Radio stations in St. Louis were expressing an interest in playing the new CD. KSHE insisted on an exclusive premier of the CD. Considering all KSHE had done for us over the years, this did not seem an unreasonable request.

When we got the finished product, we kept to our word and gave KSHE first play. They did play it, but only once. The golden age of radio was gone. It wasn't really KSHE's fault. Almost every station was playing nothing but *classic rock*. Which was just a cool name for *oldies*. New product from Mama's Pride was not going to be on the menu.

We had a release party at Sherre Birenbaum's music store — the Disc-Connection. We probably sold about 300 CDs that day. We continued to play and sell CDs. The band would even take their salary from playing and buy CDs with it to help pay back the investors.

Sadly, with no airplay and no real concerts, we never went past one pressing of 5,000 copies. We managed to pay back around 65 percent of their investment. We believed with all our hearts that we would sell tons of CDs. It just simply didn't happen.

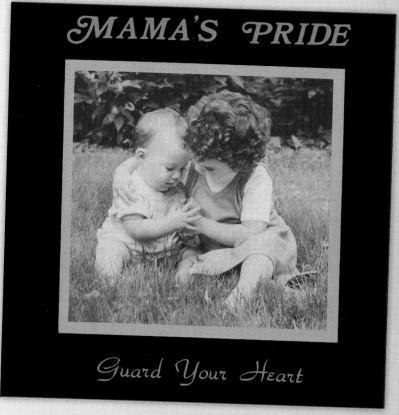

Mama's Pride continued to play for a while but we had no desire to play clubs again night after night. We knew that *Guard Your Heart* had run its course. This time we had lost money for other people, too. We did one last concert at Mississippi Nights. We took the money we made that night and bought as many CDs as we could to reimburse the investors.

The two children on the Guard Your Heart CD were the daughters of Dave Kelley (General Manager of KSHE at the time). Being a protective father he, understandably, did not want their names in the credits. They are both grown now so I would like to finally give them their due. Thank you Nora and Keegan Kelley.

After that, I kept the books and continued to sell CDs when I could. I wasn't doing much music at that point. I continued to perform with Butch Wax & The Hollywoods, but I eventually quit them. It was a fun band, but other than singing I really had no input and I lost interest. My buddy (Carol Rowley) and I quit together. I had thoughts of starting my own *oldies* band but my brother, Danny, talked me out of it.

He said, "Pat, is that really what you want to do... put together a glorified cover band?"

When I thought about it, I knew he was right.

In June of 1992 Mama's Pride had one of our coolest concerts. I received a call from Irv Zuckerman from Contemporary Productions. We were old friends and I hadn't heard from him in years. He'd heard the band was back together and wanted to know if we'd be interested in doing an opening slot at Riverport Amphitheatre.

We hadn't done a real concert in many years and I, of course, said we'd love to. He told me the headliner was looking for a small group that could do 30 minutes and get on and offstage quickly. They wanted someone experienced so they wouldn't be star struck. Irv knew that we'd been down this road many times with major acts.

I assured him we could do a solid 30-minute set. I said, "Irv, why would we be star struck... who's the headliner?"

Irv said, "It's Ringo Starr's All-Starr Band."

I thought, *Oh, my God... a Beatle!?*

The All-Starrs consisted of Zak Starkey, Joe Walsh, Dave Edmunds, Timothy B. Schmit, Nils Lofgren, Todd Rundgren, Burton Cummings, and Tim Cappello. Wow, what a lineup!

I told Irv that we'd added Tom Denman on keyboards so we had seven members, not six. He quickly said, "I'll call you right back." I tried to stop him before he hung up because that wasn't all. He called back about 20 minutes later and said that it was fine if we could be offstage in 15-20 minutes. I told him that wasn't a problem, but that there was one other thing.

He asked what... I said, "We also have a three-piece horn section."

Irv said, "You're kidding right?"

I assured him I was not kidding. The *Guard Your Heart* CD had horns and we'd added the Dogtown Horns (Ray McAnallen, Kevin Rauscher, and Richard Zempel). I told him that they were only horn players with no amps or extraneous equipment.

Irv said, "Dear God, let me call them. Now, before I call, you're not using cloggers or a marching band... this is it, right?"

Somehow he got them to agree to a 10-piece band when all they really wanted was a three- or four-piece group.

So, on June 26, we headed to Riverport Amphitheatre to open for Ringo Starr & His All-Starr Band. When the All-Starr Band got there I was standing in the back so I could see the multiple limos pull up. One after another, limos pulled up and rock stars got out. Finally, the last one pulled up and there he was... Ringo! This was not watching the *Ed Sullivan Show* in 1964 — he was getting out of a limo 10 feet away.

As he walked by, he looked over and said, "Hi, how are you?"

I'm not sure I even responded.

1961 Gretsch Chet Atkins

I brought my classic 1961 Gretsch Chet Atkins that day because I knew it'd get noticed. The first person I met was Joe Walsh, who came running out of a dressing room yelling, "Oh man, where did you get that guitar? I used to have one just like it!"

I asked, "What happened to it?"

He said, "Ugh, I gave it to Jimmy Page."

I also talked to Timothy B. Schmit. I asked if he remembered singing on our second LP. He didn't, but was very apologetic and friendly.

At one point, when we were playing "Ol' St. Lou," I looked over and Todd Rundgren was dancing and enjoying our set. I looked back at Kevin Sanders and he looked like he'd just landed in Neverland. Kevin was a huge Todd Rundgren fan, so this was surreal for him.

We were supposed to play a 30-minute set and have the stage stripped in 20 minutes. Our set was exactly 30 minutes and the stage was stripped in 15 minutes. Ringo came into our dressing room afterwards. He walked in and said, "Hey Mama's boys how are ya'?" in that legendary Liverpudlian accent. Mama's Pride was the funniest bunch of guys I've ever worked with, and they were completely speechless.

He said, "How'd ya' like to do Kansas City with us?"

Like one voice, we all said, "Yes!"

He said, "Alright, see ya' there," and left.

It was like we were bit players in *A Hard Days Night* for about four minutes.

On June 28 we pulled up to the Sandstone Amphitheater in Kansas City, Missouri. A good friend — Joey Vaccaro — had a motor home and drove us there so we looked somewhat professional. I had talked to everyone in the All-Starr Band except for Burton Cummings. He was a bit standoffish. At one point during their show he was sitting behind the stage and I could hear someone onstage playing solo Chet Atkins-style guitar. I walked up to Burton and asked, "Who's onstage playing?" (You couldn't see the stage from where we were positioned.)

He looked up at me and mumbled, "Dave Edmunds," then looked back down.

I said, "Wow, he's doing songs from *Chet Atkins Picks on The Beatles*."

He looked up and said, "Did you have that album?"

I said, "Yah, it had that beautiful 12-string country gentleman on the front!"

Burton and I talked the whole time until it was time for him to go back up. People in this business can seem aloof or (what people perceive as) conceited. Many times,

they're just tired of answering the same questions by well meaning fans over and over.
I, unwittingly, touched on a favorite topic for him.

After the show, the road manager asked me if he thought we'd be interested in going to Europe. It would be a fairly short, expensive tour. (Opening acts don't make much.) All the guys, by this time, had day jobs, families, and commitments. It wasn't really a sure thing and I never heard back.

KPS AND **A NEW DIRECTION**

The *Guard Your Heart* project really took a lot out of me. My kids were soon-to-be teenagers and with that brought all the problems every parent has to deal with. I had grown weary of trying to feign a relationship. It seemed like the wheels were coming off of my life.

The internet was really getting to be big and chat rooms were all the rage. I was emotionally lonely, so I would go into the chat rooms and talk to people. In a chat room you could be whatever you wanted to be. I had lived a very interesting life and could always garner an audience of listeners. Just being in there and talking to people who really wanted to listen to me was so healing. It stirred something in me and I felt the desire to write again.

Chat rooms were fun, but also very sad. Often times, it was people who just didn't want to deal with real life all the time. I had been speaking to a female school teacher from (I think) Wisconsin. She had stated that she was single or divorced (I don't remember) I asked her why she was in chat rooms instead of out really meeting people. She said she couldn't deal with the bar scene and being hit on by creeps.

She said, "Pat, I just want someone to talk to and this provides that." It was like someone smacked me in the face and said, "Write that down!" It was the first song I'd written in a while and it was called, "Someone To Talk To."

I continued to talk to people online and get ideas for songs. I also got involved with a recording studio called KPS. It was a new studio on Vandeventer in St. Louis. A guy named Bill Keyes headed it up. There were so many creative people down there, both audio and video. I met some new friends and rekindled some old relationships.

My old friend, Rod Sherrell, was doing his cable TV show from there. I met a guy named Doug Jones who was a computer graphics wiz. I reconnected with "Baby" Al Caldwell, a fabulous bass player. He was the first guy to introduce me to Pro Tools (a computer application for professional music and audio production). Bill Keyes bought the system and Al read the manual in one day and was recording with it the next. He was brilliant. There were scads of musicians that filtered in and out as well. Just being in that environment made you want to create.

Prior to "Someone To Talk To" I had written six songs in a ten year period. In 1996 and 1997 I wrote 26 songs. For me, that was a lot. I ended up recording 15 of those songs. I was only at KPS for a little more than a year, but it was a great year.

I had become friends with Ken Hensley of Uriah Heep. He was living in St. Louis at the time and going to the same church I attended. We worked in a small church band along with noted Christian artist Randy Mayfield. During this time Ken asked me to play dobro on a project called *Rattlesnake Guitar* — a tribute to the music of Peter Green. I agreed and flew to Chicago to lay the tracks. It was just he and I on this particular track. He played guitar and sang. I played dobro. The song was called "Hellhound on My Trail." Unfortunately, Ken took written credit for playing the dobro and my name was not included on the album.

One day my old friend, Carol Rowley, called me and asked me to come out and see her and her guitarist friend doing a duo at a cool place in Kirkwood, Missouri, called Cafe Victorian. It was such a small room that they didn't even use a PA. I sat in and did a couple of my new original songs. I felt the fever to play again.

The guitarist's name was Mike Barada and he offered me a job there with he and Carol.

Mike Barada and I at Cafe Victorian

Bob Bosch
playing along at
Cafe Victorian

I took it right away. It really gave me a platform for my new songs. At some point Carol left and it was just Mike and I. There was another guy who played before us named Bob Bosch. He would do solo for three hours or so and then Mike and I would play duo.

Eventually, Bob would just stay and play with us, too. They both were very good acoustic players and that really helped because I had not played in a while. I leaned heavily on their chops. They both had good voices, too, so we would harmonize a lot. Bob would play with us off and on and I was always pleased when he'd stay after because he had such a unique approach to music.

June of 1997 was a turning point for me. That's when I took my first trip to Ireland. For every Irish American, this is their dream vacation. I spent weeks putting the itinerary together for the trip. Like most Irish Americans, I knew absolutely nothing about the real Ireland. Between the music, the culture, and the people themselves... it was life changing. When I got back to St. Louis I wanted to do some Irish songs with Mike. Mike was a total music lover so he graciously agreed.

Dogtowners. Left to right: Me, Brenda King, and Mike Barada

About this time another old friend came in to see Mike and I. It was Brenda King, my bandmate from Butch Wax & The Hollywoods. She, of course, sat in and sang.

It sounded so good that she ended up joining us. We called the trio the Dogtowners. We played the Cafe Victorian regularly. We also played at my brother Danny's restaurant — Seamus McDaniels.

Another *moment in time* was when Bob Bosch called one day and invited me to a *Mensa* party. Mensa International is the largest and oldest high IQ society in the world. Bob was a member of Mensa and always wanted me to get tested and join. I used to tell him, "I always thought I might have a high IQ, but if I take this test and fail, I'll be bummed out... I'll just live in ignorance, then I can believe what I want."

I did, however, go to the party. Some of the people there were exactly how you would imagine them. One fella told me he could speak over 200 languages. Some, he said, were only spoken by a handful of people. I remember thinking, *if almost nobody speaks this language, what's the point?* (I'm not sure I would have blended in Mensa.)

Bob was introducing me around and introduced me to a guy who seemed sullen and quiet. When Bob introduced us he said, "This is Joe Butler, he's from Ireland." I definitely wanted to talk to Joe! As it turned out, he wasn't sullen as much as bored — his wife Jessica was the Mensa person, not him.

As Joe and I talked, he said he'd heard of Mama's Pride. He also said he had a bar in Westport Plaza called McNulty's Irish Pub. I told him about the Dogtowners. He said that he'd like to hear us sometime.

With Joe Butler at McNulty's

He never did call me so I checked out McNulty's myself. One night they were having a band in from Ireland called the Dublin City Ramblers. It was a ticketed event and you got seated with strangers, but all of us had been to Ireland so that would be the table topic. Eventually you were like friends. I loved this place and Joe was like a whole other person in his bar. He was full of life — dancing around the room like someone who'd just been given the keys to heaven.

The Dogtowners had some Fridays open and I spoke to him about it. He said he had a regular guy on Fridays and he was honor bound to keep him. The Irish have a great sense of loyalty... but do not make them mad. I don't know what that guy did, but one day Joe called and said that guy had pissed him off and all his Fridays were now open if we wanted them. I jumped on it.

We played every week at McNulty's. I could do all the Irish music I wanted to, and my own songs as well. Joe Butler was a gracious host, even when the nights were slow. He also would bring in artists from Ireland if they were in the country somewhere. The St. Louis Irish were always telling him to bring in this one or that one. He'd work hard to get them there and then half of the St. Louis Irish, who begged for the artists, wouldn't even show up. This was one of the things he complained about the most when we'd talk.

I started helping him with promoting. I even made tickets for the events. I'd do it using Photoshop and buy business card stock and print them. They were fancy (with the photo of the artist) and they were full color! The first time he saw one he said, "Bejaysus, Paddy, they look so lovely I might come meself."

Joe had a grand wit.

He often brought in Paddy Reilly. I worked with him on the last show he had with Paddy. He wanted to have it at the Sheldon, but from experience I knew he'd lose money there even though it was lovely. I talked him into renting a banquet room right down the corridor from his pub.

The Dogtowners opened for Paddy Reilly. I promoted the hell out of this show and he had a packed house. Many were people I knew and had goaded into coming to hear some quality Irish music. He made a nice profit and I was happy for him. I remember that his favorite song I did that night was a song I wrote called "Swan Hotel."

Dogtowners with Paddy Reilly

Joe loved my music and always encouraged me to do more of it. This was rare in a bar. He was always on me about making a CD, too. I'd never really thought about doing it because my only experience with doing a CD was *Guard Your Heart* and that was a daunting project!

Also around this time, I collaborated again with Ken Hensley of Uriah Heep and a group called Visible Faith. We recorded a CD with him called *Glimpse of Glory* on which I was credited for singing "Guard Your Heart" — a song written by my brother, Danny. I also played pedal steel, but was not credited for doing so.

I had done some projects at the Sheldon Concert Hall in St. Louis. It's an acoustically perfect room. In 1999, I did a *Pat Liston* show there. I had my Dogtowner bandmates — Mike Barada and Brenda King — work with me. In addition to them, I used Cindy Carpenter, Robin Holder, and Dale Tieman on background vocals; Larry Carpenter on piano; Thayne Bradford on violin and mandolin; Sandy Weltman on harmonica and bodhran; and Scott Bryan on percussion.

It was a really fun show and opened the door for more Sheldon Concerts. Mama's Pride had done a totally *unplugged* concert there in 1992 as part of the "Save the Sheldon" series.

The Dogtowners were still working McNulty's, but eventually I wanted to sing more Irish songs and more of my own. I was writing a bit, too. Mike and Brenda were very good singers, so I could hardly ask them to cut back on their vocals so I could sing more. The only remedy I could see was to go solo.

I went solo and continued to play at McNulty's. I had gone to Ireland two more times — once in 1999 and once in 2000.

My favorite St. Patrick's Day of all time was in 2000. Joe started music at McNulty's at 8:00 a.m. There was myself and another singer from Ireland. I can't remember his name but, we sang all day and a group took over as it got close to evening. The beauty was, people were actually there for the *craic* (Irish for a good time) and the music. There were no stupid drunks — it was genuinely a good time. We also played the next day at what Joe used to call *the survivors party.* It went all day as well! Joe knew how to do a party!

McNulty's was in a corridor with a lot of other restaurants and bars. Right next to the pub was a radio station — 550 KTRS. A guy that worked there named Howard Morton used to come in and see me play a lot. He was also a musician and a Mama's Pride fan. He used to set up interviews on the nights I was working at McNulty's. I would run next door before I started and do an interview to get people to come out. There was a big window facing the corridor so people could watch the on-air people. It was always fun.

One night a guy from the Westport Playhouse, which was downstairs from McNulty's, came in and asked if I would be able to open for April Wine the next night. I said, "Sure, why not?" I called my buddy, Mike Barada, because I didn't feel comfortable (at the time) as a soloist opening a concert for a full band. We did the show and it actually came off pretty well.

Joe Butler came down and watched. He had never seen Mama's Pride or me in a concert situation. There were a lot of Pride fans there, to my surprise. Joe was blown away at the response from the audience. He laughed and said, "Jaysus, now you're gonna want a raise."

Left to right: Mom, Pat Liston (my sister-in-law), Mike Liston (my older brother), Danny, and Amy Liston (niece)

Left to right:
Gene Liston (my son),
Tim Liston (Danny's son),
and Mom

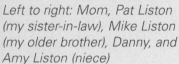

In June of 2000 I did another Sheldon Concert. I billed it as *Pat Liston & The Dogtowners*. It was simple, Mike Barada, Brenda King, and myself. There was one specialty, however. I had been talking to my mom about singing with me.

She was 84 and hadn't really done much singing in a while. Her age was starting to affect her some, but she was still very lucid. It took a lot of convincing, but I got her to agree to singing one song onstage with me. I told her I would come over and practice with her a couple of times a week until the concert. I then talked to my brothers, Danny and Mike, to see if they would like to sing with us as a, sort of, family thing. They agreed.

The day of the show we did a sound check with Mom. Danny said to Mom, "Mom, if you stray from the lyrics, we'll just follow you."

Casually, Mom said, "Okay."

As we were getting ready to sing, Danny walked over and said to Mom, "Now, Mom, these type mics are very tight ranged and you have to get right on top of them."

Well, at that, Mom turned to Danny and said, "You know, I've done this before."

Danny was suddenly eight years old and had been sent to his room. Mike and I, wisely, said nothing.

That night, the audience did not know Mom was coming up. About three-quarters of the way through, I brought her and my brothers up onstage with me. The crowd went wild when they realized what was happening. I announced the song — "Let The Rest of the World Go By" — an old song written in 1919. Mom used to sing it when she was on KMOX in the 1930s.

At the Sheldon. Left to right: Brenda King, Mike Barada, Mike Liston, Me, Mom, and Danny.

Danny and I had never been onstage with Mom nor our brother, Mike, so it was a special moment. I believe Brenda King played accordion, and Danny and I played guitars. Mom pulled it off without a hitch. I think her boys were more nervous than she was. When she finished, it brought the house down. Someone gave her roses when she was finished.

As I was leading her offstage to a standing ovation, she looked at me, then to the audience and said out loud, "Is that it?!" The audience cracked up.

I said, out loud, "Whadda you mean, you didn't want to do this at all... we don't have another song."

She, once again looked at the people in the audience, then me, and says, "Okay, it's your show," as much as to say, *you're making a mistake, but you'll have to live with it*. The audience loved it. It was a bit difficult to capture the audience after that, but (wisely) I only had a couple of songs remaining. All in all it was a wonderful night.

I was still at McNulty's every week, but this business has no guarantees except one — things will change.

Joe came to me one day and said that he was losing the restaurant. It was a long story, but the bottom line was he had to sell and was moving to Chicago. I was not happy, but I understood. I had had so many changes in my life that I just rolled with it and thought, *okay, whats next?*

I went to his house a few days later and helped him pack and took him to the airport. It was very difficult telling my buddy goodbye. After he'd gone to Chicago, the people who had his lease at Wesport Plaza managed to get the restaurant away from him in a devious fashion and he lost it all. (There has to be some serious karma for people like that.)

This was as good a time as any to start working on a solo CD. I spent the next two years putting together musicians, material, arrangements, and studio time for the project.

I bought the cheaper version of Pro Tools. I still had all the files from KPS Studios. I used some of those, but I mostly recorded new tracks. My new music was very different from Mama's Pride, but not different from who I had always been.

Choosing a rhythm section was tricky. I knew the sound I wanted. I wanted it simple, but tasty. I called my old bandmate, Dickie Steltenpohl, for bass. Dickie was the best and most creative bass player I'd ever worked with. I knew he would understand what I wanted and would have some innovative ideas.

I had befriended a drummer during my KPS Studio days by the name of Don Drewett. He had already played on some of my recordings down there. I not only loved what Don played, I loved what he *didn't* play.

The first session I ever did with Don I raved over his approach.

Don said, "I didn't really do that much."

I said, "I know, I like that... and what you did do was perfect."

I got hold of another old friend, Bill Murphy for keyboards. Bill could also play accordion and I wanted that on a few of the songs.

On guitar, I recruited Scott Nienhaus, who was living in Nashville at the time.

I also enlisted the help of Bob Breidenbach on dobro, Steve Radick on congas, Keith Hempen on congas and assorted percussion, Tim Britton on uillean pipes, Laurie Hartung on highland bagpipes, Michelle Defabio on violin, Julie Leonhardt on violin, Don Black on viola, and JoEllen Lyons on cello.

It was a daunting task, having never done a CD to this extent. Aside from amassing all these musicians, I had to get a studio, photographer, graphic designer, people to press the disc and transfer artwork for a 16-page booklet.

"Baby" Al Caldwell

I got my old friend, Al Caldwell, to mix it at Icon Studios (owned by my friend, Perry Emge). I had it mastered at Ardent Studios in Memphis by Kevin Nix. A good friend, Doug Smith, did the photography, Doug Jones helped me with graphic design and artwork... it was an education.

I was at my computer finishing up some art work. The last audio track had been laid just the day before. All that was left to do was type in the thank yous on the appropriate page. Since I had an appointment downtown and was trying to hurry, I quickly saved everything and shut my computer down. I was only going to be gone for about an hour. On the way back home I was buzzing with excitement. I was, basically, finished — I just had to transfer it, send it off, and wait for the finished product to arrive. I couldn't believe I had pulled this off and was feeling like a mini-record mogul.

I pulled around to the side of the house that was on the alley and noticed the back door was standing open. I had left through the front door. As I got closer to the house, I noticed the basement door had been kicked open. I immediately called the police. Someone had broken in during that hour I was gone. It was like they knew how much time they had. They had stolen all my stereo equipment from my upstairs office, but worse, they had taken my computer and all the hard drives. Almost five years of audio and artwork... gone!

I felt sick to my stomach. One of the police knew I was from Mama's Pride and when I told him what they had actually stolen, he was livid. My eyes scanned the room, and there, in the corner on a guitar stand, sat my priceless Martin D18. It sat there like it was saying, *I'm still here*. The cop looked over and said, "It was kids. Only a kid would have thought that wasn't worth stealing."

That Martin was worth twice all the other equipment combined. Ironically, my electric guitars were at a friend's house being serviced. One of them was my '61 Gretsch Chet Atkins. With the Martin being there and the others uncharacteristically somewhere else, it was like God was saying, *it's going to be alright*.

I cannot explain the sudden peace I felt — a peace in an absolute storm.

I turned in my claim to my homeowners insurance. They said they would pay for it all, and then dropped our insurance after 18 years with no claims. I would get my equipment back, but it certainly wasn't going to have five years of hard work on it.

I gave my friend, Perry Emge, a call right away. Remember, he owned Icon Studios and I had to dump all my songs on his hard drives after doing some recording there about three months prior to this. I called him just in case he might still have them on his drives.

When he answered I asked if he had dumped my stuff already.

He said, "Wow, that's strange. I was just this minute getting ready to erase all these drives."

I said, "But you still have them on there?!"

He said that he did, and when I told him why I was calling he freaked out!

I said, "Don't erase anything, I'm going to buy two hard drives and head right down!"

I then called my graphics buddy, Doug Jones. He still had the stuff I had sent to him. He put everything back together for me, even better than it was originally.

I had done a fair amount of overdubs since I had been to Icon Studios. So those tracks were gone forever, but every person came back in and re-recorded their parts. Some turned out even better than the original tracks. In my mind, it was nothing short of a miracle that it came together. I desperately wanted it done and delivered before April 12th.

My brother was working on a new CD as well. He had been talking to me about a great promotional idea for both of us. He'd had a conversation with Mark Klose and they had talked to Pat Hagin from the Pageant. They all agreed it would be a good idea to have Mama's Pride do a show at the Pageant. I did have to agree, a Mama's Pride concert would sell a lot of our solo CDs in one night.

I called Pat Hagin from the Pageant and worked out the deal. Pat and I agreed on Saturday, April 12, 2003. So this is why I wanted my CD to be pressed before that date. The CDs arrived the day before the concert — hard work and lots of help from friends made that possible.

PAT LISTON BLUE MIST

1. ALMOST LIKE BEING IN LOVE
   (P. Liston)
2. I GUESS WE'LL NEVER KNOW
   (P. Liston)
3. BLUE BANDANA
   (P. Liston)
4. COWBOY CLOTHES
   (P. Liston)
5. IT'S ALRIGHT
   (P. Liston)
6. SPELLBOUND
   (P. Liston)
7. BLUE MIST
   (P. Liston)
8. LOOK AWAY
   (P. Liston)
9. STRANGE ADDICTION
   (P. Liston)
10. PETER PAN WINDOW
    (P. Liston)
11. (Now that I have)PASSED THE TORCH ALONG
    (P. Liston)

Produced by Pat Liston
Mixed by: "Baby" Al Caldwell
Recorded at: Icon Studios, Dogtown Studio, The Sandbox, and KPS Studio
Mastered by: Kevin Nix at Ardent Studios, Memphis, Tennessee
Front and back Cover photography: Doug Smith
Graphic Design: Doug Jones/Lightstream Studio

When Pat Hagin and I talked about the concert he asked what I thought the turn out would be. There was a man by the name of Scott Davis who had created a Mama's Pride website in 1997. I watched it pretty closely. People visited all the time, but I didn't see as many as I'd have liked. Scott worked very hard at presenting a good site, but he couldn't do much about the number of visitors. Based on this, I told Pat Hagin that I thought maybe 400+ might attend. He agreed and said he could close the balcony off so it would look more crowded downstairs.

I got busy making posters for the event and doing any promoting I could. Mark Klose was onboard to do some advertising on K-HITS.

Mark Klose had been advertising for a week or so before the band could even start rehearsing. The day the tickets went on sale Pat Hagin called me. The Pageant had sold 850 tickets the first day! (A sell-out at the Pageant was 1,500.)

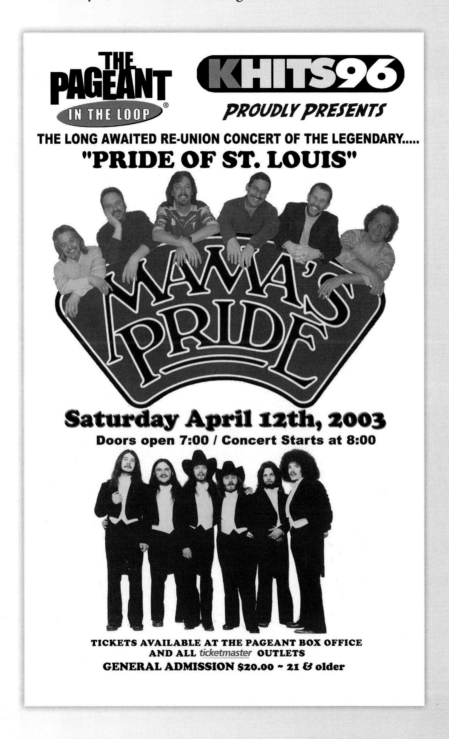

Pat knew his venue and he told me, at this rate, it would be sold out by the end of the week. I was stunned. Pat was a bit shocked himself. It wasn't that he didn't think we were good enough, it just seemed to come out of nowhere. As Pat had predicted, by Friday Mama's Pride had sold out the Pageant — one of their fastest sell outs at that time!

I called Pat and said, "My God, should we do a second night?"

Pat chuckled and basically said, "Duh." He said the only Saturday they had open was May 3rd, which would be three weeks later.

I told him, "We haven't played together in almost 11 years... we may need three weeks in between!"

So, May 3rd was booked — which by the day of the concert, sold out as well.

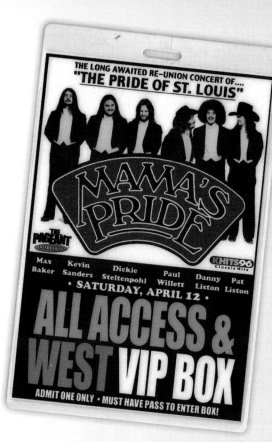

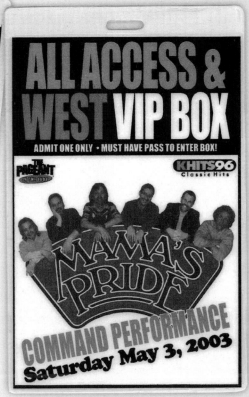

I had been putting a band together to perform songs from my new CD. Some of the guys were onstage with me at the May 3rd Mama's Pride concert: Scott Nienhaus, Bill Murphy, and Bob Briedenbach.

The band that I finally put together was, Scott Nienhaus (guitar), Bill Murphy (keyboards and accordion), Dickie Steltenpohl (bass), Don Drewett (drums), and myself.

The Pat Liston Band.
Left to right: Me, Dickie
Steltenpohl, Scott Nienhaus,
Don Drewett, and Bill Murphy

It was a really good group, but venues for original music, even with this great line-up, were few and far between. So, it was short lived.

Mama's Pride did another concert on December 20th, 2003. This concert fell short of a sellout by less than 200 people. The highlight of this concert was my brother, Danny, connecting with his newfound daughter, Angelique. He wrote a beautiful song for the occasion called "Because of You."

The following year Mama's Pride did two more concerts at the Pageant, on May 1st and the other on December 18th. Neither sold out. This caused us to decide on doing just one concert a year.

In 2004, Scott Nienhaus teamed up with a woman named Karen Crawford to do a duo. He invited me to come sit in on a few of their gigs. The harmonies were magical. We decided to put together a trio and call it Liston, Nienhaus, & Crawford. Scott had a big name in St. Louis and beyond. He had played with Firefall, Nicolette Larson, and a later rendition of the Byrds. So we decided to use our names for the band in hopes that people would recognize it and come out to see us play. We mixed original music with any rock classics that had good harmonies.

Left to right: Scott Nienhaus, Karen Crawford, and Me

We got along great. I used to get Karen laughing so hard onstage that we'd periodically get a scowl from Scott. Which is totally understandable considering it was usually during something he was singing.

I have to tell this story: I had not been with Scott and Karen long... we were tearing down after a gig. Karen didn't know me real well — other than me being the leader of Mama's Pride. While wrapping wires, she tripped on a wire or a case or something. She was going down fast, face first. I did what anyone would do, I reached out to grab her because, like I said, she was going down quickly. The next thing I know I have a breast in each hand! We immediately went to our separate corners with that *how 'bout them Bears* look on our faces. Karen's cheeks were glowing like a light house beacon on a foggy night.

I finally broke the silence and said, "Well... they're real."

All three of us busted out laughing... and Karen's face got even more red!

So, for a four-month period in 2004 I was, not only starting to play with Scott and Karen, I was doing a ton of work on our house in Dogtown to sell it (working towards buying a new one out in O'Fallon, Missouri), putting together another Mama's Pride concert at the Pageant, and doing an extremely involved basement remodel that had a curved bar (I did remodeling work to make money).

Anyway, due to all I had going, I contracted diverticulitis. Fortunately, I managed to dodge surgery and the meds cured it.

We moved into our new house in August of 2004. Most people were shocked that I moved away from Dogtown, having lived there most of my life. After doing my first CD and doing so much new writing, I was feeling restless. I was 56 years old and — for the first time in my life — was feeling old.

I was embracing every change I could grasp.

Years earlier, I had heard that getting older is doing more and more for the last time and less and less for the first time. So, I was looking for new experiences. I started working more regularly with Scott and Karen. I truly enjoyed playing out. I built a studio in the new house. I wanted to be creative on any level possible. Most people my age were moving towards retirement mode. I was looking the other direction.

The move and my desire to get back into music didn't make home life any better. Through the years I had tried, in every way I knew, to be flexible. I walked away from who I was to raise a family — I had no regrets, but our children were raised and I was not ready to head out to pasture. I felt I had more to say and more to do.

I used to watch couples laughing and talking together and seemingly enjoy each others company. Our relationship had never had that. We could have fun with other people, but rarely with just the two of us. We had always been two completely different people and after 26 years, it was starting to take its toll. I even took antidepressants for a while, but felt they only masked a deeper problem. I started drinking more at home. I sat up, by myself, at night drinking a bottle of wine or more. I was eating a lot at night as well and had put on nearly 30 pounds.

My attitude was so skewed, I remember praying several times during this time, "Lord, free me from this apathetic hell."

My mom had been in a nursing home for almost two years. I hated that. It was the most difficult thing I ever had to come to grips with. The nursing home was only two blocks from our Dogtown house, but now I was 40 miles away. Mom was slipping away mentally. Thank God for my brother, Danny, because he was with her much more than Mike and I.

It was the evening of Christmas day 2004 when I got the call from the nursing home.

"Your mother has passed."

I called Mike and Danny and we went to the home. It really affected Danny. He wanted to be there when she went. We all did.

A hospice person helped a little by saying it was common, especially for mothers, to pass when family wasn't around. It allows them to let go. I have to admit that deep down inside, I was glad she went. Nursing homes are awful places to be — people go there to die, and they know it.

Mom was in a better place... and we would meet again.

Mom was gone. My daughter, Elisha, had long since moved out. My son, Gene, was in and out. In my mind, I was basically done with what I had quit music for. Even if I was 56, I wanted more out of life.

My wife and I went to the Lake of the Ozarks every other weekend with friends. Even though it was fun, it seemed desperately close to a retirement kind of thing.

My wife insisted that I only play every other weekend — that way we had a weekend for the Lake. In reality, it was a reasonable request.

I had had a passionate void for years. I came alive in about 1996, but then retreated again and I was feeling restless. I knew that my wife and I were just going through the motions. In some ways, I think we always had. I had heard a song once called "Very Close Total Strangers" — it described us.

I kept myself very busy over the next year. I was starting production for another Pat Liston & Friends concert at the Sheldon Concert Hall in St. Louis. The show was Thursday, June 9th, 2005. I used Scott and Karen for this one. I also had Bill Murphy on accordion/keyboards, Bob Briedenbach on dobro, Tommy Martin on uilleann pipes, and Ron Sikes on percussion. It was one of my best. Everyone involved was an exemplary musician/singer. It was also very well attended — more so than my previous shows. I think that was because playing with Scott and Karen and doing the Pageant shows with Mama's Pride I was out in the public eye more than I had previously been.

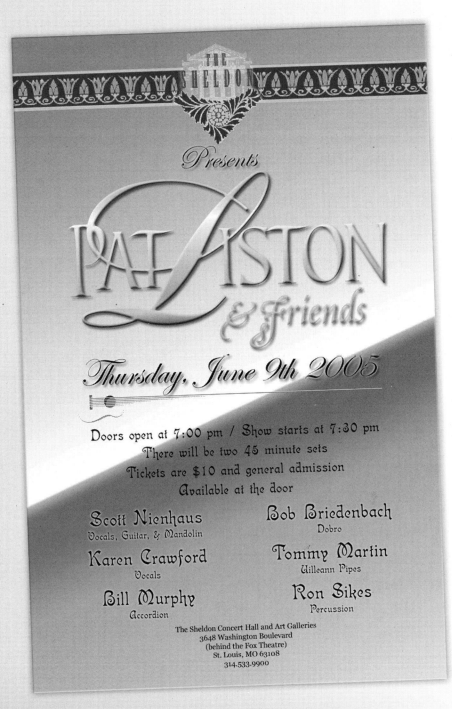

Later in 2005, I was playing with Scott and Karen at a place called Cleo's in Edwardsville. We played there every Sunday, until I started playing every other week. Then, Terry Jones Rogers, a musician friend of Scott's, had moved to St. Louis to do the alternate weeks. This was how Scott and Karen made their living and they had to work every week.

On one of my Sundays at Cleo's, a woman walked in. She was simply dressed in Levis and a flannel shirt, but she had a presence that drew my attention.

I rarely took much notice of attractive women anymore. Another characteristic that made me feel old. This woman was different. She was, to be sure, very attractive, but there was something else. Something I couldn't put my finger on — something much deeper than mere beauty.

She had steel blue eyes and was very difficult to make eye contact with because... as they say, *the eyes are the window to the soul.* At the sake of sounding overly poetic, I could see something so much deeper. Her eyes spoke volumes to me. It was like I knew her or had known her somehow. It put me in a definite quandary.

She came in several times before I could muster the courage to say hello. This was unusual for me because I was married and I was not a player on any level. So, why would I be uncomfortable talking to her? I just felt I needed to talk to this woman for some reason. I had never in my life felt a draw like this.

One night she came in and I saw her talking to a good friend of mine, John Gagliardo. I could tell by the way they spoke they knew each other pretty well. John and Rhonda Gagliardo were Mama's Pride fans that I had recently gotten to know very well. I walked over to John after the woman had walked away and asked him who that was.

He said, "Oh, that's Dawn. She's a bartender at a place I play my pool league. Why?"

John knew I was married and never asked about anyone — I left every job as soon as we were done. So, I guess it seemed strange for me to ask him who she was. About that time she walked back to his table and John said, "Dawn, this is Pat Liston... Pat, this is Dawn."

The next few minutes are still a bit sketchy.... I spoke some unintelligible words and went straight to the bar. I asked Jen, the bartender, for a shot of tequila. She said, "Who's this for?" having never seen me do a shot of anything.

I said, "It's for me... my mouth's not working."

She looked at me as much as to say, *and this is gonna help?* I threw back the shot and when I turned to leave the bar, Dawn was right behind me!

She said, "Are you okay?"

We walked over to John and Rhonda's table and sat down. I did what I always do when I'm uncomfortable... comedy!

Dawn laughed at everything I said. Not in that accommodating way, but real laughter. The more she'd laugh, the sillier I got. I had her in tears. I went back and did our last set, but when I was done playing, I packed and left. I wasn't stupid, I was having way too much fun. This was a young beautiful woman and I was feeling things I hadn't felt in years.

In February of 2006, I started thinking about another Sheldon Concert — something bigger. I wanted to add real strings and some more Irish influence. I got together with

a woman named Mary Sweetin. She was a violinist I met through another violinist friend, Michelle DeFabio. Mary was to arrange the strings on all the songs that were to use strings.

I was so excited. I had five string players: Mary Sweetin on violin, Justin Meaux on violin, Michelle DeFabio on violin, Deberah Haferkamp on viola, and JoEllen Lyons on cello. In addition, I had Linda Elliott on harp, Bob Briedenbach on dobro, Bill Murphy on accordion/background vocals, Tim Britton on uilleann pipes, and Ron Sikes on percussion. And, of course, Scott Nienhaus and Karen Crawford.

What I didn't tell anyone was, the encore was going to be epic!

We worked so hard on the encore that we would have done an encore even if nobody applauded!

But they did.

We came back out and did "The Parting Glass" — a lovely Irish ballad. We did the version from the movie *Waking Ned Devine*. When it got to the end of the song, I spoke about my dear friend, Joe Butler, and his love for Irish music. Sadly, Joe had passed away the previous July. I tagged it by saying he loved the ballads, but he truly loved it *steppy*. The band, at that point, went in to "The Witches Reel," another song featured in *Waking Ned Devine*. It was a Irish Reel that got the audience fired up!

About the time they thought it could get no better, the side door opened and out came three Irish dancers in full regalia! The crowd went crazy!

I had previously talked to my good friend, Jennifer Bartley, who has a dance academy called, the O'Faoláin Academy of Irish Dance. I had seen her and her daughter dance before. We decided on her daughter (Carolyn Bartley) and two other girls from the academy, Annie Rogers and Amanda Warner Peck. They looked beautiful and considering they couldn't hear anything onstage, because of an inept sound tech, they did a wonderful job. As I said, the audience went nuts! Even with the confusion onstage, Carolyn took control and winged it. She plowed right through the mistakes and confusion and brought the house down.

The crowd wanted more... we didn't have another song. I brought all the musicians out onstage. I knew I had to calm things down so, Bill Murphy and I had worked out a Jimmy Webb song just in case — just Bill playing piano and me singing. The song was called "If This Was The Last Song." I told the musicians that it was for them. It's a touching song that, basically, says *if this were the last song, I would want it to be about you.*

A sweet, melancholy ending. It was my best show at the Sheldon. Sadly, it was to be my last there. The rent had gotten too expensive for me and they took no interest in returning my calls — again, things change.

Five days later we were off to Jamaica. My daughter, Elisha, was getting married. She did all the wedding plans, because she was no longer living at home, but again… it was in Jamaica. Sounds fun, but with all the wedding stuff, it seemed like the four days we spent there came and went immediately.

It was an absolutely beautiful wedding, but it came right in the middle of my big Sheldon concert and a CD project that I was doing simultaneously.

My daughter Elisha's wedding day.

While doing the Sheldon concert preparations, I was working on a *live* Mama's Pride CD. We had recorded four different concerts at the Pageant. Three had Andy Beeny and one had Jim Bigget doing the recording. I had the studio in my home so I did all the mixing and editing from there. It took months to wade through everything.

Obviously, I had several versions of each song. I put them all in order and Kevin Sanders came in on one occasion and helped me to choose some of the best performances. Some of the recordings were flawed, so it was tricky fixing and editing things. Al Caldwell helped me a lot and did the final mix.

We had the great Oliver Sain sit in one night at the Pageant on organ and Max sang the old blues classic — "Mother Fuyer." That was on the CD. Oliver had cancer and looked pretty fragile that night, but it was a sweet moment.

Sadly, only five months later, on October 28th, 2003, our dear friend, Oliver, lost his fight with cancer.

Mama's Pride with Oliver Sain at the Pageant, 2003

On another night, the legendary Johnnie Johnson sat in on a song Danny wrote called, "Oh My Soul." Danny was really excited to have that on the CD. He came to the studio one day to hear it. To his dismay, Johnnie came in on the wrong chord at the beginning of every verse.

Johnnie was 80 and really hadn't gone over the song. The verses came in on the four chord and Johnnie would play the one chord, or tonic, at the beginning of each verse. Danny was heartbroken because it was very obvious that it was the wrong chord. I told him to give me a week. It's the digital age and things like this can be fixed.

Now, whether they could be fixed by me, I wasn't sure, but it was worth a try. I went to places within the song where Johnnie was playing a four chord and cut and pasted it at the beginning of the verses. I used different ones so it wouldn't sound like I'd done that. It was a little tricky because Johnnie is constantly moving melodically, but when it was blended back into the mix, it sounded great.

Danny was thrilled because it was *his* song and he wanted Johnnie playing.

I took a few weeks off to focus on the Sheldon Concert and my daughter's wedding, but then went right back at it.

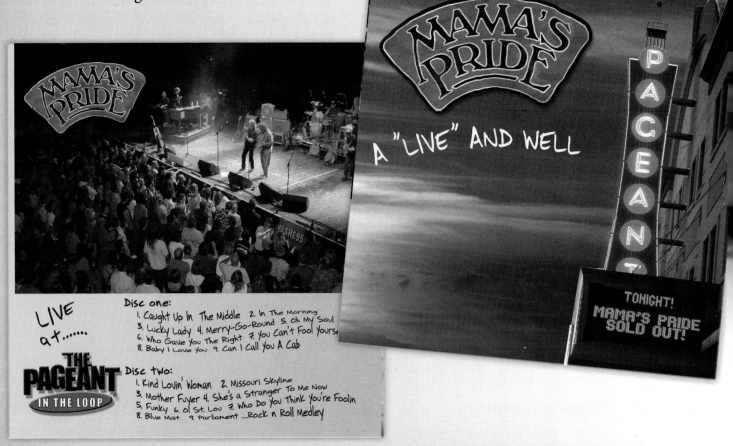

LIVE
at.......
THE PAGEANT
IN THE LOOP

Disc one:
1. Caught Up In The Middle   2. In The Morning
3. Lucky Lady 4. Merry-Go-Round 5. Oh My Soul
6. Who Gave You The Right 7. You Can't Fool Yourse
8. Baby I Love You 9. Can I Call You A Cab

Disc two:
1. Kind Lovin' Woman 2. Missouri Skyline
3. Mother Fuyer 4. She's a Stranger To Me Now
5. Funky 6. ol St. Lou 7. Who Do You Think You're Foolin
8. Blue Mist   9. Parliament ....Rock n Roll Medley

MAMA'S PRIDE
A "LIVE" AND WELL

PAGEANT

TONIGHT!
MAMA'S PRIDE
SOLD OUT!

Mama's Pride had a Pageant concert coming up on Saturday, June 24th. I wanted it finished for that show.

Once again, the CD was finished and delivered the day of the show!

The Sheldon was done, my daughter was married, the *live* CD was finished, and Mama's Pride had another Pageant concert under their belt. Back to reality...

I have to admit, I couldn't wait for the next time I played Cleo's. I kept denying how unhappy my life was and how much fun I'd been having there talking and laughing with Dawn and her family. I knew she was a lot younger than me so I figured that made it just good clean fun because, other than being funny, I saw nothing in me she could possibly want.

Dawn didn't come in every time I was there, but almost. I kept trying to deny it, but I was feeling something very deep for her and over those passing weeks and months it only got stronger.

Finally, in mid-November of 2006, I told my wife I wanted a divorce. For most people I knew, this came as a shock. They knew nothing about Dawn. Even the people in Illinois who saw us laughing and talking at Cleo's were surprised.

The truth be known, up until this point, Dawn and I had never even been alone anywhere. There was no torrid affair... I just fell quietly in love.

I lost almost every friend I had in St. Louis. People (especially church people) struggle with things like divorce. No one really wanted to know what happened, they just wanted me to stay married. I am a people person and have always had a ton of friends. It is a very odd thing to see almost every person you know turn against you on some level. Turn against you without even asking what might have happened. I was met with either judgment or indifference... I'm not sure which is worse.

My counselor, Fleet Rand, was about the only person in the whole ordeal in St. Louis who had my back. It taught me a lot about what a friend looks like.

Eventually, Dawn and I started attending a church called New Testament Fellowship in Alton, Illinois. (It's now called Enjoy Church.) Pastor Daren Carstens and his wife, Laura, were very compassionate. Between them and Fleet Rand, they helped to heal a lot of wounds.

200 The following year I won Best Male Vocalist in the *Riverfront Times* for 2007. It seemed, musically, that things were already changing. Though I was honored, it struck me funny that after all these years, I was just getting this accolade now. I never knew who wrote my review, but I always thought it was one of the best reviews I'd ever gotten.

Best Vocalist (Male)
Pat Liston
www.patliston.com

For Pat Liston, next year will mark a quarter-century after the founding of Mama's Pride, St. Louis' answer to Little Feat, though only their die-hard fans know that. The band's two classic albums have been locked in Atlantic vaults for years and still haven't seen proper reissue. Liston's band may yet do another reunion show, but if you want to hear one of the finest country soul singers in the Midwest, you'll have to catch one of his solo gigs (or his acoustic trio, which teams him with Scott Nienhaus and Karen Crawford). Liston has an Irish soul: He wails and moans with Celtic blues, carries an ageless folk melody with his gently rasping tenor (which sometimes recalls Stephen Stills, sometimes Wilson Pickett) and phrases with unrestrained, even torrential emotion.

...... Riverfront Times 2007

A LIFE IN REWIND AND A NEW CD

My music, and my passion for it, grew by leaps and bounds. I hadn't done much on my new CD up until this point and now I was working away. Dawn had inspired several songs, as I knew she would. I realized that all my love songs up until now had been largely fantasized. Even if they were *about* someone, I had to romanticize the song in order to make them seem real.

Now, my love songs were real — word for word. I had found my soulmate and life had changed. Although it was about to change in a way I'd have never imagined in my wildest dreams.

Dawn was having some issues with her thyroid and feeling sick to her stomach. She was also putting on weight that didn't make sense to her. These were all things that the doctor told her might happen while on the thyroid medication.

It was April of 2007. Dawn had had a doctor's appointment scheduled for some minor outpatient surgery. Then, the day before her surgery, the doctor called.

Dawn looked rattled after getting off the phone and said to me, "They canceled my surgery."

I panicked, thinking something was wrong. "Why did they cancel?"

The next sentence that came out of her mouth was absolutely, categorically, the last thing I'd ever have imagined her saying...

"Because one of us is pregnant!"

I sat there stunned.

In a moment of complete bewilderment all I could think to say was, "Which one?"

She looked me square in the eye and said, "Keep that sense of humor, you're gonna need it."

Pregnant. Pregnant? I was 58 years old.

She made an appointment for an ultrasound. To our absolute shock she was not only pregnant, she was 17 weeks pregnant! She had been going to doctors during this time taking blood tests, urine tests, you name it, and no one had noticed this?

The nurse asked if this was our first child.

Dawn said, "No, I have two grown children." The nurse, who said she had been doing this for 14 years, bust out laughing. She turned to me, as if to ask the same question.

I quickly said, "You don't even wanna know."

The nurse said, "You're far enough along that I can tell you the gender, unless you don't want to know."

I piped up and said, "No. Tell us. God knows we don't need anymore surprises!"

"It's a boy."

We tried not telling anyone right away. We told Scott and Karen, but swore them to silence for the time being. The following week we played Cleo's. Dawn always drank beer if she drank. Jen, the bartender who'd given me that shot of tequila, set a beer on the bar for Dawn.

Dawn, awkwardly, said, "Umm, I think I'll have a glass of red wine."

Jen was young, but she was a woman. She went over to Karen and said, "Is Dawn pregnant?"

Karen stammered... but that was enough. By the end of the night everyone in the place knew.

Dawn continued to bartend, but her boss told her he wanted her to *manage*. This basically meant she lost all her tips — which for her was a sizable amount. He said he did it so she could sit, being pregnant and all. She knew better. She stuck it out though.

It was Labor Day, September 3rd, 2007.

We were going to her mom's house for a little family gathering. Dawn said, "Maybe I should take some extra clothes just in case." I thought, *in case of what... the baby isn't due until October.* (But being older and wiser than I once was, I only thought it.)

We had not been at her mom's any amount of time when Dawn was feeling things that gave her pause. Her mom, who had formerly been a nurse, insisted that we go to the hospital.

As soon as we got there and they checked on her situation, they said, "We're checking you into a room." The fact that it was Labor Day seemed ironic.

She had a very hard time with the delivery. Any man that reads this and has been in that situation knows how helpless you feel. Some women get mean or angry during labor. Dawn didn't. She was sweet and held my hand through most of it. Well, she almost squeezed the blood out of it, but I understood.

On Wednesday, September 5th, 2007, he arrived. We had decided on Liam Thomas for his name. As Dawn was holding him, I felt the need to ask again, "What will his name be?"

She looked at me for a while then asked, "Can we call him Thomas Liam?"

I said, "Absolutely."

Tom was Dawn's twin brother's name. He had lost his life in an automobile accident at 26 years old. I was honored to call our son Thomas. It was like her brother had delivered him to us. He was very tiny, being a bit early, but perfectly formed.

Yes, life was changing at a rapid pace. It made me recall having prayed — less than two years prior — for a freedom from apathy. Well, obviously God heard me and had a wonderful sense of humor!

The following November, I asked Dawn to marry me. I know, it's supposed to go the other way around, but life gets busy! I figured my chances were good, I was already moved in and we had a child.

We were in the Ozarks staying at a friend's house on the lake. I took her out to a restaurant called Andre's. It was a Monday during the off season and the place was practically empty. So it was kind of cool. Thomas was in a pumpkin seat right next to me when I asked... for moral support and intimidation.

She accepted.

2007 went out with a bang! On December 8th Mama's Pride did our 8th show at the Pageant, and a sell-out to boot. It had settled into an annual Christmas type event. Then on New Years Eve, Dawn and I went to Tan-Tar-A in the Ozarks. I was playing with Butch Wax & The Hollywoods again, bringing in the new year!

I spent the better part of 2008 trying to get the new CD done. With a new baby, things went slowly on that front. Dawn helped me immensely on the artwork and calling to get the best pressing prices, etc. I didn't have a studio anymore, but I had my Pro Tools set up at Sean's (Dawn's brother) house. I also used Jupiter Studio in St. Louis for a few things. I already had some tracks laid from my old studio in O'Fallon, too.

Jim Gaines mixed it for me at Bessie Blue Studios in Stantonville, Tennessee. Dawn, Thomas, myself, and my cousin Adrian went down there together. Adrian came to help some with Thomas.

It was a typical *Pat Liston rush job.* Poor Jim Gaines had to mix 12 songs in four days. After the mix, we all drove to Mississippi. We were right on the border and my Mom's home town of Rienzi, Mississippi, was less than 40 miles away. We managed to find my favorite Mississippi cousin, Peggy (Baker) Connor. It was a very nostalgic trip. I had not been there since I was about 12.

We only stayed in Rienzi for the day. We left for Memphis the next day to get the mixed songs mastered by Brad Blackwood at Euphonics Masters. We took the opportunity to visit Graceland while we were there, too. We drove back to St. Louis and had Brad mail the masters back to us.

When we got back to St. Louis we finished up the artwork and 20-page booklet. The photography, artwork and graphics were done by Chuck Sheets, Doug Jones, Keith Hempen, Barb Moyer, Ruth Tate, and my wife, Dawn.

For the musical portion I used: Dickie Steltenpohl (bass), Scott Nienhaus (guitars, mandolin, and background vocals), Karen Crawford (background vocals), Don Drewett (drums), Terry Jones Rogers (background vocals), Bob Briedenbach (dobro), Bill Murphy (accordion), Keith Hempen (percussion), Steve Radick (percussion), Jim Stevens (alto saxophone), John Mondin (guitar), Tim Britton (uilleann pipes), John Logan (acoustic guitar), Carolyn Bartley (percussive hard shoe Irish dance), and Tommy Martin (uilleann pipes).

The booklet had pictures and lyrics as I always do. I also wrote an evaluation of how I saw part of my life leading up to this moment. This is it:

> *To My friends, family, and fans,*
>
> *Never think that one random act in life cannot change your life and the lives of others profoundly.*
>
> *I wrote a song that was on my last solo CD called "Look Away" that, in my mind, needed a 12 string Rickenbacker guitar. I called Scott Nienhaus in Nashville, who was from St. Louis, because he played a 12 string Rickenbacker guitar. I sent him the song and some other songs from my, then upcoming solo CD, "Blue Mist". He liked it so much*

that he came to St. Louis and played on the CD and then decided to move back here.....

..... because I wrote a song called "Look Away" that needed a 12 string Rickenbacker guitar and Scott played one.

While he was here he met Karen Crawford and they started living together, playing music together..... because I wrote a song called "Look Away" that needed a 12 string Rickenbacker guitar and Scott played one and played it on my CD and moved back to St. Louis.

I went to see them play one night and sat in. A guy named Russ Sanders was there and said we should all play together, that he owned a bar called Cleo's and would hire us on Sundays..... because I wrote a song called "Look Away" that needed a 12 string Rickenbacker guitar and Scott played one and played it on my CD and moved back to St. Louis and met Karen and played music with her and I sat in with them. We got together as a trio and started playing, which included the bar "Cleo's" on Sundays

..... because I wrote a song called "Look Away" that needed a 12 string Rickenbacker guitar and Scott played one and played it on my CD and moved back to St. Louis and met Karen and played music with her and I sat in with them and Russ saw us and wanted to hire us to play at Cleo's on Sundays. A woman named Dawn, who worked six nights a week, came into Cleo's one Sunday because it was her night off and Scott, Karen, and I were playing. Dawn enjoyed the band and came in almost every Sunday after that. I was smitten by her as though I'd known her in another life. She said she felt she'd known me before as well,

this, because I wrote a song called "Look Away" that needed a 12 string Rickenbacker guitar and Scott played one and played it on my CD and moved back to St. Louis and met Karen and played music with her and I sat in with them and Russ saw us and hired us to play at Cleo's on Sundays and Dawn came in because it was her night off. Dawn and I fell in love and eventually knew we needed to be together forever, because we'd felt we, somehow, had been already. As time went on and Dawn and I were together, Dawn got pregnant and we brought Thomas Liam into the world

...... because I wrote a song called "Look Away" that needed a 12 string Rickenbacker guitar and Scott played one and played it on my CD and moved back to St. Louis and met Karen and played music with her and I sat in with them and Russ saw us and hired us to play at Cleo's on Sundays and Dawn came in because it was her night off and we fell in love. In this time we have been blessed with new family and met countless friends that are near and dear to us; people who have stood beside us through thick and thin; people whose lives have, no doubt, been changed as well

..... because I wrote a song called "Look Away" that needed a 12 string Rickenbacker guitar and Scott played one and played it on my CD and moved back to St. Louis and met Karen and played music with her and I sat in with them and Russ saw us and hired us to play at Cleo's on Sundays and Dawn came in because it was her night off and we fell in love and brought Thomas Liam into the world. I've written so many songs since I met Dawn that I had to do this new solo CD. You can sit and give a listen, and, now, better understand these events

.....all because I wrote a song called "Look Away" that needed a 12 string Rickenbacker guitar and Scott played one and played it on my CD and moved back to St. Louis and met Karen and played music with her and I sat in with them and Russ saw us and hired us to play at Cleo's on Sundays and Dawn came in because it was her night off and we fell in love and brought Thomas Liam into the world and have been blessed with new family and met countless friends that are near and dear to us..... people who have stood beside us through thick and thin.... whose lives have, no doubt, been changed as well.

One song, just simple lyrics and melody that, in my mind, required a 12 string Rickenbacker guitar, brought about the greatest change that I have ever had in my life. It changed Dawn, brought Thomas Liam here (he'd been waiting so long), changed Dawn's family, my family, and showed me who my friends were and who my friends were not. It changed Scott, Karen and everyone they know. The ripple-effect will, now and forever, be felt because of a simple song. Remember each day, that what you do affects many, sometimes without your knowledge. God has a plan, and, as He puts it, "My ways are not your ways." .... Amen!! God is truly the only one who successfully multitasks!! Now go *out and do something.... anything. It doesn't have to be a song: The whole world is a melody. Grab a note. Do something and change lives. God calls us His "workmanship." The Greek word for workmanship is "poema," from which we derive the English word "poem." You are a poem.... His poem. Be what you were meant to be and bring about the wonderful changes that you are meant to cause.......*

God bless you,
Pat

That came to me one night at a gig while talking to my friend Dawaine Null. I said it all to him that night while just talking. He said, "Dude, you need to write that down somewhere." So I did.

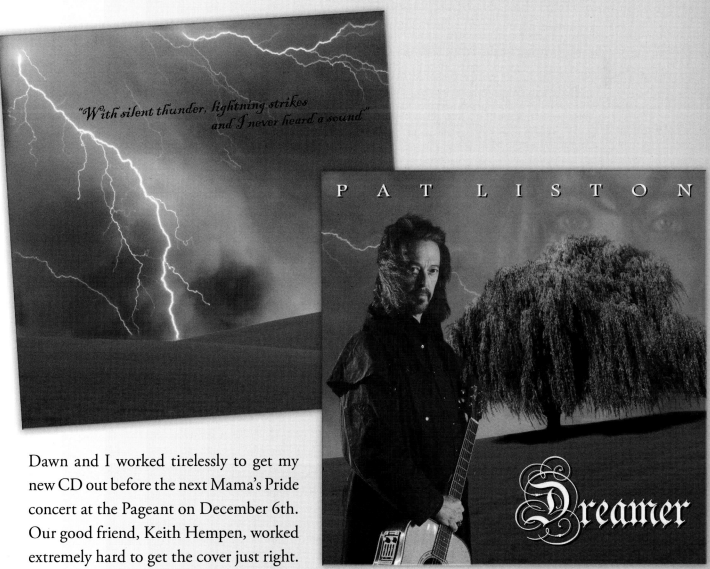

Dawn and I worked tirelessly to get my new CD out before the next Mama's Pride concert at the Pageant on December 6th. Our good friend, Keith Hempen, worked extremely hard to get the cover just right. In usual fashion, my second solo CD — *Dreamer* — arrived the day of the show.

Another blessed event that happened in June of 2008... my daughter Elisha gave birth to my first grandchild, Chase Jayden. Arriving nine months after her brother Thomas!

Also in 2008, Mark Klose called me in August about the K-HITS 96 Rock 'N' CholesteRoll show on October, 4th, at Jefferson Barracks. He was wanting to see if I could do a solo, or stripped, version. Dawn had more than proven herself in booking so I, wisely, handed it off to her. She was never afraid to ask for good money.

We decided to do a small group with my brother, Danny, and myself. We used Scott Nienhaus on guitar, Dickie Steltenpohl on bass, and J.D. Wheeler on percussion. We did a lot of altered Mama's Pride songs, given the lineup. It actually went over very well and gave Danny, Dickie, and I a chance to get creative with some old songs.

The crowd gave a very warm reception considering Max, Kevin, and Paul weren't there. We opened for Kansas and Michael Stanley. Two bands we had worked with back in our heyday.

The first solo CD, *Blue Mist* got two good reviews — one by Jess Marich in *Shake* magazine out of Nashville, and one by John O'Regan in *Irish Music* magazine.

Pat Liston - Blue Mist
Dogtown Records

Pat Liston made this record against all odds. After getting the masters robbed (along with many other belongings) he managed to get back-up files and finish the project. That's destiny. The album is so refreshing that I have to belive in such things. Liston wrote all the tunes. He flavors them with sounds that hearken back to the best of the seminal creative forces of rock, folk and pop. I sometimes think I'm hearing a George Harrison solo track, or a David Crosby guitar thing, or maybe *Badfinger*. There's Clapton slidey-stuff and *Byrds* sounds coming from Scott Nienhaus' guitar. It's all in here and more. Even slight hints of country. You know that always was one of the elements of rock & roll. This music has a lilt to it. It's certainly not wimpy but it isn't a "rock-out" boogie kind of thing either. It's melodic and catchy. Edgy? Yes, but not overly so. Pat and his cohorts make St. Louis their home. If you find yourself in that town, you ought to try to catch them performing. I'd like to.
Jess Marich

THE DEFINITIVE VOICE OF IRISH MUSIC WORLDWIDE

MUSIC

Volume 10, No. 10 July 2005
Price €2.95 £2.50 (Stg)

PAT LISTON
BLUE MIST
DOGTOWN RECORDS PL6509

A native of St. Louis in Missouri, Pat Liston has been involved in playing and writing music for over three decades. Founder of mid 1970's rock/soul band Mama's Pride signed to Atlantic Records with his brother Danny and toured with The Allman Brothers, Charlie Daniels, Lynyrd Skynyrd et all. More recently, he has turned his attention to Irish music complimenting his family heritage, and mixed it with his own styles and idioms. The result is Blue Mist which is a collection of self-penned songs firmly in the domestic US Folk/Rock vein but a hidden Celtic lineage. Almost Like Being in Love resembles John Lennon circa Double Fantasy and I Guess We'll Never Know is a bittersweet love song set in Dublin, Bill Murphey's accordion and Tim Britton's uilleann pipes adding the Celtic flavour. Look Away has the righteous anger of a Dick Gaughan and the political snap of Billy Bragg, while Blue Bandana and Cowboy Clothes sound straight out of Texas campfires and the Mama's Pride classic Blue Mist gets a chilling revisit. Michael Cooney's uilleann pipes herald "Now That I Have) Passed The Torch Along an evocation of the past and future generations. The work of a seldom-heralded talent, Blue Mist offers a master class of Irish American folk-rock.

John O-Regan

Now the new CD, *Dreamer,* was also getting attention — once again by Chris James.

With 11 songs on my first CD, 12 songs on the new one, and a few random Mama's Pride songs, I was starting to feel cramped in a vocal trio.

Scott and Karen had excellent voices, so you could hardly ask them to cut back so I could sing more. I was approached by a woman named Carolyn Haupt at a Butchwax gig

Pat Liston - Dreamer
Self Produced

Pat Liston is probably best remembered as the writer and lead vocalist from *Mama's Pride*, a St. Louis band that had two successful albums in the 1970's, "Mama's Pride" and "Uptown & Lowdown". "Dreamer" is Pat's second solo CD, following "Blue Mist" from 2003. Acoustic guitars and fantastic harmonies, coupled with strong, flavorsome songs are the ingredients. This new album advances the direction he displayed so well on that first outing. The music is immensely accomplished and tuneful. Liston's stylistic approach harkens memories of Crosby, Stills & Nash, *Poco, Eagles* (when they focused on acoustics and harmonies) and groups that ilk. Liston wrote all the songs, played guitars and received brilliant assistance from a cross-section of St. Louis' best musicians, most notably the superb guitar work of Scott Nienhaus. The vocal harmonies on this record are infectious and impressive. All through the CD, Karen Crawford joins Pat and Scott for a three-part vocal stack that stands up with the best. Pat sings "seein' each other revives a simpler time in our lives." This music is like that. A better era is recalled, a time when people sang and played music that was not synthesized product. That concept should never go away. This group of cohorts can certainly do the same thing in live performance that you hear on the record - without tape loops, sequences and dance steps. This here's real music from seasoned veterans. Pat performs often in the St. Louis area, doing solo acoustic and occasional band performances.
Chris James

who wanted to hire just me for a birthday party. I had the particular night off and she offered very good money. I accepted and did my first solo gig since the McNulty's Irish Pub days.

Because of how well the solo gig went, Dawn and I started talking about the possibility of me going solo permanently. Terry Jones Rogers was complaining about needing to work more and I needed more work as well. I didn't blame Terry, after all, it was I who created this dilemma by only wanting to work every other week in the first place. I started playing more with Butch Wax & The Hollywoods. I was actually, at this point in time, working more with Butch Wax than I was with Scott and Karen. I had too many irons in the fire and decided, after almost five years, my time with Scott & Karen had come to an end.

I did my last gig with Scott and Karen on Sunday, December 28th, 2008, at Chez Marilyn in Alton, Illinois. It was a good run and we did sound awfully good together. And the chain of events that came about because of my collaboration with them, changed my life forever. God Bless you both.

I started playing at my brother Danny's restaurant — Seamus McDaniels in O'Fallon, Missouri — every once in a while. It was around this time that Dawn said she wanted to be my booking agent. It seemed perfect, except for one thing... she'd never done it before. But in addition to being a bartender, Dawn was also in real estate for a while. I thought, *what's the difference... selling houses, selling me.*

She talked about the price she was going to charge. I stopped her right there. I reminded her that I'd been in this business a long time and places are not gonna pay that for a soloist. She argued, "...but you're not just a soloist, you're from Mama's Pride — the lead guy." I told her I understood her logic and appreciated that she thought I was worth that money, but I'd been around longer and knew better.

She said, "Let me make some phone calls."

I agreed to that. She came back to me later in the day and said, "You were right, I didn't get that money."

As I was getting ready to put my arm around her and consolingly say, *It's okay, honey, I've been in this business for years...* she piped up and said, "I got more!"

I didn't really know what to say. How can you feel bad about being wrong when you're making more money and your wife has just proven that people do think you're worth it?

I kissed her and said, "Okay, Partner. Get to work." And that's exactly what she did.

Dawn booked nine gigs that January, one of which was Cleo's. I mean, we *had* to do Cleo's and as Karen always said, "Ya' gotta love it, it's Cleo's!"

I had asked Dawn to marry me, that was the easy part. Now, the problem was, when? We got three marriage licenses before we finally managed to get it done. We decided we'd have a small wedding, then later do a big one. We contacted our friend and pastor, Daren Carstens, at Enjoy Church in Alton, Illinois, and decided to get married on Thursday, April 30th, 2009.

In attendance was Dawn's mom, Barb, and her brother, Sean; John and Rhonda Gagliardo; Jerry and Brittany Harvey; Pastor Daren; Dawn, myself... and Thomas. It was lovely... and the big wedding... well, we never quite got around to it.

Dawn started booking me 12 to 15 times a month. I was a working machine. I did almost 200 dates in 2009. There were about 10 Butch Wax & The Hollywoods dates mixed in. Mama's Pride did our 10th concert at the Pageant on December 5th. Dawn also booked Mama's Pride at Wildwood Springs Lodge in Steelville, Missouri. It was attended by a large number of my *Paddy Pack* people, all wearing their shirts.

Dawn was always coming up with new ideas. We had a group of folks that used to attend my gigs regularly that coined themselves *the Paddy Pack*. Dawn put on a few shows at our house that she called *garden parties*. It usually consisted of mostly Paddy Pack people. These were ticketed, too. She also came up with an idea to book a one-time event with Max Baker, Danny, and myself, calling it, cleverly, MP3.

Also, in 2009, Mike Steinberg and Thomas Crone approached Danny and I for a documentary they were wanting to produce. It was going to be a two-fold documentary about Mama's Pride and Pavlov's Dog. They did a very good job and had a release at the Tivoli Theater in St. Louis on Friday, November 20th.

I closed out 2009 with a New Year's Eve date with Butch Wax & The Hollywoods at Tan-Tar-A Resort at the Lake of the Ozarks. Dawn and I always loved this date because I only sang and didn't have to set up any equipment. It was almost like a paid date night.

In 2010 Dawn started booking some private parties, which paid more and had a captive audience that usually wanted to hear all my music. She continued to be the *Booking Banshee* as I called her. She booked Scott Nienhaus and I as a duo on several occasions as a ticketed event and they were always a success. At the end of April she booked Mama's Pride once again for two nights at Wildwood Springs Lodge. The whole Wildwood Springs experience was something Dawn and I loved. This particular show was our son Thomas' first real band experience. He keyed in on *uncle* Kevin and his drums.

On September 11th, 2010, Dogtown had its first Dogtown Street Musicians Festival. The closing ceremony was to honor a notable Dogtown musician. They chose for their first one to honor my mom.

Johnny Corbett, a childhood friend of mine, was in charge. His mom, Louise Corbett, was very good friends with my mom and Johnny decided on my mom as the first recipient. This honor touched both myself and my two brothers deeply.

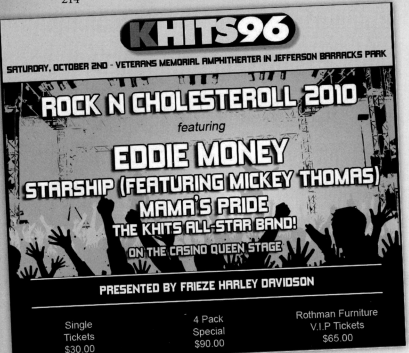

On October 2nd, 2010, Mama's Pride was back at K-HITS 96 Rock 'N' CholesteRoll show. This time it was the full band opening for Eddie Money and Starship with Mickey Thomas. The concert went over great. Mama's Pride seemed to be getting more attention these days.

Dawn booked me twice that month playing solo at Wildwood Springs Lodge. The first one was opening on October 15th and 16th for Marshall Tucker. The only original member was Doug Gray, but it was really nice to see him again.

Me, Richie Furay, and Michael Martin Murphey

RICHIE, MICHAEL, & ME, ...DANNY, ...AND OTHERS

The second one she booked was really special. Leon Russell was supposed to play on October 30th and I was going to open for him. Leon had to cancel because of a big show with Elton John in Europe. I was really disappointed. Bob Bell, the owner of Wildwood Springs, was scuffling to get something to fill that date in. Bob and Dawn talked a lot about it. Dawn wanted to stay in the loop because whatever it was, she wanted me involved.

Bob decided he wanted it to be a songwriters night — three songwriters onstage together — me being one of them. Well, I love this kind of thing, but I loved it even more when we were told that the other two people were going to be Michael Martin Murphey and Richie Furay of Buffalo Springfield and Poco fame.

I had never met or worked with either of them. I know they had to be wondering who I was and where I fit in. The night was nothing short of magical. Both Richie and Michael are Christians and we prayed together before we went onstage, something I had not done in quite some time. Well, that set the tone for the evening. It was far and away one of the best shows I was ever involved in.

I continued to play a lot by myself. I was actually starting to prefer it. On May 7th, 2011, Danny and I did a show together at Wildwood Springs Lodge — just the two of us. We alternated songs like I had done with Richie Furay and Michael Martin Murphey. It was a very cool show. We did old and new songs. Danny even did his original version of "Can I Call You a Cab" which was much more bluesy.

It was a very laid back performance. Danny even brought up the Lonesome Hill Gang — the Jacobson family — an *in-house* bluegrass band that also works at Wildwood Springs Lodge. It was another magical moment at Wildwood.

Dawn booked me continuously, always trying new things. On August 20th of that year she had an idea to do a Liston Family reunion concert at the Sheldon Concert Hall. My cousin, Kari Liston, along with Jeremy Segel-Moss, would open the show, then my brother Danny's group would play and then I would have a group to close it out. The concept was good, and Danny and Kari did great, but we lost money and my portion of the show was sorely lacking. It was not one of my more memorable events. We went to Chicago the following day to play at a big festival and the promoter stiffed us. It was a very rough weekend... but, it happens.

Dawn booked Mama's Pride again for an outdoor show that July that was called Cruzin '66 Cave Jam. It was held in Pacific, Missouri. It was over 100°F, but the show went over very well and, as always, Dawn got the band very good money.

I played about 150 gigs in 2011, some private, some concerts. In December, as always, Mama's Pride played the Pageant. It was our 12th concert there... and we closed out the year at Tan-Tar-A with Butch Wax & The Hollywoods again.

❧

2012 was a very busy year as well — almost 180 gigs!

J.D. Blackfoot called me in March and wanted to know if I could join my brother, Danny, on his new CD to do some background vocals.

We went to a church building in St. Louis city because of the acoustics. After we did the vocals, J.D. asked if I would like to do a little slide guitar work on the CD. I agreed and played on three songs. It was a fun project.

The CD was called *The Legend of Texas Red*.

In May I went in to MusicMasters Studio for Scott Nienhaus and Terry Jones Rogers to do some background vocals on their new CD. There was a large group singing background.

We had gone through it a few times and finally Greg Trampe, the engineer, said, "One of the females is singing an odd high note."

He went through each person to see which one was the culprit. It seemed all their parts were correct.

He said, "It seems like an odd overtone or something." That's when it hit me...*overtone?*

I said, "Umm, Greg, it may be me."

He said, "No you're singing a lower note, this is a higher note."

I said, "I know... listen."

I sang my note and Greg said, "Oh, my God, you have two notes coming out."

I'd forgotten that my voice does that sometimes. Everyone had a good laugh and I laid out on that one note.

On June 14th I opened solo for Poco at Mile 277. It was a packed house and a grand time. I worked solo at Mile 277 the night before and Rusty and Mary Young came in. The four of us sat around afterwards talking. I finally spoke with someone who has more stories than me.

On July 4th, Mama's Pride returned to Wildwood Springs Lodge. Bob Bell and Dawn thought we could try a summer gig there. It went quite well and was another great Wildwood experience.

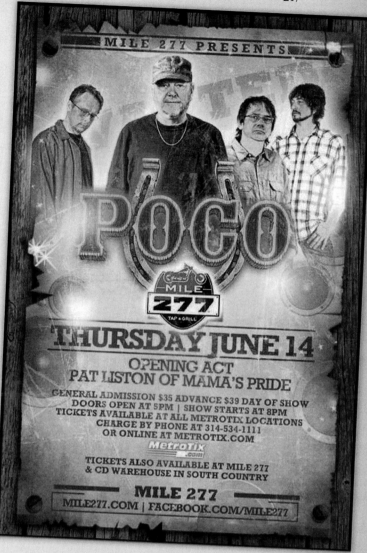

Me and Rusty Young (of Poco)

KSHE Rock Hall of Fame induction plaques. Left to right: Max Baker, Guy Favazza, Danny Liston, Kevin Sanders, Me, and Paul Willett.

40 YEARS, HALL OF FAME, AND #1

In the fall of 2012 KSHE radio contacted Danny and told him that they had decided to induct Mama's Pride in to the KSHE Rock Hall of Fame. We were to be the 12th group and the first St. Louis band they had inducted. It was quite an honor and very touching to be recognized in this manner by KSHE.

Danny contacted me and we all decided that the upcoming Pageant concert on Saturday, December 1st, would be the best place to do the induction. Danny and I did a taped interview with long-time friend and radio personality, Guy Favazza. This interview would be used on the KSHE Real Rock Museum website and would be played on the night of the concert during our break.

We did a *live* group interview on KSHE radio the day before the show. During this interview Rick Balis, program director at KSHE, presented the six of us with plaques commemorating the induction. They also played the video for us after the interview. It was very moving — we all were teary-eyed. Rick Balis told me, personally, that we were the only consideration that year and that the vote was unanimous.

In addition to this, KSHE had compiled all their song requests through the years and did a countdown of the top 95 song requests of all time. My composition, "Blue Mist" won the #1 slot.

Between the two marked achievements, it was almost more than I could handle. I had written that song in 1971 and it was 2012 — 41 years later it was being honored as KSHE's all-time most requested song.

The night of the Pageant was great. It, of course, was sold out. The fans knew the induction was forthcoming at the show. There were KSHE on-air personalities there (past and present) to do the induction onstage. Mark Klose and John Ulett did the presentation along with Ted Habeck and Guy Favazza. It was humbling to be honored in this way and especially by four close friends — three of whom dated back to our beginnings.

It was a wonderful, but strange, night for me. I've always been of the mind that when you start reflecting on the past you start drawing a close on the future. I've always felt that if all I have is one day left on this earth, I still have a future and another shot at something.

So, although this was a very sweet night, it made me somewhat uncomfortable. Too often people my age and younger spend an inordinate amount of time reminiscing instead of looking forward.

I felt so strongly about it that night, that when I came out by myself on the second set to do the song "Maybe" — as I usually do — I changed my mind.

I began talking to people about music and what I felt it's all really about. I told the audience that I felt there were four parts to a song... 1. writing it, 2. recording it, 3. performing it... and the fourth part was the part I couldn't do, only they could do it — 4. *receiving it*.

I asked them to remember the first time they heard "Blue Mist." They didn't reflect... it didn't remind them of any other time, but that very moment. They *received* it, absorbed it and experienced a whole new melody... heard a brand new story they had never heard before.

"This," I told them, "is what music is about."

I don't know how many actually heard what I said, or assimilated it if they did. I told them I was going to do a brand new song for them to *receive*. I played a song I had written for my little boy, Thomas, called "If I Had My Way."

There was polite applause, but most just didn't seem to get what I was trying to explain. Maybe it was too large of an environment to do such an intimate song? Large facilities are rarely conducive to anything intimate.

All in all it was a good night. Mama's Pride played all the songs of the past that people came to hear. The fans were absolutely electric! But once it was over, I was glad to get back to my solo gig. I love writing and performing and interacting with the audience. My solo gigs are smaller and allow me a better platform to accomplish that.

WILD AT HEART, TOMMY SHAW, AND THREE DOG NIGHT

Now I was ready for 2013. I'm always ready for the next experience.

I had been pondering my next CD. My wife, Dawn, had been trying to get me to do the next one by myself. We had considered a *live* CD, but there were always a lot of issues with this type of live CD. Audience noise was a major factor because I had a few ballads for the CD. All you need is one outsider that doesn't care that you're recording and they could ruin an entire night of recording.

The concept of doing an entire CD of just me, no overdubs, no vocal harmonies — just me — made me uncomfortable. My wife was convinced this was a good idea. I even spoke to my brother, Danny, and he was in total agreement with Dawn — that it was a great concept for my style of music. Okay... if my wife is telling me to do it and my brother is telling me to do it... then, maybe I should.

I spoke with Dawn and decided that if I was going to do this, I was going to do it in a studio in front of a live audience. At least, that way, I had quality sound and the audience was, basically, hand-picked. We decided we'd do it three nights in a row with three different groups of people.

The only studio that I was familiar with that was big enough to hold 25 to 30 people seated was MusicMasters in St. Louis. I had known the owner, Greg Trampe, for a long time. He was excited to do the concept. We sold tickets for the three nights — February 21st, 22nd, and 23rd. We sold out all three nights very quickly.

But there are always curves.

My throat started hurting a few days before the first night. Then a snow storm hit on the 21st, so we had to cancel that night. The studio was already booked on the 24th so we couldn't push it back. We simply decided to do just two nights. People were disappointed that were supposed to attend on the 21st, but there was nothing we could do. My throat miraculously healed for the two nights of recording.

I recorded the same 20 songs each night so that I would have two different versions to choose from. I recorded straight through, no second takes and no overdubs. I decide to use 10 songs for the new CD — *Wild At Heart*.

The following week I played with J.D. Blackfoot at the Sheldon Concert Hall. I performed on the songs that I did on his CD. It was fun and well attended.

1. Let It Go
2. Maybe
3. Steel Blues
4. Last Farewell
5. If I had My Way
6. Never Say Never
7. Man In The Middle
8. If You Have Not Love
9. Someone To Talk To
10. Hero

All Songs Written By Pat Liston

Produced by Pat Liston
Engineered & Mixed by Greg Trampe
Recorded at Music Masters, St. Louis, MO
Mastered by Kevin Nix at Ardent Studos, Memphis, TN.
Front cover photo: D. Gausling of PBC Studios, Bethalto, IL.
Traycard photo: Pat O'Malley
Back booklet photo: Dawn Liston
Booklet Photographers: Karen Guercia, Dawn Liston, & Pat O'Malley
Graphic Design: Doug Jones

In early April I got a call from one of Mama's Pride's ex-managers, Charlie Brusco. Charlie now managed the group Styx, among others. He wanted Mama's Pride to play on the Styx show that was due to play St. Louis in May. Naturally, I handed it over to Dawn. She contacted Live Nation, the promoters of the show, and worked out a deal.

On May 18th Mama's Pride opened for Ted Nugent, REO Speedwagon, and Styx at the Verizon Wireless Amphitheater in St. Louis. Mama's Pride had not done a multi-act show in many many years. It was wonderful seeing Charlie Brusco again, but it was not one of our best performances.

Dawn and I met Styx afterwards. We were talking in their dressing room with Charlie Brusco. Styx was the highlight of our night. They were, unlike the other acts that day, so nice and engaging.

Dawn mentioned to me, as we were walking out of the dressing room, she really wished we'd gotten a picture. I grabbed her hand and turned around and went back in and asked Tommy Shaw if he'd mind taking a picture with us. He handed Dawn's camera to his daughter, Hannah, and had her take the picture. I have to say, I have met some really nice people in my years, but Tommy Shaw was one of the very nicest of them all.

Tommy came up to me and spoke earlier, commenting on how much he liked our band. The other two acts wouldn't even make eye contact backstage. This concert reminded me of all the things I hate about this business — all the *rock star hoopla*. I don't miss that part.

The following October, Dawn booked me opening two nights for Three Dog Night at Wildwood Springs Lodge. I really enjoyed this show because I have always liked their music. I knew there would be a few folks there who had seen me before so I wanted to have a new song for them. I wrote a song that I'd been wanting to write for a while, and the Verizon Amphitheater experience had made it even easier to write. The song was called "My Good Old Days Are Now."

I always have people coming up and saying, *Remember the good old days?* Those days were not always that good. The music business people in my past almost ruined music for me. Those days made me bitter toward music for many years. The song was written from the heart of my life. I do feel my good days are now for many reasons. My perspective is different — what I once overlooked in my youth I see more clearly.

A funny side note: Dawn knows that my last song of the night is always "Blue Mist." As I was performing, I was trying to figure out where to place the new song. I decided, while onstage, that I should close with the new one after "Blue Mist."

After "Blue Mist" Dawn came onstage and started breaking down, not realizing I was going to do another song. The place was packed (sold out). I looked at her and said, "I'm going to do another song."

She gave a bewildered and embarrassed look and said, "Well, ya' coulda told me!" The crowd laughed and I did the last song.

I talked with Danny Hutton and Cory Wells after the show. They were very nice. I had Thomas with me and he had just turned six. I introduced Thomas to Danny Hutton and without my knowledge Thomas said, "I like you guys, you're good."

Danny smiled and said, "Thanks, are we better than your daddy?"

Thomas paused, then, with a very straight face, said, "No."

Danny laughed out loud and said, "Good answer, Thomas!"

I DON'T KNOW WHAT'S NEXT, BUT THERE'S ALWAYS SOMETHING.

My wife, Dawn, and I have five children between us and four grandchildren. She is my absolute soulmate. I am blessed with so many wonderful friends. I play music for my living. I am not rich financially, but I am rich beyond my wildest expectations.

Though I have experienced so many wonderful things in my life, I am still not a *look back* type of guy. I live in the present and look forward to the future. Often I talk to people even younger than me who sound like they are done. I hope to never be *done* until I breathe my last breath. I want to finish this book, do another CD, continue writing and performing, and who knows what else.

This portion of the book is exactly why I hesitated to do a book.

As I've said, reflecting on your life often seems to mean you're gearing down or headed to pasture. I am doing neither — God created us to be creative, and to continue on the path. How sad it would be to stand before God in the next life and hear Him say, "Pat, I had more for you to do and experience... why'd you stop?"

I don't know what He has in store... but, from experience, I know, He's always had something. Mom raised my two brothers and I that way and it's always played out in my life.

I wrote a song for my mom called "Mama's Pride & Joy." I've only sung it out once. The bridge is, basically, what I remember Mom telling Danny and I growing up:

> Can you hear, the people in the dark,
> As they sing along with you?
> They'll see God's flame,
> If you just light the spark,
> By telling them what God has given you.

He has given me much... and continues to bless me with riches greater than gold or fame.

As a child I remember seeing the *Wizard of Oz*. There was a scene where Dorothy came to a crossroad going down the Yellow Brick Road toward the Emerald City. As she heads towards *the prize* — the *brass ring* — I used to think, "I wonder where that other road goes?"

I was always drawn to the road less traveled... I still am.

The following Artist History, Soundtrack, and Discography lists were meticulously researched and compiled by my good friend and classic rock savant, John Sebben.

PAT LISTON ARTIST HISTORY

1964 – THE IMPACTS
Pat Liston – *guitar (later vocals)*
Larry Welsh – *drums*
Ronnie "Maynard" Schwarz – *vocals*
Tom Zuzenak – *alto sax*
Bill Booth – *guitar*
unknown – *tenor sax*

(INTERIM)
Pat Liston – *guitar, vocals*
Larry Welsh – *drums*
John Colletta – *guitar*
Mike Roggers – *bass*

1965 – THE SKEPTORS (MARK I)
Pat Liston – *rhythm guitar, vocals*
Larry Welsh – *drums*
Mike Roggers – *bass*
Joe Pousosa – *lead guitar*
Tom Stallone – *trumpet*
Paul Kerner – *sax*

1966 – THE SKEPTORS (MARK II)
Pat Liston – *guitar, vocals*
Larry Welsh – *drums*
Mike Roggers – *bass*
Bill Noltkamper – *keyboards*
Tom Stallone – *trumpet*
Vince Sala – *sax*
Joe Leppart – *trombone*
Terry Sparks – *occasional front singer*
Mike Diehl – *Search '66 front singer*

1967 – THE MELLA FELLAS
Pat Liston – *guitar, vocals*
Larry Welsh – *drums*
Michelle Cardillo – *lead vocals*
Bill Noltkamper – *keyboards*
Gary Bourgeois – *bass, backing vocals*
Tom Stallone – *trumpet*
Vince Sala – *sax*
Joe Leppart – *trombone*
Tim Evans – *baritone sax*

1968 – SOULFUL ILLUSIONS

Morris Vaughn – *vocals*

Henry Miller – *vocals*

William Staples – *vocals*

Benjamin Mitchell – *vocals*

Pat Liston – *guitar*

Danny Liston – *drums*

Don L. Wade – *drums*

Rudy Coleman – *bass*

1970 – BOBBY & THE INNKEEPERS

Bobby Shorter – *keyboards, vocals*

Dave Cordova – *sax*

George Subia – *drums*

Jimmy Loya – *trumpet*

Pat Liston – *guitar*

Laine – *bass*

1970 – CHUCK FREEMAN & THE DRIVERS (ONE GIG)

Chuck Freeman – *vocals*

Pat Liston – *guitar*

Danny Eisenstein – *bass*

Don Miller – *drums*

Gil Avila – *trumpet, keyboards*

Roy Avila – *sax*

1970-71 FRENDS & BROTHERS

Gil Avila – *trumpet, keyboards, congas, vocals*

Roy Avila – *saxophones, flute, keyboards, congas, vocals*

Al Romero – *bass, vocals*

Manny Rich – *drums, valve trombone, vocals*

Pat Liston – *guitar, vocals*

1972 – CLEAN DIRT (SIDE GIG)

Jay Marino – *guitar*

Pat Liston – *guitar*

Lanny Bowles – *drums*

Denny Braun – *sax*

Brian Clarke – *bass*

1972-73 MAMA'S PRIDE (MARK I)

Pat Liston – *guitar, vocals*

Danny Liston – *guitar, vocals*

Max Baker – *guitar, vocals*

Mike Gordon – *drums, vocals*

Gary Bouregois – *bass, vocals*

1973 MAMA'S PRIDE (MARK II)

Pat Liston – *guitar, vocals*

Danny Liston – *guitar, vocals*

Max Baker – *guitar, vocals*

Mike Gordon – *drums, vocals*

Gary Bouregois – *bass, vocals*

Kevin Sanders – *drums, vocals*

1973 MAMA'S PRIDE (MARK III)

Pat Liston – *guitar, vocals*

Danny Liston – *guitar, vocals*

Max Baker – *guitar, vocals*

Mike Gordon – *drums, vocals*

Gary Bouregois – *bass, vocals*

Kevin Sanders – *drums, vocals*

Frank Gagliano – *keyboards*

1973-74 MAMA'S PRIDE (MARK IV)

Pat Liston – *guitar, vocals*

Danny Liston – *guitar, vocals*

Max Baker – *guitar, vocals*

Gary Bouregois – *bass, vocals*

Kevin Sanders – *drums, vocals*

Frank Gagliano – *keyboards, vocals*

1974-76 MAMA'S PRIDE (MARK V)

Pat Liston – *guitar, vocals*
Danny Liston – *guitar, vocals*
Max Baker – *guitar, vocals*
Kevin Sanders – *drums, vocals*
Frank Gagliano – *keyboards, vocals*
Joe Turek – *bass, vocals*

1976-77 MAMA'S PRIDE (MARK VI)

Pat Liston – *guitar, vocals*
Danny Liston – *guitar, vocals*
Max Baker – *guitar, vocals*
Kevin Sanders – *drums, vocals*
Joe Turek – *bass, vocals*
Paul Willett – *keyboards, vocals*

1977 MAMA'S PRIDE (MARK VII)

Pat Liston – *guitar, vocals*
Danny Liston – *guitar, vocals*
Max Baker – *guitar, vocals*
Kevin Sanders – *drums, vocals*
Paul Willett – *keyboards, vocals*
Dickie Steltenpohl – *bass, vocals*

1978-80 MAMA'S PRIDE (MARK VIII)

Pat Liston   *guitar, vocals*
Danny Liston – *guitar, vocals*
Max Baker – *guitar, vocals*
Kevin Sanders – *drums, vocals*
Dickie Steltenpohl – *bass, vocals*
Jeff Schmidt – *keyboards, vocals*

1980-82 MAMA'S PRIDE (MARK IX)

Pat Liston – *guitar, vocals*
Danny Liston – *guitar, vocals*
Max Baker – *guitar, vocals*
Kevin Sanders – *drums, vocals*
Dickie Steltenpohl – *bass, vocals*
Jim Vogts – *keyboards, vocals*

1988 – THE PHLAMING PHLEGMATICS (MARK I)

Pat Liston – *guitar, vocals*
Kevin Sanders – *drums, vocals*
Vince Corkery – *bass*
Rob Bernstein – *keyboards*
Dave Black – *guitar*
Thayne Bradford – *backing vocals*
Fred Lang – *backing vocals*
Wayne Givens – *backing vocals*
Gerald DeClue – *alto sax*
Marla Feeney – *baritone sax*
Dan Smith – *trumpet*
Cary Sheley – *trombone*
Mike Karpowicz – *tenor sax*

1989 – THE PLAMING PHLEGMATICS (MARK II)

Pat Liston – *guitar, vocals*
Gerald DeClue – *alto sax*
Marla Feeney – *baritone sax*
Dan Smith – *trumpet*
Cary Sheley – *trombone*
Mike Karpowicz – *tenor sax*
rhythm section: Street Corner
    Billy Barnctt – *guitar, background vocals*
    John Coatney – *drums, background vocals*
    Bill Montogmery – *bass, background vocals*
    Jeff "Doc" Taylor – *keyboards, background vocals*

1991-92 BUTCH WAX & THE HOLLYWOODS

Gene Ackman – *keyboards*

Pat Liston – *guitar, vocals*

Bob Hammett – *guitar*

Mike Tate – *bass*

Mark Kersten – *drummer*

Tom O'Brian – *tenor sax*

Kevin Rauscher – *trumpet*

Carol Rowley – *vocals*

Brenda King – *vocals*

1992 – MAMA'S PRIDE (MARK X)

Pat Liston – *guitar, vocals*

Danny Liston – *guitar, vocals*

Max Baker – *guitar, vocals*

Kevin Sanders – *drums, vocals*

Dickie Steltenpohl – *bass, vocals*

Tom Denman – *keyboards, vocals*

Paul Willett – *keyboards, vocals*

The Dogtown Horns:

Ray McAnallen – *trombone*

Kevin Rauscher – *trumpet*

Richard Zempel – *saxophone*

1997-2000 – THE DOGTOWNERS

Brenda King – *accordion, vocals*

Mike Barada – *guitar, vocals*

Pat Liston – *guitar, vocals*

1999 – VISIBLE FAITH

Ken Hensley – *vocals, keyboards, guitar*

Danny Liston – *vocals, guitar*

Pat Liston – *vocals, guitar*

Jerry Hamm – *guitar*

Hunter Spruenger – *bass*

Preston Vadin – *drums*

2003 – THE PAT LISTON BAND

Pat Liston – *guitar, vocals*

Scott Nienhaus – *guitar*

Bill Murphy – *keyboards, accordion*

Dickie Steltenpohl – *bass*

Don Drewett – *drums*

2004-2008 – LISTON, NIENHAUS & CRAWFORD

Pat Liston – *guitar, vocals*

Scott Nienhaus – *guitar, vocals*

Karen Crawford – *vocals*

2009 – MP3 (ONE-TIME EVENT)

Pat Liston – *guitar, vocals*

Danny Liston – *guitar, vocals*

Max Baker – *guitar, vocals*

SOUNDTRACK

10 – Hound Dog (Presley, Elvis – 1953)

10 – Don't Be Cruel (Presley, Elvis – 1956)

10 – Love Me Tender (Presley, Elvis – 1956)

10 – My Baby Left Me (Presley, Elvis – 1959)

11 – Drifting & Dreaming, Sweet Paradise (Lewis, Ted – 1925)

11, 179 – Let the Rest of the World Go By (Haymes, Dick – 1919)

12 – Silver Strings (unknown)

12 – Hit the Trail and Ride (unknown)

17 – Wild Weekend (Rockin' Rebels, The – 1963)

17 – Nadine (Berry, Chuck – 1964)

19, 21 – La Bamba (Valens, Ritchie – 1958)

19 – Perfidia (as performed by the Ventures – 1960)

19 – The Cheater (Kuban, Bob & The In-Men – 1966)

22, 23 – I Got You (I Feel Good) (Brown, James – 1965)

23 – Prancin' (Turner, Ike & Tina – 1962)

23 – Money (That's What I Want) (as performed by The Kingsman – 1964)

23 – Shake a Tail Feather (The Five Du-Tones – 1963)

23 – Louie Louie (as performed by The Kingsmen – 1963)

23 – You Can't Judge a Book by the Cover (Bo Diddley – 1962)

23 – Sleep Walk (Santo & Johnny – 1959)

23 – Hang On Sloopy (The McCoys – 1964)

23 – High-Heel Sneakers (Tucker, Tommy – 1964)

23 – Do You Love Me (The Contours – 1962)

23 – Fever (Little Willie John – 1956)

23 – Hold It (Doggett, Bill – 1958)

DISCOGRAPHY

ALL SONGS WRITTEN BY PAT LISTON UNLESS NOTED

1. "HELP ME" B/W "JUST ONE LOOK" – MORRIS VAUGHN . . . . PG. 29-30
1967
Gatetown Music – NO 2105
produced by S. Byrd
recorded at Archway Sound Studios – St. Louis, MO

Pat Liston on guitar:
    A. Help Me (Morris Vaughn) . . . . .pg. 29-30
    B. Just One Look (Morris Vaughn) . . . . pg. 29

2. *TRUTH OF TRUTHS* – VARIOUS ARTISTS . . . . .PG. 54-57
1971 (2 LP)
Oak Records – OR 1001
produced by Ray Ruff

Pat Liston on vocals:
    B5. David to Bathsheba (Val Stöecklein) . . . . .pg. 54-56
    B7. Prophecies of the Coming Messiah (Alan Henderson) . . . . pg. 54
    D7. Prophecies of the Coming of the End of the World
        (Alan Henderson, Ray Ruff) . . . . pg. 54

3. UNRELEASED PAT LISTON SOLO ALBUM. PG. 57-59

1972

1. Young & Free . . . . pg. 49, 59
2. I'll Be There in the Morning . . . . .pg. 58-59
3. Because of You . . . . pg. 59
4. Kathy . . . . pg. 59-60
5. Mobile Blue (Mickey Newbury) . . . . pg. 59
6. Remember the Good (Mickey Newbury) . . . . pg. 59
7. Empty Chairs (Don McLean) . . . . pg. 59
8. Say It's Not Over (Val Stöecklein) . . . . pg. 59
9. I Wonder Who I'll Be Tomorrow (Val Stöecklein) . . . . pg. 59

4. MAMA'S PRIDE – MAMA'S PRIDE . . . . PG. 92-100

October, 1975

ATCO Records – SD 36-122

produced by Arif Mardin

recorded at Criteria Recording Studios – Miami, FL

A1. In The Morning (Danny Liston, Max Baker) . . . . pg. 73, 90, 100

A2. Who Do You Think You're Foolin'
(Gagliano, Turek, Liston)

A3. Blue Mist . . . . pg. 19, 61, 73, 219, 223

A4. Laurie Ann . . . . pg. 76

A5. Missouri Skyline (Sanders, Baker, D. Liston, P. Liston)

B1. Ole St. Lou (Sanders, Baker, Turek, D. Liston, P. Liston) . .pg. 92, 116, 169

B2. Kind Lovin' Woman (Max Baker, Danny Liston)

B3. Where Would You Be . . . . pg. 100

B4. Young & Free . . . . pg. 49, 59

single: "Blue Mist" (long version) b/w "Blue Mist" (short version)

US: ATCO Records – 45 – 7040, 1975

single: "Blue Mist" b/w "Missouri Skyline"

Turkey: Atlantic Records 76500, 1976

UK: Atlantic Records K 10709, January 30, 1976

5. UPTOWN & LOWDOWN – MAMA'S PRIDE . . . . PG. 103-110

February, 1977

ATCO Records – SD 36-146

produced by Jim Mason

recorded at Davlen Sound Studios – Sherman Oaks, CA

A1. Can I Call You A Cab (Danny Liston) . . . . pg. 104, 107, 132, 215

A2. She's a Stranger to Me Now . . . . pg. 106, 107, 110

A3. Lucky Lady (Max Baker, Pat Liston)

A4. You Can't Fool Yourself

B1. The End of Our Road (Strong-Penzabene-Whitfield) . . . . pg. 110

B2. Merry-Go-Round (Pat Liston, Danny Liston) . . . . pg. 73

B3. Now I Found You (D. Liston, P. Liston, Baker, Sanders)

B4. Long Time (Danny Liston) . . . . pg. 104

additional musicians:

Timothy B. Schmit – *backing vocals*

Joe Lala – *percussionist*

Lenny Castro – *percussionist*

Dennis Dreith – *saxophone*

Jerry Jumonville – *saxophone*

single: "Shes A Stranger To Me Now" b/w "Shes A Stranger To Me Now" (mono)

ATCO Records – 7081 (promotion copy – not for sale)

unreleased:

Wandering Man (Joe Turek) . . . . pg. 108

When Will You Learn (P. Liston, D. Liston, Baker, Sanders) . . . . pg. 110

6. UNRELEASED HENRY PAUL DEMO . . . . PG. 131

1978

Mama's Pride was backing band

7. "MAYBE" B/W "MONKEY'S GUN" – MAMA'S PRIDE

1980

Tapestry Records – TR004

produced by Jack Bielan (A), Pat Liston (A, B)

8. ETERNAL MYSTERY – VARIOUS ARTISTS

1981

KBK / Earth City Sound Studios – MK 18-1216

produced by Kent Kesterson

recorded and mixed at KBK/Earth City Studios – St. Louis, MO

includes two tracks each by Randy Baird, Fairchild, Freedom, Mama's Pride, September

  includes Fairchild on background vocals:

  Connie Fairchild, Gary Scott, Michael Newman, Johnny Rodenhaus, David Toretta

9. SEPTEMBER FIRST – SEPTEMBER

1981

Sugar Records – SRJ-811

produced by Wayne Boosahda

recorded and mixed at KBK/Earth City Studios – St. Louis, MO

  A2. Sorry (Russ Kirkland)
  Mama's Pride credited as part of "Crowd"

10. GUARD YOUR HEART – MAMA'S PRIDE

1992

St. Louis Records – MP 10172

recorded at Icon Studio – St. Louis, MO

produced by Jim Gaines

  1. Caught Up In The Middle (D. Liston, P. Willett)

  3. Chance of a Lifetime (D. Liston, P. Willett)

4. Somebody to Love (D. Liston)
5. Sail On . . . . .pg. 116, 163
6. Que' Linda (P. Liston, P. Willett) . . . . pg. 164
7. Angel Missing Out Of Heaven (D. Liston, P. Willett)
8. Maybe. . . . . .pg. 132, 134, 163, 217
9. Who Gave You The Right (D. Liston) . . . . pg. 164, 165
10. Song Of Hope (D. Liston, F. Gagliano) . . . . pg. 165, 166
11. Love Can (D. Liston, P. Willett) . . . . pg. 165

additional musicians:

Mark Biehl – *soprano saxophone*
Pete DeLuca – *saxophone*
Tom Denman – *keyboards, organ*
Niall Gannon – *bodhran, fiddle, tin whistle*
Mike Liston – *performer [newscast]*
Rusty Parker – *percussion*
Ed Savoldi – *baritone saxophone*
Elliot "Doc" Simpson – *trumpet*

"Song of Hope" children voices: Allison Finn, Dorothy Johnson, Elisha Liston, Erin Lang, Eugene Liston, Jasmine Parker, Jessica Lang, Josh Lang, Lauren Willett, Natasha Johnson, Rachel Baker, Richard Steltenpohl, Sarah Reel, Sean Liston

11. RATTLESNAKE GUITAR: THE MUSIC OF PETER GREEN – VARIOUS ARTISTS . . . . PG. 172

1997

Viceroy Music – VIC2-8021

1-14 – Hellhound On My Trail (traditional)
performed by Ken Hensley . . . . pg. 172

12. A GLIMPSE OF GLORY – KEN HENSLEY & VISIBLE FAITH . . . . PG. 175

1999

H.I.S. Records – 9090317

Pat Liston as guest lead vocals:

4. Guard Your Heart (D. Liston, P. Willett) . . . . pg . 165, 175

241

2003

Dogtown Records – PL 6509

produced by Pat Liston

recorded at: Icon Studios, Dogtown Studio, The Sandbox, and KPS Studio

    1. Almost Like Being in Love

    2. I Guess We'll Never Know

    3. Blue Bandana

    4. Cowboy Clothes

    5. It's Alright

    6. Spellbound

    9. Strange Addiction

    10. Peter Pan Window

    11. (Now that I have) Passed the Torch Along

additional musicians:

    Don Black – *viola*

    Bob Breidenbach – *dobro, lap steel*

    Tim Britton – *uilleann pipes*

    Michelle Defabio – *violin*

    Don Drewett – *drums*

    Laurie Hartung – *highland bagpipes*

    Keith Hempen – *congas, djembe, percussion, shaker, tambourine*

    Julie Leonhardt – *violin*

    JoEllen Lyons – *cello*

    Dan Maloney – *slide guitar*

    Bill Murphy – *accordion; synthesizer*

    Scott Nienhaus – *guitars, mandolin, backing vocals*

    Steve Radick – *congas*

    Dickie Steltenpohl – *bass, backing vocals*

14. A "LIVE" AND WELL AT THE PAGEANT – MAMA'S PRIDE . . . . PG. 195-197

2006 (2 CD)

Carideas Records

produced by Mama's Pride

recorded at The Pageant – St. Louis, MO

1-1. Caught Up in the Middle (Danny Liston)

1-2. In The Morning (Danny Liston & Max Baker)

1-3. Lucky Lady (Pat Liston & Max Baker)

1-4. Merry-Go-Round (Pat Liston & Danny Liston)

1-5. Oh My Soul (Danny Liston) with Johnnie Johnson . . . . pg. 198

1-6. Who Gave You The Right (Danny Liston)

1-7. You Can't Fool Yourself

1-8. Baby I Love You (Ronnie Shannon)

1-9. Can I Call You A Cab (Danny Liston)

2-1. Kind Lovin' Woman (Danny Liston & Max Baker)

2-2. Missouri Skyline (Kevin Sanders, Danny Liston, Max Baker &
Pat Liston)

2-3. Mother Fuyer (Riley King) with Oliver Sain . . . . pg. 197

2-4. She's a Stranger to Me Now

2-5. Funky (Lester Chambers)

2-6. Ol St. Lou (Kevin Sanders, Danny Liston, Joe Turek, Max Baker &
Pat Liston)

2-7. Who Do You Think You're Foolin (Frank Gagliano, Joe Turek &
Danny Liston)

2-8. Blue Mist

2-9. Parliament....Rock n Roll Medley (Kevin Sander, Danny Liston,
Max Baker, Pat Liston & Dickie Steltenpohl)

(Chuck Berry)

(Richard Penniman)

15. DREAMER – PAT LISTON . . . .**PG. 203-207**

2008

produced by Pat Liston

recorded at KPS Studios, Blue Mist Studio, Jupiter Studios, Lupe Soup Studio

   1. Bad Risk

   2. Make Believe You're My Girl Tonight

   3. Open My Eyes

   4. Dreamer . . . . pg. 138

   5. A Long Way From Neverland

   6. Easy To Love

   7. Simpler Time

   8. Love Of Convenience

   9. Swan Hotel . . . . pg. 175

   10. My Daddy Knew The Cisco Kid . . . . pg. 4, 5

   11. Double Edged Sword

   12. Willow

additional musicians:

   Carolyn Bartley – *tap dance*

   Bob Breidenbach – *dobro*

   Karen Crawford – *backing vocals*

   Don Drewett – *drums*

   Keith "Bongo Boy" Hempen – *casaba, congas, guiro, organ, tambourine*

   John Logan – *acoustic guitar*

   Tommy Martin – *uillean pipes*

   John Modin – *guitar*

   Bill Murphy – *accordion, organ*

   Scott Nienhaus – *guitars, backing vocals*

   Steve Radick – *congas, shaker, tambourine*

   Terry Jones Rogers – *backing vocals*

   Dickie Steltenpohl – *bass*

   Jim Stevens – *saxophone*

16. THE LEGEND OF TEXAS RED – J.D. BLACKFOOT . . . .**PG. 216**

2012 (3 CD)

Pat Liston as choir/chorus, slide guitar

244

17. UNIVERSAL MIND – WAYNE GIVENS

2012

produced by Wayne Givens

    3. Beautiful Lady – Pat Liston as guest lead vocals

    4. The Answers – Pat Liston as guest lead vocals

    5. Promises – Pat Liston as guest vocals, pedal steel guitar

UNRELEASED SONGS *(AS OF SEPTEMBER 2016)*